A thousand miles up the Amazon, surround-
ed by dense jungle, is the Brazilian city of
Manaus. Today Manaus
just fifty years ago, whe
ber boom was at its hei
more swinging than Lo
than Paris, more violen
Coast...a city complete with museums, electric street-cars, and a two-million dollar
opera house. Manaus, capital of the jungle
state of Amazonas, was built by rubber,
greed and slavery — and the tale of its rise
and ruin is one of the most dramatic, little-
known episodes of recent history.

This is the story that Richard Collier tells
in *The River That God Forgot*. It begins in
the early years of this century at a time when
two-thirds of the entire world's rubber supply came from Manaus — *and when each ton
of latex exported cost seven native lives.*

Even then the days of Brazil's rubber barons
were numbered. In one of the greatest *coups*
of commercial espionage in history — brilliantly described here by Richard Collier —
British officials had already succeeded in
smuggling the precious rubber-tree seeds
out of Brazil — and into Malaya. But before
Far Eastern rubber could compete with

1924 and passed a peaceful country childhood in Surrey. At 18 he joined the R.A.F.
and as a services war correspondent traveled extensively in the Far East. After his
return to England, he edited *Town and
Country* magazine for several years and then
became a roving free-lance correspondent
throughout France, Italy and the British
Isles. Mr. Collier is now married and lives
in his childhood home, which is the subject
of *A House Called Memory*, one of his many
popular books. They include also *The City
That Would Not Die* and *The Sands of
Dunkirk*.

*The River
That God Forgot*

The River

The Story of

by RICHARD

That God Forgot

the Amazon Rubber Boom

COLLIER

E. P. Dutton & Co., Inc.
New York / 1968

LIBRARY OF CONGRESS CATALOG CARD NUMBER: 68–12451

First Edition

To the memory of
WALTER
ERNEST
HARDENBURG
Son of Liberty
1886–1942

*Rubber dazzled them, as gold and diamonds have
dazzled other men and driven them forth to
wander through the waste spaces of the world.
Searching for rubber, they made highways of
rivers whose very existence was unknown to the
government authorities, or to map-makers.
Whether they succeeded or failed, they left
everywhere behind them settlers who toiled,
married and brought up children. Settlement
began; the conquest of the wilderness entered
on its first stage.*

—THEODORE ROOSEVELT

There is no sin beyond the Equator.

—PORTUGUESE PROVERB

Contents

Photographs

following page 128

following page 176

PART ONE

The Secret Seed

EVEN AS DAWN broke over the Amazon Valley, in Manaus, Brazil, almost 1,000 miles upriver from the Atlantic, the nightclubs were jammed to suffocation. Slowly as steely pink light flooded three million square miles of evergreen hardwood forest, the city's thousand streetlamps glowed paler. But as yet, in this most isolated of all twentieth-century capitals, few men were stirring. On the wide boulevards, only the slippered shuffle of servants, bound for market with palm-leaf baskets, broke the brooding silence.

But in the narrow side streets converging on the docks, from night spots like the Phoenix, the High Life, the Garden Chalet and the wickedest of all, called the Pension of the Mulattos, came sounds savage and strident that now, in August, 1907, heralded every sunrise over Manaus: the crash of broken glass, the harsh laughter of women, a blaring cacophony of cakewalks, polkas and outrageous, high-stepping cancans.

Across the Cathedral Square now one man came alone, a tall, swarthy, black-bearded Peruvian, impeccable in white linen, a fine Havana cigar jutting from his massive jaw. Though sciatica was a cruel torment in his right hip, pain had never yet deterred 43-year-old Julio César Arana from an unrelenting purpose. Already, one block from the dockyard gates, he could see his destination, shaded by giant mango trees, its legend "Short Order Fries—Drinks of All Nations," picked out in glaring lights: the nightclub called The Terrible Ones.

Briefly, conscious always of the dignity that set him apart from other men, Arana braced himself, leonine head held high, white well-manicured hands gripping the silver-topped cane that sup-

Caracas

Canal
Zone

PANAMA Panama

PACIFIC
OCEAN

VENEZUE

Bogotá

Buenaventura Cali COLOMBIA

ORINOCO

A
N
D
E
S

Pasto

ICANA R.

IUAPÉS R.

Güeppí

La Chorrera
El Encanto

CAQUETÁ R.

JAPURÁ R.

Quito

NAPO R.

PUTUMAYO R.

SOLIMOES R.

ECUADOR

Iquitos AMAZON R.

A

MARAÑON R.

YAVARI R.

JURUÁ R.

Yurimaguas
Rioja
Lamud
Chachapoyas
Tarapoto
Cajamarca

HUALLAGA R.

UCAYALI R.

GREGORIO R.

ACRE R.

Port

M
T
S

PERU

ACRE TERRITORY

ABUNÁ R.

Villa
Bella

MADRE DE DIOS R.

BENI R.

Riberalta

Lima

BOLIV

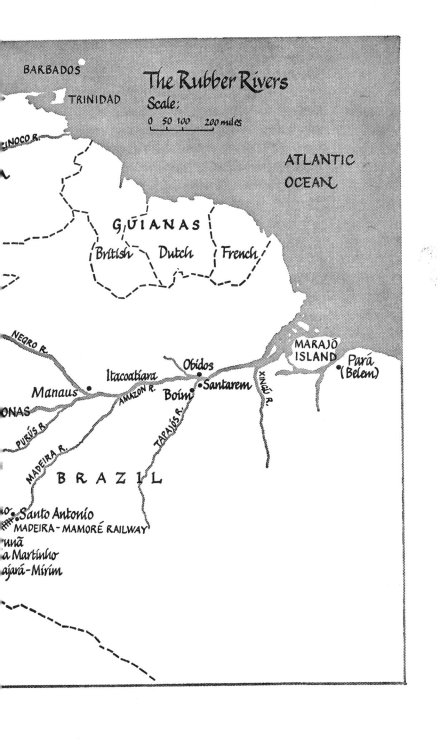

The Rubber Rivers

Scale:

0 50 100   200 miles

BARBADOS

TRINIDAD

ORINOCO R.

ATLANTIC
OCEAN

GUIANAS

British   Dutch   French

NEGRO R.

Manaus

Itacoatiara

Obidos

Santarem

MARAJÓ
ISLAND

Pará
(Belem)

AMAZON R.

Boim

XINGÚ R.

AMAZONAS

PURÚS R.

TAPAJÓS R.

MADEIRA R.

BRAZIL

Santo Antonio

MADEIRA - MAMORÉ RAILWAY

uná

a Martinho

ajará-Mirim

ported him. Then, with one thrust of his powerful shoulders, he breasted through the nightclub's swinging doors.

An awed silence fell upon the room. The sad burden of the pianola's "O Sole Mio" ground to a standstill. In this Brazilian cosmopolis, there was scarcely a man or woman who did not fear the advent of Julio César Arana, the Peruvian rubber baron, a secretive, iron-willed man who was known to live only for his work and his family. And Arana, his eyes taking in the tawdry throng, thought, as he had so often thought before: This city is doomed. It's time to get out.

At this hour, the air in the honky-tonk was thick and scarcely breathable: a nauseous compound of Rio Branco cigarettes, chicken soup and Enigma perfume. At a score of marble-topped tables lounged men of all ages and descriptions, from teen-age boys to spry seventy-year-olds, colored stones adorning their fingers, hissing sibilantly for sweating waiters to refill their glasses with Cordon Rouge champagne. Clinging to them, or crowded round the tumbling dice of the backgammon board, were the women of all nations: Wanda, the Pole, Amalia from the Balkans, Yolanda Ricci from Italy. In their gowns of blue, green and salmon-colored Surah silk, they looked like gaudy butterflies basking in the bright sunlight of Manaus' prosperity, their teeth set, as fashion decreed, with diamonds, black lace fans poised negligently, shoeshine boys at work on their trim feet. As Arana watched, one woman leaned forward to scrawl her fee, for the benefit of a drunken client, in a pile of wet spilled sugar.

It was almost a symbolic gesture. On this thirteenth day of August, 1907, the Amazon held the monopoly of the wild rubber the world demanded for its motor tires—300 million virgin forest trees dotted across two million square miles—and Manaus was a money-minded city. As capital of Amazonas State, one of twenty that had made up the sixteen-year-old Federal Republic of Brazil since its independence from Portugal, it was the pulsing heart of this monopoly; in the year just past—£14 million worth of wild rubber, ferried down the Negro River tributary on which Manaus stood, had paid off fully 40 percent of Brazil's annual debt. From hoarding after hoarding blazed a lottery slogan that might have served as the city's yardstick: *Vale quem tem* (You're worth what you've got).

In recent months, 5,000 men a week had flooded upriver from Pará (now Belém) on the Amazon delta, lured by the biggest boom since the Klondike, which was currently exploding the economies of the six Amazon Valley nations—Portuguese-speaking Brazil, and the Spanish-speaking republics of Peru, Bolivia, Colombia, Venezuela and Ecuador. Even the great steel tycoon, Andrew Carnegie, it was said, had lamented: "I ought to have chosen rubber."

But it was no desire to convert Manaus' free spenders that had brought Arana thither: his concern, as always, was both personal and private. One man bolder than the rest shouted, "Hey, Don Julio, how about a drink?" but one glance of Arana's cold hooded eyes silenced him. Moving delicately, despite his bulk, avoiding the dive's ornate porcelain spittoons, the Peruvian made a beeline for a table in the room's far corner. The sight he had seen numberless times over the past three years now met his eyes again: his young brother, Lizardo, disheveled and ashen-faced, passed out cold on the marble top. With arms entwined about the young man's neck was a woman of the town, solicitous yet watchful of her chances.

Grimly Arana fought to keep his anger in check. To him his sleek, pomaded younger brother, in his natty belted plaid jacket and jaunty bow tie, was a symbol of all that ailed this city. Three years earlier, at a salary of £2,500 per year, Julio had appointed him manager of his Manaus branch, yet despite the pressures of business Lizardo time and again arrived late at the office, fuddled with champagne, his white linen collar soiled with rouge. Yearning to strike him, Arana still maintained his frozen calm. So long as the Peruvian remained remote and aloof, no man could penetrate his armor.

Not deigning to speak, he glanced at the street woman. One peremptory jerk of his head was enough; she melted discreetly into the crowd. His dark piercing eyes bored into Lizardo; his voice was pregnant with unspoken menace: "Get out of here *now* and clean yourself up. I want to see you in the office in half an hour—better, make it twenty minutes."

Still dazed with liquor, Lizardo groped from a haze of hangover to mutter an abashed apology. Fumbling to fix his collar and tie he sent a waiter speeding for ice and black Brazilian coffee.

Without vouchsafing him a further glance, Arana shouldered back through the crowd, out into the city's gathering heat.

Behind him the voices and the laughter rose again, but uncertainly now; the pianola once more jangled into life, but with an air of seeming bravado. In the twenty-three years since Julio César Arana had arrived on the Amazon, few men had opposed him and lived to talk about it.

As Arana, a scarf of cigar smoke trailing behind him, passed beneath the blue-washed cathedral walls, walking east toward his office on Marshal Deodoro Street, the air was already as warm and moist as the breath from a steam kettle. Now over sixteen square miles, the legendary city of Manaus was awaking once again to find its voice.

This morning, as always, Manaus was one of the noisiest cities on earth—as if to convince itself that the jungle, only two miles from the city's center, was not a tight black ring of vegetation that hemmed it in on all sides. Conscious of the urgent equatorial thrust of earth against the pavements, street vendors set up as lusty a clamor as children whistling in the dark: the haberdasher's wooden clappers, the cake seller's haunting pipes, the tailor's horn, the iron spoon of the tinsmith. Lottery-ticket sellers bawled, "Get rich . . . get rich!" vying with the shrill paean of roosters behind mud walls. Other more urban sounds smote Arana's ears . . . the labored creaking of the water cart laying dust and the ice cart plying from house to house . . . the uncertain quavering and scraping of cellos, flutes and violins as the children of the rich practiced their scales.

Above the sounds rose one more strident than all the rest: the clangor of Manaus' bottle-green electric streetcars, sponsored by Charles Ranlett Flint, whose United States Rubber Company purchased fully a quarter of all the city's rubber. Though cities as renowned as Boston, Massachusetts, still made do with horsecars, Manaus' cars had girdled the city's sixteen miles of track in a dawn-to-dusk service for seven years now. Built to the jungle's very edge, the track would have served a city of a million, but on this August morning Manaus saw the million population explosion as just around the corner.

It was still only fifteen years since 30-year-old Eduardo Gonçalves Ribeiro, the republic's youngest-ever State Governor, had swept to power on a rising tide of rubber to strike the keynote in the symphony of Manaus. A diminutive dark-skinned dictator, whose twisted dreams embraced both women and power, Ribeiro had early seen the city's resources as limitless, and with reason. A 20-percent export tax on every kilo of rubber sometimes enriched the State's treasury by £1,600,000 a year.

A former military engineer, Ribeiro, almost overnight, had wrought an astonishing transformation on the jerry-built shantytown that had been Vila de Barro do Rio Negro—site of an ancient fort erected by the sixteenth-century Portuguese colonizers. Streets one hundred feet wide were carved across the swamps of the Negro River, laid out on an east-west gridiron pattern, intersected by boulevards running as straight as arrows to the jungle's edge, paved in cobbles shipped from Portugal at five shillings apiece. Electric lamp standards replaced the sad smoky kerosene lamps of the past. In step with them along the broad avenues marched a green rampart of shady trees, clipped as if barbered: figs, crotons, jacarandas, sweet-smelling eucalyptus from Australia.

By July, 1904, when Julio Arana first opened his Manaus office, Ribeiro, before strangling himself in a fit of erotic mania, had spearheaded an achievement already hailed as "an amazing tribute to the energy of man." From the somber forests and malarial marshes had mushroomed one of the world's most exciting cities:

a visionary's dream of hospitals, churches, banks, office blocks and covered markets, along with a £500,000 Palace of Justice and forty-five primary schools. Its citizens were assured of over two million gallons of pure water daily and three hundred of them were linked by the first telephone system the Amazon had ever known.

But Ribeiro's tortured spirit had envisaged not only utility but beauty. Along with the fine public buildings went splendid parks and municipal gardens, dotted with summerhouses and cool arbors, their ornamental lakes spanned by rustic bridges. On stifling evenings, twice weekly, the city's elite flocked to the park's green-and-gilt bandstands for concerts by the governor's band—then moved on to the Grand Hotel Internacional, known as "the finest in Christendom," for ices and champagne.

Besides these, Manaus now supported a racecourse, a bull ring, thirty-six fashionable doctors, twenty-four bars, twenty-three high-class department stores, eleven fancy restaurants, nine modistes, nine gentlemen's outfitters, seven barbershops, seven billiard saloons and seven bookshops. It was with truth that Ribeiro had boasted: "I found a village—I made of it a modern city."

It was a civic pride Julio Arana shared along with 36,000 other Manaus citizens, though typically one in twenty, like Arana himself, had their roots elsewhere: Parisian milliners, bankers from Stuttgart, merchants out of Lisbon, Liverpool engineers. Oblivious to the dripping equatorial humidity, they liked to stress that temperatures over 100 degrees were unknown in their adopted city, with 77 degrees as the mean annual temperature. "A climate like the south of France" was a favored comparison, and loyalists turned to France, too, for another clincher: out of 1,200 youngsters entering a recent Parisian contest, a Manaus-born lad had taken first prize for health and physique.

Fiercely proud of their jungle metropolis, the locals liked to quote the German explorer, Baron Friedrich Heinrich Alexander von Humboldt, who had prophesied almost a hundred years earlier: "There [in the Amazon Valley] sooner or later, the civilisation of the world will be found." Under the striped awnings of the pavement cafés on the broad Eduardo Ribeiro Avenue, men said it was only a matter of time before Manaus, surpassing Rio de Janeiro, became the new capital of Brazil. At one recent banquet a local bigwig had summed up the view of thousands: "No adult heart can feel that Manaus is anything less than fabulous."

In many ways the city was a rich man's folly. From the intersection of Municipal Street with Eduardo Ribeiro Avenue, Arana saw now the apogee of that folly, cresting the hill a hundred feet above sea level by San Sebastian Square: the blue-and-gold-tiled dome of Manaus' fabulous opera house glittering beneath the high bright sun. Every facet of this gleaming pile, even its very existence in the jungle almost 1,000 miles from the ocean, was somehow larger than life. Its iron framework had been shipped from Glasgow; the 66,000 tiles covering its cupola from Alsace-Lorraine. Within, from a domed sky-blue ceiling, picked out with angels and pink cherubs, hung Venetian crystal chandeliers, whose candlepower illumined brilliantly an audience of 1,600. In the reception foyer, rich golden drapes and tall vases of Sèvres porcelain were offset by soaring cream and coral pillars of Carrara marble, flanked by carved jacaranda wood chairs so heavy it took two men to lift them.

First mooted before Ribeiro had even taken office, as a mere £3,600 project, the opera house, like much of Manaus, had seen its priorities go awry. Constructional delays had been as endless as the contractors' bills—which mounted steeply as Ribeiro doled out free passage money to technicians, even laborers, from all over Europe. From Paris to Manaus came the Comédie Française's scenic artist, Crispim do Amaral; from Manaus to Rome sped commissions to Italy's leading painter of sacred murals, Domenico de Angelis. And from London, before the theater walls had even risen, came a hundred crates of carved and costly furniture.

None of this had troubled Ribeiro unduly. Some locals felt that a cupola of solid gold not tiles befitted Manaus, but the governor went one better—"When the growth of our city demands it," he had declared before the theater was even open, "we'll pull down this opera house and build another." By January 6, 1897, opening night, when the curtain rose on the Grand Italian Opera Company in Ponchielli's *Gioconda*, the modest £3,600 project had stripped the State Treasury of £400,000—and costs would go higher yet. To lure opera companies of note up the Amazon, the state was paying out £20,000 in subsidies each year, and after 1900, when yellow fever struck down nine members of Giulia Ragi's Operette Company, richer inducements were needed. Now few maestros finished a Manaus season without a gold-encrusted baton as souvenir. For divas there were costly marquises and earrings set with diamonds and pearls.

It was small wonder that by May, 1906, Manaus, beset by debts, needed an urgent loan of £3,200,000 from the French bankers, Société Marseillaise—though typically, four months later, they squandered £19,000 of it on one buffet supper for the visiting President of Brazil.

To the sober purposeful Arana it seemed that Manaus' 6,000 homes sought to put even the opera house to shame. In the fashionable streets round San Sebastian Square sumptuous two-story mansions now bulked everywhere, set in trim gardens behind high stone walls, faced with colored *azulejo* tiles from Portugal—primrose, azure, apple-green, rust-red—sparkling like precious stones under the sun. Built on the European pattern with high ceilings, noble stairways and ornate scrolls, they made few concessions to climate: even the flat roofs, crowned with classical statues and heavy vases, belied the torrential months of Amazon rain. And few cities offered such a riot of European styles, from Turkish minarets through Swiss chalets to English Tudor, fashions that changed arbitrarily from year to year.

Commissioning a German baronial palace to house his string of racehorses, one rubber baron, Commandant Frotta, changed it to an American colonial mansion then found the result so stylish that he moved into one wing. It was the same at all levels. One of Ribeiro's successors, José Cardoso Ramalho, took such exception to the half-completed governor's palace that he could not stomach the sight of it. Authorizing £6,000 worth of dynamite, he set engineers to blow it sky-high.

Interiors were lavish, too—a world away from the simple old-style decor of the apartment above Julio Arana's office, with its plain whitewashed walls, wicker furniture and simply-woven, palm-fiber hammocks. The new rich took their ease in fabulous £60 hammocks richly decorated with featherwork, or in rocking chairs lined with marocain. Predinner drinks were sipped from silver champagne goblets, set on Carrara-marble-topped tables with bases of solid gold. At black-tie dinner parties, guests chatted comfortably round tables built to seat fifteen, eyes riveted on the darting silvery motions from the built-in fish tank many hostesses now installed as a table centerpiece.

Nor was the display confined to what guests could see and envy. Many living rooms were rich with oil-painted murals, but master bedrooms were lined in silk, with solid English suites of cinnamon and cedarwood shipped 5,000 miles from Maples of London. Bathrooms were gay with colored tiles and mosaics, and most had succumbed to current fashion: a shiny porcelain tub with golden lions' heads roaring hot and cold water in place of taps.

Yet still the houses were rented, not freehold—for most, like Julio Arana himself, saw Europe as their ultimate future. Almost 2,500 of Manaus society took first-class return passages to Europe each year, keeping abreast of fashion; children went to convent schools in Paris or Lausanne as automatically as soiled linen was sent to Lisbon for laundering. Even an official Chamber of Commerce handout claimed for Manaus "the gay spirit of Parisian life," for *Le Matin* appeared on every newsstand and all banquet menus were in French. With its literary societies, art galleries, lecture halls and two thriving newspapers, Manaus could boast more culture than many of Europe's provincial cities.

If the citizens could not go to Europe, they brought Europe to Manaus. Rubber alone had lured men to the Amazon, and few were disposed to set down tap roots: despite valiant state efforts to encourage agriculture, primary crops like cotton, rice, tobacco, even coffee went uncultivated. In twenty rubber-rich years not one fishing company had been organized along a river teeming with fish. Geared to a merchant's boom-or-bust economy, which disdained the soil and manual labor, the people showed a characteristic scorn of local produce. As the black tide of rubber flowed toward the sea, the staples of all nations flowed back up the river as imports: Danish butter, German sauerkraut, English sausages, mortadella from Milan. No truck farmer could stay long in business: Manaus preferred its potatoes from Portugal, its cauliflowers shipped in brine all the way from Brussels.

Now, in 1907, it was hardly surprising that Manaus' prices had soared four times higher than those of New York City. A packet of cheap envelopes was priced at 3s. A servant going to market paid 25s for a scrawny chicken and sixpence for each hen's egg. An average-sized mullet at the fish market cost £1. Druggists were asking and getting £2/10 for a shilling bottle of quinine.

It was a city of dandies and belles. For beaux, spotless white linen suits, white suede shoes, Chile hats and Irish linen shirts, ordered from "Old England" or the Havana House, were the height of fashion. Manaus had become known as "The White City." A dandy might have twenty ornate walking canes topped in gold or silver and as many flowered vests and diamond tiepins. For their laces, cambrics, crocodile handbags and Rue de la Paix gowns the women had a bewildering variety of choice: milliners like Madame Bonneterre, fancy stores like Paris in America or the Russian Simon Lifitsch's Au Bon Marché on Municipal Street.

At balls or at evenings at the opera they were an unforgettable sight, parading the reception foyer or the orangery that spanned the terrace, egret feathers in their sleek dark hair, twirling their peekaboo lace parasols. Even in a temperature of 99 degrees they sported long velvet trains held up by golden loops, and diamonds glittered on their fingers.

Diamonds were the city's status symbol: one jeweler was later to estimate that in 1907 Manaus' diamond consumption was per capita the largest in the world. Even junior clerks with frayed shirt cuffs and scuffed boots flaunted £100 diamond rings. Day-to-day purchases were made from the Italians, Roberto and Pelosi on Municipal Street, from The Big Door, The Black Diamond or The Golden Globe, but on gala occasions extravagant husbands and lovers looked farther afield. The grand gesture was a cable to Paris, bespeaking a brand-new toilette with matching jewels from Cartier's.

Now at the peak of the boom all Manaus seemed compelled to spend as if £50 were two shillings, though while the money lasted none should want. The city's leading funeral parlor, Empreza Funeraria, went on record, "This firm will provide coffins free to persons of well-known indigence." A man tipped twelve shillings to have a parcel carried three blocks, or flung a golden sovereign to a boatman as largesse for a five-minute journey. A café waitress, presenting a bill for a light lunch, might get a £10 tip with a diamond thrown in.

So unbalanced was the spending that indigence seemed likely any day. If Colonel Aleixo was the first to light his cigar with a blue-black 500-milreis note, then worth £30, other "colonels," as rich sugar daddies were known, were swift to emulate him—or to try to cap the folly. Dismounting from their carriages at the Garden Chalet's open-air terrace, tycoons would refresh their high-stepping Arabs with a brimming bucket of Cordon Rouge champagne. Once, infatuated with a pretty French cabaret singer, two Dutchmen rented the opera house for a night, so that she could sing for them alone.

Others were as prodigal. One colonel, swaggering aboard a liner just arrived from England, commandeered an entire consignment of hats destined for a local merchant. Impatiently cramming on hat after hat he shied all that did not fit or please him over the rails until the harbor was a bobbing sea of headgear —then, electing to keep the last, he paid for three dozen. Another bent on cornering the city's one Mercedes-Benz hire car for himself and a woman of the town worsted all rivals with an unprecedented £400 offer. Their journey: a three-hundred-yard haul from the opera house to an adjacent bar.

There was a darker side to this. Whole sections of the city—
Itamaraca Street, Joaquim Sarmento Street, Epaminondas Avenue
—were given over to brothels, whose daily newspaper advertisements unblushingly described them as "pensions—service French
style." Opening for trade at 4 P.M. their tariff rates for new
inmates were as rigid as a customs' shed: for an evening with a
thirteen-year-old Polish virgin, imported from Warsaw by agents
making once-yearly trips, the fixed market price was £70. But
"moth-girls" who had become the reigning queens, like "Trinidad," with her bolero hats and her little black poodle Zizi, could
command prices all their own. One night's pleasure might cost a
client a £1,500 diamond necklace. To offer too little was to risk a
girl scornfully snatching a £100 note to light her cigarette.

Such women as these—from Moscow, Tangier, Cairo, Buda-
pest—Manaus took to its heart; even good-time girls had a small
army of courtiers. In life, many men had known the favors of the
dark, vivacious Aria Ramos, whose poignant violin solos were the
highlight of every carnival. In death, following a fatal shooting
accident, they mourned her, then by common consent took steps
to immortalize her. At her funeral the Order of Service featured
not only hymns but also Aria Ramos' favorite waltz, "Going to
the Sky." Soon after, in Manaus' St. John's Cemetery, there arose
a lifesize statue of Aria on a pedestal, violin at her breast, the bow
drawn back for the first strains of this same waltz.

For all its sophisticated facade, Manaus was a frontier city: a
wide-open town where no man who valued his wife's honor let her
go unescorted to church. Article 52 of the city's ordinances was
significant: "The use of guns and arrows on the streets of Manaus
is forbidden." Alongside fashionable tiled mansions huddled
stinking slums, where rainwater barrels, topless cisterns and
stagnant puddles were a potent breeding ground for the yellow
fever carrier, the dreaded tiger mosquito. One sanitarian's report
—that 98 percent of all dwelling houses harbored some species of
mosquito—went a long way toward explaining a malarial death
rate of three hundred a year.

Despite Manaus' disclaimers, the forest was never far away. All day long the sky above the city was dotted with vultures, wheeling like scraps of charred black paper in the downdraft of a fire; nine years back the municipal code had granted official protection to these scavengers, whose rustling feasts on the mounds of garbage lining the streets helped keep disease in check. Daily, even newspaper advertisements betrayed the jungle's proximity: "Bitten by a Bushmaster—Saved from Death by Dermol Skin Ointment."

Though its streets were fine and paved, jungle smells lay trapped between the city's buildings. As Julio César Arana swung into the narrow canyon of Marshal Deodoro Street, the merchants' quarter where his office was sited, these smells were all about him: sweat, sugarcane rum and spoiled fruit, Brazil nuts, rosewood oil and timbo vine. Other smells that made part of a riverine city were pungent on the moist air: roasting coffee, varnish, oakum, cinnamon, sassafras, ginger and tonka beans.

Above all, Manaus smelled of rubber, the rubber on which its prosperity rested. This morning the uneven cobbles of Deodoro Street were still sticky with the white smears of half-dried liquid latex. Those who relished it compared the smell to "fine old Virginian Ham," its detractors belittled it as like "water dashed on a recent fire." Most potent of all was the aroma wafting from the cool dark warehouses standing open to the street, where the big oblong balls, or *peles*, of cured black-brown rubber lay stacked: smoked-ham-shaped lumps that bounced and joggled as if alive, until crammed into 300-pound pine boxes for shipment to the docks of Liverpool and New York.

Again Julio Arana thought, It's time to get out of Manaus. This city's forgotten rubber, it's forgotten everything but big spending—and the boom can't last forever.

It was 6 A.M. At No. 41, on the eastern side of Deodoro Street, where the brass plate spelled out "J. C. Arana Brothers, Manaus," Arana turned into the tranquil half light of his ground-floor office-cum-warehouse. Electric fans whirred noiselessly in the thick air, drowned by the muted clack of Adler typewriters. From the corner of his eye Arana saw Lizardo, installed in the manager's glass-sided cubicle, dealing shakily with that morning's mail. But now as he settled to his own desk, it seemed to him that all his worst forebodings had been vindicated. Propped neatly against his desk set was Manaus' leading daily, *Amazonas*, with a somber item of news:

> The cultivation of rubber is now carried on methodically in about 140,000 acres of Asia . . . [soon] it is quite evident that we shall not be able to stand this competition.

When Julio César Arana was twelve years old, there took place 470 miles from Manaus, near Santarém on the Amazon, a theft so audacious it left the Brazilian authorities gasping. Neither Julio nor his childhood sweetheart, Eleonora Zumaeta, could realize it then, but this theft of 1876 was one day to rob the Amazon Valley of the prosperity that had so long sustained it.

Six years earlier, in 1870, Clements Robert Markham, a zestful 46-year-old official of Britain's India Office, had reached a radical decision in London: the reckless felling of rubber trees that was everywhere taking place in tropical forests must somehow be checked. As Markham saw it, every steam vessel afloat, every train, every factory employing steam power, needed rubber—for valves, washers, pumps, buffer springs. The time had come to align these wild rubber trees into orderly plantations, to prevent their ultimate destruction and ensure a permanent supply.

But in which kind of rubber tree should the British invest? For sixty years past they had pinned their faith in the one tree indigenous to Asia, the Assam rubber tree, the botanists' *Ficus elastica*, which flourished in all the forests bordering the Brahmaputra River. But the wild tribes who harvested the ficus, urged to bypass quality for quantity, hacked and slashed at the bark like vandals so that the white sticky latex should flow more freely into holes scooped in the earth. Already this ruthless spoliation had destroyed whole groves of trees.

But was the Assam the best tree to preserve for posterity? Experts summoned to Markham's Whitehall office could not at first be sure. Rubber of a kind was at that time harvested from upward of a hundred different plants—and all were alien to India. The State of Ceará, in Brazil's arid northeast, set much store by the bulbous-rooted manicoba tree. Mexico swore by the Castilla, which thrived only in hot dry soil, like its shrubby gray-green guayule. On the Belgian Congo, a rich harvest was reaped from the tacky, pitchlike sap of the landolphia vine.

Not until 1872 did one of Markham's experts, James Collins, former curator of the British Pharmaceutical Society's Museum, come up with a decisive analysis. The Brazilian Castilla, found also in Panama and Colombia, was superior by far to Assam rubber—but most promising of all was an unidentified species of wild Brazilian rubber tree, of the botanical genus *Hevea*. Its product, called "Pará fine Hard," after the Amazon port, fetched an average price of 3s a pound—and Britain alone, at a cost of £720,000, was importing almost 3,000 tons each year.

From this moment, the die was cast. Somehow Brazil's monopoly, accounting for half Britain's annual imports of rubber, must be wrested from her grasp.

There was precedent for this. In 1854 Markham himself, aged thirty and working with three agents, had made a breakneck flight across the snows of the Andes, bearing specimens of the wild cinchona tree, whose bark yields quinine, from the forests of Peru. Transplanted to plantations in India and Ceylon they had flourished so successfully that the cost of quinine had been slashed to one-sixteenth of its former price.

Markham lost no time. In May, 1873, the problem passed to 59-year-old Dr. Joseph Hooker, director of the Royal Botanic Gardens at Kew, on the outskirts of London. A tall, shaggy-haired, bespectacled widower, nicknamed "Lion," Hooker had had long experience of suiting the plant to the climate; he had arrived back from a climbing trip in the Himalayas in 1847 with the first giant azaleas and rhododendrons Britain had ever seen. Hooker had for some time past been in touch with a correspondent on the Amazon at Santarém, only 400 miles from the Atlantic.

"I will," he assured Sir Mountstuart Grant Duff, the Under-Secretary of State for India, "beg him to send to Kew a considerable quantity of the seeds."

It was a venture affording much margin for error. Though Markham had ordered the immediate siting of plantations near the Brahmaputra, confident that wild Brazilian rubber would soon succeed Ficus, no one knew which kind of Hevea yielded the coveted "Pará fine Hard." Even had they known with certainty, few would have selected Hooker's Santarém correspondent, Henry Alexander Wickham, for the cloak-and-dagger enterprise.

The son of a London solicitor who had died when he was four years old, Wickham's whole career bespoke lack of parental guidance. As a spoiled harum-scarum lad, whose mother Harriette, a Sackville Street milliner, could do little with him, he had shown scant aptitude for anything save fishing and pen-and-ink drawings. At twenty, following two years' art training, he had for years drifted through the wilds of Nicaragua and Venezuela, ultimately, by way of the Orinoco River and its tributaries, arriving on the Amazon.

A handsome six-footer, Wickham, at thirty, was a self-important dreamer who reveled in his chosen role of pioneer. Invariably he "camped," not "stayed," at a hotel; his special pride was a waterproof watch that survived even fording a river on horseback. But to date Wickham's pioneering had paid few dividends. By 1873, two years after settling at Santarém with his mother and his 27-year-old bride, Violet, he had done little more than build three successive houses to combat the torrid climate and struggle to raise a variety of unrewarding crops—sugar, tobacoo, tapioca, even rubber.

Despite his long-standing correspondence with Hooker, to whom he dispatched seeds and cuttings with notes on propaga-

Julio César Arana (*Author's Collection*)

Manaus boasted an opera house which cost £400,000, where maestros were lured to play with gold-encrusted batons. (*Richard Collier*)

Among the splendors of Manaus were ornate houses like the Palacio Scholz (*above*), built only two miles from primeval jungle, and an American-donated streetcar system (*below*) surpassing those of many cities in the United States at the time. (*Upper photo: Richard Collier; lower photo: Author's Collection*)

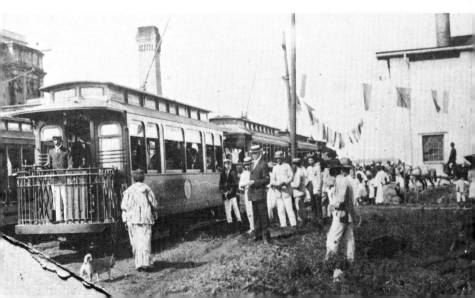

A city of dandies and belles, Manaus patronized modistes as stylish as the Atelier Palmyra (*above*) and jewelers like Roberto and Pelosi (*below*) to satisfy the world's highest diamond consumption. (*Photos: Author's Collection*)

tion potential, it seemed likely he would fail in this top-level assignment as he had failed in everything else.

But Wickham's streak of gentle obstinacy was to stand him in good stead. As a patriot he was willing enough to benefit the British Empire, but even a patriot must eat. What, he now replied to Hooker, would be his scale of remuneration? But it was fourteen months before Clements Markham could convince his masters that without financial outlay there could be no plantation industry. Not until July, 1874, did Markham report wearily to Hooker: "They have agreed to pay Mr. Wickham £10 for every 1,000 seeds."

To outwit the Brazilian authorities, Wickham decided that he himself must spirit the seeds to Pará and onto a Liverpool-bound steamer, persuading the captain to secrete them in his cabin. "But," he confessed frankly to Hooker in October, 1874, "although the sum offered by the Government appears sufficiently liberal, you will perceive that it will not pay me to go into the better districts to collect seeds in small quantities . . . if I may be guaranteed an order for a large number, I am prepared to collect the finest in the best localities and despatch them . . ."

Six months later, in April, 1875, he received through Hooker the India Office's go-ahead: he had authority to collect upward of 10,000 seeds, no questions to be asked about how he came by them. But it was then too late for forage for that year's seed. "There is now, therefore, nothing to be done but wait for next season's fruit. . . ."

But Wickham had used the time lag to advantage. On the Tapajós River, whose steel-blue waters meet the Amazon at Santarém, the courteous monosyllabic man was already a familiar figure along the rubber trails. By nature a gentle, unsuspicious people, the Brazilians by this time saw his questions and copious notes as routine. And in this era the Amazon swarmed with botanists, men like Alfred Russel Wallace, a former schoolmaster, and the Yorkshireman, Richard Spruce, indexing the 20,000 exotic plants that thrived along the mighty river.

"Why are you collecting so many seeds, Doctor?" the rubber

men, who took him for a man of learning, asked frequently, but their questions were good-natured, and Wickham, smiling and nodding, giving nothing away, bided his time.

On the night of March 6, 1876, Wickham, at the trading post of Julio David Serique, sixty-five miles up the Tapajós in the settlement of Boim, scribbled a historic note to Hooker: "I am now collecting rubber seeds . . . along the river, being careful to select only those of the best quality . . . I hope soon to leave with a large supply for England."

Days earlier had come Wickham's luckiest break of all. Early in February, along with other Santarém planters, he had received an eleventh-hour dinner invitation aboard the S. S. *Amazonas*, 1,057 tons, an ocean liner on her way upriver to inaugurate a new Liverpool–Upper Amazon run. Admiring the blue lights that dressed the ship, Wickham had passed a lively evening with Captain Murray, her commander, and the shipping line's two supercargoes.

Then, as March dawned, astounding news reached Santarém. Anchored off Manaus, Captain Murray was at his wit's end. After stripping the liner of every bale of merchandise, the rascally supercargoes had sold it for a fat profit and then decamped. The *Amazonas* was left without one stick of cargo to return to Liverpool.

Penniless, Wickham was still rich in resource. By the next steamboat a message sped upriver to Murray, offering a bold solution: as a Government of India agent, Wickham had powers to charter the vessel for her return voyage and he meant to use them. He himself was proceeding by canoe up the Tapajós to Boim on a secret assignment. Murray must bring the *Amazonas* down with all haste for a rendezvous off Santarém.

That the odds were still against him, Wickham knew. All that March day the riverbank at Boim buzzed with activity, as village girls of the Tapuyo tribe skillfully wove the openwork split-cane baskets that Wickham had commissioned, carefully packing the oily brown-dappled rubber seeds between layers of dried wild banana leaves. But this oil content, Wickham knew, could turn them rancid within weeks, destroying their vital power of germination.

For days now Wickham and his India helpers had not rested, forced to work when the sun was at its zenith and the seed capsules reached a peak point of ripeness. Alert for the sudden popgun report as the exploding capsule showered seeds forty yards from the tree, they had grubbed painstakingly to retrieve them from the black carpet of humus that was the jungle floor.

But to leave nothing to chance, and to make up a staggering total of 70,000 seeds, Wickham had been forced to send other Indians scouting the forest, paying cash for all they could locate —and how fresh their harvest might be he could not know. Nor did he know how he could conceal such a cargo from the customs inspectors at Pará. In truth, the Brazilians had no law against the export of rubber plants—but 70,000 seeds would surely mean an approach to Rio for guidance? Whatever happened, their fate would be the same. Confiscated or delayed, they would never survive to germinate in Kew's hothouses.

But fortune was favoring Wickham beyond his wildest dreams. Unknown to him the Amazon forests harbored fully seventeen varieties of wild Hevea—yet by chance he had struck on the one tree that was the rubber barons' mainstay, the botanists' *Hevea braziliensis*. Thriving in the high forest land that shelved inland from the river, its silvery trunk, akin to a poplar's, soared upward for a hundred sheer feet. On its upper branches small green three-cleft leaves, with silky white undersides, gave place at the tip to panicles of green, sweet-scented flowers. And in Wickham's openwork baskets, as he paddled back for the rendezvous with Captain Murray, were packed fully 70,000 potential top-grade Heveas.

At 3 A.M. on Saturday, June 10, Dr. Joseph Hooker hovered uneasily on the brink of sleep in the first-floor bedroom of the director's red-brick Georgian house overlooking Kew Green, Surrey. An insomniac who drove himself through a 16-hour day, Hooker's accepted panacea was to recite poetry in his head until he dropped off, but the events of this night, he later recalled, banished all thoughts of sleep. Disturbed by a sudden staccato rattle, he had started up in bed. Beneath the chestnut trees that fringed the moonlit green, someone was tossing pebbles at his white-sashed bedroom window.

Hastening downstairs in his nightshirt, the botanist was astonished to find a total stranger in a wide-brimmed tropical hat, clutching an old Gladstone bag, who introduced himself as Henry Alexander Wickham. The Amazon seed snatch was now accomplished fact—and the theatrical Wickham had been unable to resist announcing it in this dramatic fashion.

In the director's study, lined with rare flower prints and Wedgwood medallions, Hooker, in the cold small hours of this Saturday, heard the impetuous Wickham babble out his story. For not only had Wickham brashly chartered the *Amazonas* all the way to Liverpool, stowing his crates of precious seeds in her forehold, but at Pará, aided by the British Consul, Thomas Shipton Green, he had so hoodwinked the Brazilian customs chief that the ship had not even been searched.

"All we have," Wickham had declared smoothly, with something akin to truth, "are exceedingly delicate botanical specimens specially designate for delivery to her Britannic Majesty's own Royal gardens of Kew."

From the quayside, he had noted with satisfaction that Murray, following orders, kept up a full head of steam as an emergency measure. But even this precaution had been unnecessary. The customs, delighted to help a man of science on a special assignment for his Queen, gave their immediate clearance.

On Friday, June 9, the *Amazonas* had at last reached Le Havre, and the impatient Wickham, leaving the ship, had crossed the Channel posthaste to London. There, long after midnight, he had hired a hansom cab to Kew. In his Gladstone bag were precious samples of the seeds, but the remainder, packed in five hundred-weight of crates, were still aboard the *Amazonas*, which was due to dock at Liverpool later that day. What Wickham urged now was the despatch of a special night goods train to collect them.

Readily Hooker assented. As early as 6 A.M. on June 14, the

gardeners of Kew, checking on duty in their regulation blue serge suits and wooden clogs, passed through the little green curator's gate to find an unprecedented sight. The propagating house called 17A gaped open to the chill morning air—and dumped unceremoniously on the paving stones outside was a motley collection of rejects: frail mauve orchids, flame-colored hibiscus, dwarf carnauba trees. Hooker and his curator, John Smith, were assuring Wickham's precious freight every chance of survival.

Anxious days followed for Hooker and his staff. On the fifteenth, all 70,000 of Wickham's seeds were sown; four days later some were already sprouting through the moist black humus. By July 7, Hooker's deputy, William Thiselton-Dyer, was noting: "Many hundreds are over fifteen inches high and all are in vigorous health." In truth Wickham had done better than he knew, for though less than 4 percent of his seeds survived the magnitude of his haul had ensured that by July's end fully 1,919 seedlings awaited urgent transmission to Asia.

Shipped aboard the *Duke of Devonshire in* "Wardian cases"— miniature hermetically-sealed greenhouses invented by a medical research worker, Nathaniel Ward, which nourished the plants by means of their own condensed moisture—the plants left London docks in the care of gardener William Chapman on August 12, 1876, bound for Colombo, Ceylon, and the Peradeniya Botanical Gardens.

In these thirty-eight steaming Wardian cases reposed the potential ruin of the Amazon—and the makings of a new industry whose total cost to Britain was £1,505/4/2d.

Not that the Amazon Valley realized it then or for many years thereafter. The mercurial happy-go-lucky Brazilian temperament fought shy of facing up to facts—and most, as the coldly purposeful Julio Arana saw, were loath to face up to them even now, in 1907. Manaus' Chamber of Commerce hailed the first news of Wickham's theft with contemptuous guffaws: the climate of Asia would prove uncongenial, the curing process would go awry, the seedlings would wither and die. Not until eight years later, in

1884, did they clamp down a nugatory £60 tax on every kilo of rubber seed exported.

It was in this year that 20-year-old Julio César Arana, of Rioja, a sandstone town above a flower-carpeted valley in the foothills of the Peruvian Andes, first turned his thoughts to rubber. Only 75 miles away was the thriving port of Yurimaguas, on the Huallaga River, and many tales filtered up this Amazon tributary of the fortunes that were piling up along the rubber trails. The Amazon was more than booming; men said it was exploding! Arana wanted two things from life: to marry Eleonora Zumaeta and to possess wealth and power. And rubber might prove the key to both these ambitions.

Handsome, quick-witted young Arana, whose assured manner early won him the courtesy title "Don Julio," notoriously had his way with any girl he fancied—but with Eleonora Zumaeta, whose parents' house adjoined his own on Rioja's Plaza Principal, it had been a different story. At eleven, Arana was almost a fixture on the party wall, signaling urgently to Eleonora or throwing her bouquets of flowers he had gathered from the valley. Mostly the petite, vivacious girl, three years Julio's senior, disdained even to notice him; his flowers withered on the patio where they lay. Rarely, in relenting mood, her keen blue eyes flashed him a smile before she tossed him a sprig of wild cherries from her father's tree.

From the first she was the one person before whom Arana was ever humble. The better to serenade her, he grew skilled with the guitar, the accordion and the concertina. At primary school, his favorite teacher was now the professor of poetry, Leopoldo Cortez, who after hours sometimes agreed to criticize the acrostics Julio composed in her honor. Then came a bitter blow. At fifteen, she won a scholarship to the Convent of San Pedro in the Peruvian capital of Lima, five hundred miles away across the Andes. It was then an unheard-of journey for a girl to undertake, but Eleonora, escorted by her uncle, Cecilio Hernandez, bravely embarked on the six-month trek—on horseback, often on foot, across the majestic snow-splashed peaks. Arana, twelve years old, steeled himself for a long wait.

At fourteen, he quit school to work in his father's business. Martin Arana, like most of Rioja's solid citizens, was a hatmaker, for every home was virtually a small hat factory, where the family fashioned the soft pliable straw hats from the leaves of the screw-pine tree. Some were so delicate and flexible that an expert worked on them for a month at a time; folding into the pocket like a silk handkerchief, they retailed at £40. Others were peon's sombreros, priced at 50 cents, no more than a day's work. As a barefoot teen-ager, Julio learned first the painstaking task of making hats, then the high adventure of peddling them—on rugged icy journeys with his father, a hundred miles over the mountain passes to Chachapoyas and on to Cajamarca.

Later Martin Arana, a stooping, introverted man, was to recall: "In those days Julio was so energetic that muleback was nowhere near fast enough for him. When the going got rough he was always jumping off to help the mule, trying to finish the journey quicker."

In truth, Arana's restless, churning ambition craved an outlet he could not find. At fifteen he tried to enlist as a volunteer in the war against Chile until a memorable drubbing from his father brought a change of heart. Balked, he now took a job as a secretary in Chachapoyas—with Martin's full approval. Secretly Martin was proud of his son: if the boy learned bookkeeping and office routine he thought there was nothing he might not achieve.

At seventeen, back in Rioja, Julio was running his own small hat store in the marketplace when electric news reached him. Eleonora Zumaeta was coming home, the first Rioja girl ever to complete her schooling and then go on to win a teacher's diploma. The whole town declared a fiesta in her honor.

Arana was overcome. He had countless poems stored away to read to her, and more closely to resemble a poet he had let his hair grow long and wavy, like Professor Cortez'. But that evening, when he contrived to spirit her away from the revelers for a tender moment in the patio, Eleonora took one glance at him and stiffened with distaste. "What is the matter?" Julio faltered.

Eleonora shook a decided head. "It's your hair," she said flatly. "Whatever possessed you to let it grow like that? I can't bear men with long hair."

Julio swallowed miserably and thought that her delicate white skin and blue eyes had never looked more desirable. His favorite poem, which began, "O morning star . . . enchantress of all who behold you," for the moment went unread. But next day, early, Julio made hasty tracks for the nearest barbershop.

From this time on, Arana's courtship of Eleonora was relentless, implacable and single-minded. But sadly he had to acknowledge that what set her apart from other girls in his eyes was a potent factor weighing against him: her proud free spirit. Deeply involved with study and teaching and musical festivals, Eleonora had no time or inclination for courtship. She held a trump card then dealt to few Peruvian women: she could support herself by teaching and so retain her independence. She wanted a career, not the trammels of marriage with a small-town trader. Thus Arana's mind was resolved. There was a world beyond Rioja; to win her he must set out to conquer it.

Now Arana's journeys on the rubber rivers became a matter of monthly routine. But at first, until he had prospected the terrain, he stuck to the trade he knew. As a confident eighteen-year-old hat salesman, he traveled for the first time down the tawny 3,900-mile length of the Amazon, the great moving inland sea, its ultimate banks in places sixty miles apart. From Iquitos, in Peru, he traveled by steamboat past Manaus to Pará, only ninety miles from the Atlantic Ocean, and the brash noisy towns that were rising like shooting stars along the river taught him much about men.

Arana himself liked best to recall his triumphs over the openhanded improvident Brazilians with the story of his first visit to Pará. Haunting the pavement cafés with a selection of his finest hats, he made the initial mistake of approaching men who drank alone—and found his refusal rate depressingly high. By degrees it dawned on him that not only was he rating his goods too low, he was overlooking the Brazilians' love of ostentation.

"If you had a hat worth £5," Arana would relate, "you asked a Brazilian £25, and you asked him when he was drinking with a friend. Not only would he pay the £25, to prove he could afford it, but the friend would buy one, too, for that same reason."

Work done, he sat closeted in cramped hotel rooms, pouring out his heart to Eleonora. By 1884 she had moved on to Yurimaguas to open the first state school and to her grandmother's house, where she lodged, letters from Julio flooded in by every mail. At last, sensing that she wavered, he set out for Yurimaguas to lay siege to her heart, and now fate conspired to aid him. In the night the riverboat struck a hidden balk of timber and sank like a stone.

For the first time but not the last, Julio Arana fought for his life, battling the Amazon's remorseless four-mile-an-hour current. From the darkness came the pitiful cries of the drowning, and Arana, grappling to salvage his choicest samples, was sucked under by a terrifying vortex of water. Somehow, his powerful arms cleaving the whirlpool, he struggled clear, then, to conserve his strength, clung tightly to an overhanging tree while the breath labored back into his lungs. At last, coolly, with measured stroke, he swam to the bank with his samples intact.

Already in Yurimaguas the bells were tolling, the news borne upriver by the smoke signals of the tribes, and among the dead they mourned was Julio Arana. Yet when he arrived at Eleonora's house dripping but alive, she greeted him calmly; only for a fleeting second had she believed that he was dead. But as they worked side by side in the kitchen, drying and ironing the sodden hats, Eleonora was forced to examine her motives for the first time. Why had her heart seemed to stop when the first news came—and why had she firmly disbelieved it from then on?

Meanwhile, as always on his journeys, Arana kept on reading, anything that was nourishment for his restless driving brain: mythology, drama, poetry, above all, of rubber and its history. He had a great hunger to bend the world to his will, and knowledge could be power. Aboard the three-tiered river steamboats on which he traveled, old-time Mississippi stern-wheelers that the passengers called "birdcages," Arana sat apart from the others, hating the night-long poker games, the drinking, the vulgar, sweaty good fellowship. He sat reading, eternally reading, and as he turned the pages, rubber, as it had seized the minds and imaginations of other men, began to take hold on his.

It had been in 1745 that Charles Marie de La Condamine, a scientist assigned to South America by King Louis XV of France to measure a degree of the meridian, had reported to the Parisian Academy of Sciences on the strange uses to which Ecuador's Omagua Indians put the white sticky sap of the tree called *cahuchu:* the tree that weeps. Bottles, boots, even hollow balls and syringes, were fashioned from this strange substance, which was to pass into the French language as "caoutchouc" (rubber).

As far back as 1495, Columbus' Spaniards in Haiti had seen the natives playing with elastic balls, but De La Condamine's report now focused the attention of Europe and its scientists. All through the eighteenth century, Portugal was importing quantities of rubber hats, capes and bags from Brazil, though the sticky substance remained a curiosity, used primarily for primitive playthings. As late as 1770, Dr. Joseph Priestley, the discoverer of oxygen, wrote a minor footnote to the history of the gum: sold in half-inch cubes for three shillings apiece, it was ideal for erasing lead-pencil marks. Thought to hail from the East Indies, it was known from this time on as "India rubber."

Despite its intriguing potential, rubber's progress, for seventy years thereafter, was marked by meteoric ups and downs. In the 1830's, "rubber fever" briefly hit the United States, as the populace clamored for overshoes made of the magic new gum from the Amazon. Britain set more store by rain capes, which Charles Macintosh, a thrifty Glasgow chemist, had evolved in 1823, using naphtha, a waste product of the local gas works, as a solvent to convert rubber into a pliable coating for fabric. Yet though manufacturers esteemed rubber for purposes as diverse as beer-engine pumps, fire hoses, catheters and fishing boots, its uses were still but a drop in the bucket. Not until the winter's day in 1839 when Charles Goodyear, an ailing, sallow-cheeked inventor, accidentally touched a gum-and-sulfur mixture to a hot stove lid in a Massachusetts village store to find it charred like leather was the riddle of rubber finally solved.

From a maverick substance which froze iron-hard in winter, then melted to a malodorous glue in summer, Goodyear had evolved vulcanized or weatherproof rubber—and from this historic moment the Amazon rubber rush was on.

By 1888, one year after 24-year-old Julio had at last stood with Eleonora before the altar in the Church of Our Lady of the Snows, Yurimaguas, the future seemed boundless. The costly wedding present, which perilously reduced his savings, a gold bracelet inset with a sapphire, now seemed more than justified. Six thousand miles away in Belfast, Northern Ireland, a prosperous bushy-bearded veterinary surgeon, John Boyd Dunlop, anxious to help his ten-year-old son Johnny win a local tricycle race, had perfected the pneumatic rubber tire.

For Arana, these next years confirmed his cherished belief that he was a man of destiny. Never once did it strike him that his preoccupation with rubber could alienate him from Eleonora; for her he had embraced this strange new life. Along with one of his brothers-in-law, Pablo Zumaeta, a virile red-haired giant of eighteen with sparkling blue eyes, he opened a trading post at Tarapoto, a forgotten 6,000-strong community on the rubber-rich Huallaga River. Though he and Eleonora made their home twelve miles away, in the foothills town of Lamas, Julio did not at first neglect her. Each day he rode through the forests to the trading post; each night at dusk he rode back.

It was a primitive pioneer life. Along these rivers some rubber trails were so isolated only the goodwill of wandering hunters saw mail or messages delivered. On shallow tributaries, some ports had no steamboat service for six long months of the dry season. The only talk was of rubber prices, always months out of date, and attacks by Indians who resented the coming of the rubber men to their forest domains. Soon after setting up at Tarapoto, this hostility almost cost Arana his life.

It was the second time he had battled for survival in this alien land. Had it not been a Friday his chances would have been slim, but on Fridays the bachelor Pablo always rode back to spend the weekend with Julio and his bride. It was nearing sundown, and as their horses labored up the steep incline from forest to foothills, between bluffs crested with wild pine, there was no sound but the jingle of bridles, the horses' muffled breathing. Julio, riding ahead, had no warning of what was to come; briefly, he glimpsed two copper-skinned bodies, smeared with crimson paint, arcing like swimmers from the bluff. Then their impact drove the breath from his body; he hit the rocky trail with a spine-jarring thump.

Dimly he heard the thin high snickering as his horse reared, and the thunderclap of hooves, but the heavy poncho he wore against the mountain cold had ridden up to smother him and pinion his arms. Then abruptly the flailing pressure of bodies eased and he saw Pablo, spurring forward, vault from his pinto at a gallop to rush into the fray. Scrambling to his feet he and Pablo stood shoulder to shoulder and there was a brief and bloody bout of fisticuffs before the Indians fled as fleetly as they had come.

From this encounter, Julio bore away two resolutions. He wanted men around him united by blood ties, men who, whatever their shortcomings, he could literally trust with his life, and in the years that followed he was to find work not only for Pablo but for five more of Eleonora's relatives and for his own brothers Francisco and Lizardo. For nothing, neither Indians nor white men nor disease nor the latent horrors of the jungle, would deflect him from what he had set out to do.

Almost twenty-five years of Arana's life were devoted to the jungle, and from first to last he hated it. In Rioja, the changing seasons merged into a long golden spring day, the temperature never above 78 degrees, the air clean and cool from the mountains. Along the rubber rivers, the air was torrid and sulfur-smelling; a damp shadowy twilight blotted out the sun. Sand flies raised purple-black blisters on Arana's hands and face; the shrill cries of jungle birds fretted his nerves. The air was an eternal vapor bath of heat whose monotony was inescapable: even the ceaseless hissing of rain on the river from November through February did nothing to abate it.

Within days a leather toilet case sprouted a green, downlike mold. Half an hour after firing, a nickel-plated Smith and Wesson revolver needed an oil bath to dislodge the rust. Worst of all was the stupefying boredom that drove men to the brink of madness. On the Upper Amazon a steamboat's whistle brought every man in the township screaming into the street, greeting fresh provisions and mail from home with volley after volley from their Winchesters.

But personal considerations did not stop Arana now. The Amazon Valley was a veritable spiderweb of waters, more than 1,100 major tributaries—"those great moving roads," Pascal had called them. Some, like the Purús, 2,190 miles long and the 1,500-mile Negro River, were larger than the Rhine. The 1,800-mile Madeira itself fanned into ninety lesser tributaries. On many such waterways, the Yavarí, the Purús, the Acre, Julio was the pioneer trader, supplying everything from canned goods for the rubber men to French cologne for their half-breed mistresses, accepting rubber as yet unharvested as his final payment. And always he stipulated that the price obtaining was the market price on the date of the agreement.

Sometimes the price of rubber had slumped by the time the shipment reached Europe, but more often, in these boom years, it had risen. Thus Julio netted a 400-percent profit on the goods he had advanced. And month after month the "black gold" flowed down these rivers to the white city, Manaus, whose splendid natural harbor on the Negro River had made it the Amazon Valley's great distributing port and export center.

Still Arana was not satisfied. His probing spirit sought to explore every aspect of rubber. One day in 1809, a few months after the birth of his daughter Alicia, he announced decisively to Pablo: "Get ready for a trip. We're going into this rubber business in earnest."

Pablo was puzzled. Indolent by nature, he often found Arana's insatiate ambition beyond him. The Tarapoto trading post was doing well, if not spectacularly; he could not see the object of becoming more deeply involved. Arana now enlightened him. Near Yurimaguas he had bought a small rubber trail to exploit on his own behalf. But first he and Pablo were bound for Ceará, in northeastern Brazil, to recruit a force of tappers.

Arana chose shrewdly. In these years, there were workers and to spare in Ceará. From the pitiless 800,000 square miles of Brazil's great dust bowl, often beset by drought for eight months on end, the rubber barons recruited most of their labor: the people known throughout Brazil as the *flagelados*, the scourged ones. In this barren land, where nothing grew more than thirty feet above its thirsty roots, the highways to the coast were choked with mass exoduses of 400,000 people, begging from door to door in clouds of blinding dust, willing to take ship anywhere where food and work abounded.

In 1877, again in 1888, *flagelados* had flocked to the Amazon Valley, happy to travel third-class on the lower deck, their hammocks slung among the cattle pens. On his river journeys, Arana had often seen them: hollow-cheeked, gap-toothed men clad in checkered cotton shirts and pantaloons, with weather-beaten straw hats, lining the rails with lewd gestures to every passing vessel. But the streets of Manaus rarely saw them. To prevent them from jumping ship the steamboats anchored a mile offshore.

Few *flagelados* then realized they were exchanging one bondage for another. At Yurimaguas, each of the twenty rubber tappers whom Arana and Pablo signed on were already £30 in debt for their passage money from Ceará. Along the wooden jetty, where canoes and barges tied up, they marched to Arana's white-painted trading post perched on poles above the river: a store pungent with dried salt fish, coffee and paraffin, its beams a small forest of machetes, rifles and fishing lines. It was here they collected their three months' supply of goods—food, a Winchester and ammunition, buckets and calabashes for latex—worth perhaps £4 in all. But in Arana's bulky ledgers, each tapper was debited for upward of £70—a debt he could wipe out only by selling Arana rubber he had yet to harvest.

But Arana had studied the system along the riverbanks; he knew he was safe enough. Few men in the ensuing three months could collect enough rubber to cancel their debts—and by then they needed fresh supplies. There was no time to hunt or fish or raise crops outside their flimsy palm-leaf huts; the winning of rubber swallowed up every daylight hour. Come the next load of supplies, the debt mounted higher yet. Rarely did any man repay what he owed; few, as long as they lived, saw hard cash for their labors.

Dawn was the hour when Arana's tappers first hit the trail: it was then, following the first oblique incision of the soft iron machete, that the latex flowed most freely. Armed with hundreds of small tin cups, like beggars' bowls, they inched painfully from tree to tree, hacking at underbrush and lianas, striving to reach trees set a hundred tantalizing yards apart through deep jungle. Sometimes, clamping the cups in position, they worked in darkness so intense only the light of kerosene head lamps, clamped on their heads like old-fashioned vizors, revealed the latex, welling silently like white emulsion. Ahead lay six hours of this labor, for though most tappers' trails were roughly elliptical, they wound as far as a mile inland, dotted with as many as two hundred trees, and the way was a stumbling, blundering purgatory over narrow log bridges spanning malarial creeks.

But in time the tappers knew every inch of their 100-acre beats as if they had traversed them blindfold. They knew which trees were "five gallon cows," virgin trees still rich in latex, and which were "caimans," worn-out trees, their bark coarse and gnarled. By 11 A.M., a first circuit of the trail saw them back at their jungle homes for a hasty snack of dried meat and coffee, but by noon they were on the trail again—this time to collect the morning's latex in galvanized two-gallon buckets.

Then, in the smoke huts near their shelters, they built smudge fires of oily nuts from the urucuri palm and the choking, curing process began. Armed with long, broad-bladed wooden paddles, they dipped the blades into a calabash of coagulating latex, twirling them through the dense, bitter-smelling smoke. A dozen turns and a thin layer of fine rubber was forming. Again they plied their paddles, and slowly the skin of rubber masking the paddle grew thicker, until the calabash was dry. All this ate up three hours' time and called for up to 1,500 arm movements.,

Day by day the morning's tapping, the afternoon's curing, went on—until the time when every tapper hefted the solid black balls of cured latex, weighing up to two hundred pounds, onto burlap shoulder saddles and stumbled to their canoes for the long journey downriver to Arana's trading post. Few had any clear idea of what rate of pay was due to them, or that when top-grade wild rubber was 4s a pound, Arana paid them a maximum of fivepence but more often a penny. And fewer still could fathom why Arana wanted the rubber, for none had ever seen a bicycle, let alone an automobile.

The system had piled up dizzy fortunes—but it was still too slow for Arana. Worse, he found that the tappers visiting the store sought to forget their bondage in drink and quickly grew quarrelsome. The ugly climax was a night when the storeman refused them credit and Arana, busy checking off supplies on a launch at the water's edge, faced a drink-crazed stampede of tappers intent on casting him bodily into the river. Again it was Pablo's brawn that saved the day, but Arana had had enough.

"We've got to try something bigger," he told Pablo firmly. Within a week, despite his brother-in-law's bewilderment, he had sold out, transferring the tappers' debts to another trail owner.

Still Pablo could not see it. It was the classic pattern for getting rich all along the Amazon. A man used his profits to buy more land, indent more labor, and in time created an empire. But Arana, dissatisfied, sought a faster way to fortune. The experts said an average tract of forest contained eighty nonrubber trees to every wild Hevea—a criminal waste of man-hours. Foremost in every tapper's mind was the thought of flight, which meant hirelings with Winchester .44's posted in day and night shifts, on the lookout for fugitives. The most willing tapper could not produce more than twenty-five pounds of smoked rubber in a twelve-hour day. And even a fine 100-foot-high wild rubber tree in its prime yielded little more than three pounds of rubber a year.

From December to June, when the rains came, a gleaming gray expanse of water 150,000 miles square carpeted the valley. Monkeys, snakes and birds took to the tall timber. In these months the latex of the wild rubber trees would not congeal. Day after day, the tappers lounged in their hammocks, smoking, dozing, dreaming of far-off freedom, their debts mounting still higher.

To Arana the economics made no sense. The higher the tapper's debts the greater his servitude—but each man, balanced against the purchase of the estate, had cost him an outlay of £100. All through the rains he must supply them with trade goods. Each month, his own debts to Manaus' wholesale merchants went higher still; some, charging 12-percent interest, gave credit of up to £40,000. In turn, the merchants owed money to the banks and rubber importers in New York and London, but these were men at the pinnacle of power, thinking big, living big. Someday, Julio Arana vowed, he would walk with these men.

And by August, 1907, Arana had tangible proof that he had made it. His Manaus office on Marshal Deodoro Street now bristled like a campaign headquarters with colored wall-size maps of his territories. "See," he would tell newcomers haughtily, his thumb jerking upward, "here are *my* rivers," for on six of them he held squatter's rights over an area larger than France, rights enforced by the constant patrols of twenty-three armed trading launches, designed and built for him in Liverpool and Port Glasgow.

Already in his own lifetime he was a legend, a man whose giant step into the big time drew others to the far-flung rivers. Most of them never came back, their trunks growing thick with the dust of years in the attics of Manaus' Grand Hotel, but there were always newcomers who knew their luck was in. As far away as Pará, men told enviously of how Arana in 1896 bought out his then trading partner, the sophisticated Frenchman, Carlos Mourraille, becoming overnight head of a powerful firm of importers and merchant bankers. The heavy boxes of gold sovereigns lining his office were an unfamiliar commodity, but Arana, after long nights of study, mastered both accountancy and banking.

His prodigious industry, his contempt for Manaus' free-spending "colonels," led journalists to dub him "The Abel of the Amazon." From 1896, the year he moved his family to a fine ten-room house at Iquitos, on the Peruvian Amazon, he had made his credo plain. Though a family group of twenty-four often sat down to dinner, no business contact ever got past his threshold. The nearest thing to luxury was a cow grazing on a waste plot to ensure fresh milk for his children. And in place of glittering *azulejo* tiles, Arana faced his house with the motto, carved in stone, that was now his watchword: "Activity, Constancy, Work."

Awed, men avowed that Julio Arana was unconquerable: one incident just prior to the Iquitos move became legend. Arana's family, then at Yurimaguas, saw little of him, but each time he returned, Eleonora found him harder, more withdrawing, oppressed by the cheapness of life. Still the urge to triumph over his environment gave him no rest, and for eight months he ranged the Yavarí River, "the river of death," doling out goods and money in exchange for unharvested rubber, gambling on the European market price, piling up his fortune.

One morning he had the queer sensation that the steamboat deck was melting beneath his feet. His legs grew weak and limp. A strange torpor spread upward from his ankles to his belly and his ribs seemed clamped by an inescapable vise. He retained enough presence of mind to jab his thumbnail clinically into his thigh. Though the flesh pitted deeply he felt nothing. Arana knew the long months of canned food and dried beans were taking their revenge. Beriberi—which men called "Yavarí fever"—had set in.

Doggedly he battled the disease with filtered water and lemon juice, but his powerful arms dwindled like sticks. One night, too weak to crawl from his hammock, his belly so bloated he could barely draw breath, his skin wet with exuding lymph, he felt death come very close. Aboard the steamboat the only sounds were the sleepy curses of late-night poker players, using castor-oil beans for chips, the rhythmic splash of the ten-pound lead: "*Veinte . . . dieziocho . . .*": only eighteen feet of water between the keel and the sandbanks below.

One of the cardplayers spoke matter-of-factly, quite close at hand: "Our friend Arana is going to die tonight."

Another voice dissented: "I think tomorrow night—he'll last till then." At once a third interposed: "Will you bet on that? I'll give you ten to one on his dying tomorrow morning."

Immobile, the life ebbing from him, Arana heard the odds mount steadily: the Brazilians' inveterate love of gambling made the wager too good to miss. Yet their words galvanized his once-powerful frame like electrical therapy. If only to prove these know-alls wrong, he was going to live. One day later, when the steamboat reached Yurimaguas, he was so weak that they bore him gently ashore in his hammock, but he was still breathing. Though there was no doctor nearer than Iquitos, over 200 miles away, slowly, as Eleonora treated him with infusions of forest herbs, he came back from the edge of eternity.

It was six months before Arana was cured and he had to learn to walk again with the tumbling steps of his second daughter, four-year-old Angelica. But once more he had cheated death. In 1907, recalling those men who had prematurely written him off, Arana realized that he had outlived them all.

But now a change came over him. To his contempt for death was added a contempt for life and for his fellows. One man who knew him still recalls: "If you tried to get too friendly, it was like a shutter coming down." His intimates were sycophants and hangers-on: men like Carlos Rey de Castro, Manaus' Peruvian Consul General, whose work on land concessions with the Peruvian Government was so useful Arana's company allowed him a running debt of £4,600.

Yet small men who courted favors were rarely permitted a dignified refusal. One trader, seeking an extension of credit, stood pleading in the Manaus office until he realized Arana was slowly advancing on him, shaking with contemptuous laughter, his eyes, as always when angry, half-closed. A sudden thrust of Arana's iron-hard belly sent the man tumbling backward. With a second thrust, he teetered to the threshold. One more, and he sprawled ignominiously in the dust of the street.

One thing embittered Arana above all: the belief that Eleonora had turned against him. Though once they had been so close they talked over every projected deal, perversely, when the long illness was past, they drew apart. "Get out of rubber," Eleonora had urged then. "Get out before it's too late. Believe me Julio, there's no future for you up the Yavarí."

Arana was too stubborn to see that only concern for his health prompted this counsel. He judged her contrary and feminine, and though her pleading changed subtly to nagging, it was of no avail. Events would not decide his fate, he controlled his own destiny, and though he, too, had plans to quit the Amazon, he would not admit even this much to Eleonora. From 1896 she never ceased to reproach him, but Julio, changing the name of his firm to "J. C. Arana Brothers," went on to build up valuable trading connections in Lisbon, Paris, Manchester, above all, London.

There was no doubting Arana was right: the world was clamoring for rubber. Now, in 1907, twelve years had passed since the historic Paris-Bordeaux car race, when the "lunatic invention" of the Michelin brothers, André and Édouard, had proved that vehicles on pneumatic tires were no longer a dream. It was the dawn of the Motor Age, when men in goggles and ladies in dusters, pancake hats, chic tulle veils tied beneath their chins, were as much a part of the landscape as the swirling clouds of blue smoke their Darracqs and De Dion Boutons trailed behind them. To be sure, gasoline was 6d a gallon, but this hardly troubled crowned heads like King Edward VII, with his claret-colored Mercedes, or King Leopold of the Belgians, who humored his mistress Cleo de Mérode by outfitting his touring car with high-mounted, tulip-shaped seats of red morocco leather. Soon United States car production would reach an all-time peak of 63,500 cars and many cars used £50 worth of tires each year, buses £200.

Arana knew he could not pull out yet, though by degrees he was getting ready to do so. As the first stage he had transplanted his family from the Amazon, booking them passages on the Booth Line steamship *Ambrose*, en route, via Madeira, to a rented villa in Biarritz. Now the Iquitos house stood empty; for almost three years Arana himself had been a fixture in the austere apartment above his Manaus office, working from 6 A.M. to 1 P.M., snatching brief breaks for meals at the nearby Grand Hotel. Though the family, from 17-year-old Alicia to Luiz, aged two, had not been long gone, he already sensed reproach in their letters and messages: when their birthdays fell due he now cabled money to buy toys. As recently as June 2, their wedding anniversary, he had cabled a gift of money to Eleonora, too.

Years ago he had always arrived back from steamboat trips bearing presents with much thought behind them: toys from the bazaar, fluffy kittens, parakeets, even tame herons. Now the children seemed hurt because amid the biggest gamble of his life he forgot to inquire about the health of their black poodle Gypsy. Arana thought they would never realize it was for their sake he slaved like this, to spare them the grinding years of travail he had known.

But at last, he believed, he had hit on the solution that would soon enable him to join them in Europe and spelled security for them all: the most venturesome act of filibustering since Henry Wickham had snatched the rubber seeds. With the aid of 600 hired gunmen he had little by little annexed 12,000 square miles of disputed territory.

At 8:30 A.M. the trees on Manaus' Cathedral Square cast long shadows. Across the harbor a faint breeze stirred; the air was cleaner and cooler than at any other time of the day. On Eduardo Ribeiro Avenue the sweet-toned Swiss municipal clock, raised on a column of pink and silver stone as ornate as a wedding-cake decoration, tolled the half hour.

Soon the sun-slashed pavements on the eastern side of the streets would grow empty. Men, if they walked at all, hugged the western side, though within minutes the backs of their white linen jackets grew dark with sweat. On fashionable streets, all sound muted to a gentle antistrophe: the gentle creak of rocking chairs as the ladies of the house took their ease, the swishing of wet brooms as servants bent to their chores.

At No. 32 Marshal Deodoro Street, the Chamber of Commerce building, more than a hundred rubber barons had gathered for their daily morning meeting. Across the elaborate zebra-striped flooring of the main salon, patterned in dark acapú wood and yellow cherry, they gossiped in little knots beneath the whirring fans, sipping demitasses of coffee, Brazilian style—"as black as night, as sweet as a kiss, as strong as love, as hot as hell" was the approved formula.

Many, like Arana, had been working since 6 A.M. and this, until an early lunch at 11 A.M., was the one break from their desks. Dining early, at 5 P.M., they often worked on until 9 P.M. or later. And no man even took coffee before first checking the day's prices on the bulletin board—this morning, top-grade wild rubber stood around 4/9d a pound—and on current shipping movements. Five ships were this day docking; the *Lanfranc* from Liverpool and the *Basil* out of Galveston would sail on that evening's tide.

Moving from group to group this morning, Julio Arana, as always, felt a secret surge of pride. Among those present were names he had revered since he was a small-time river trader: tycoons who, in the stampede of the nineties, had sight unseen bought vast tracts of land, staking everything on the hunch that they had cornered "black gold," not worthless jungle. From Ceará, in a year of drought, the dark burly Manoel Vincente Carioca had himself fled upriver to work as a rubber tapper; somehow he had contrived to wipe out his debts, using his savings to open a small Manaus store. Now, though he still walked with the tapper's "jungle slouch," the 46-year-old Carioca was overlord of four hundred tappers, owning so much land on the

Gregório River its extent was mere guesswork. Pressed for a figure, Carioca just smiled and shrugged: he knew only that it took a steamboat seven days to cover the frontage.

He, too, spoke of the Gregório as *"my* river," but Arana knew that he was Carioca's equal.

Such men were monarchs more absolute than most Eastern kings; to enter their water highways was akin to piracy, and the limits of the trails lying behind those highways had been charted with blood. On the Madeira River one rubber baron, proud of the fruit and vegetables he raised, sent a fusillade of shots across the bows of every passing craft—not to challenge their progress but to halt them so that he could dower them with fresh garden produce. But not all were so benevolent. On the Madre de Dios River, one merchant had currently evolved a diabolical way of augmenting his labor supply: a stud farm that kept six hundred Indian slave girls for breeding purposes.

With the power of kings, many spent like kings. The tall blond Alfredo Arruda, whose trails stretched for thirty-five miles along the Yumary River, had lavished a small fortune on fronting his Manaus town house in translucent Carrara marble. Tough old Luis de Silva Gomes, whose ten-million-acre estate on the Purús yielded five hundred tons of rubber each year, was still so jealous of his financial standing that a detective trying to protect him from fraud got short shrift. Waiting on Gomes, the investigator broke the news that a cocotte the colonel didn't even know had pledged his credit for a £1,400 diamond necklace at The Big Door jewelers and was preparing to decamp. Gomes was out-raged—not by the swindle, but by the suggestion he ought to prosecute.

"And have everyone doubt my credit?" he stormed. "Rather than that she can have a £14,000 necklace."

Yet nearly all were now outspent by the Austrian Consul, Waldemar Scholz, whose severe pince-nez and prim waxed mous-taches belied his profligate life. A onetime Stuttgart provision-store clerk, who had spectacularly made good as an importer, Scholz, within years, had blossomed into a twelve-room riverside

palace on Municipal Street, equipped with marina for yacht and
speedboat, a tame lion and phaetons and hackneys mounted by
liveried lackeys. Determined that Enrico Caruso should honor
Manaus' opera house, Scholz was as well known for his fruitless
long-distance cables to the singer as for his notorious Babylonian
parties*—when town girls like Trieste-born Sarah Lubousk and
her friend Janette took shower baths of iced vintage champagne
while the male guests crouched and lapped.

Not all were so flamboyant. At first glance Joaquim Gonçalves
Araújo—known always as "J.G."—was still the modest clerk,
with graying, close-cropped hair, who for thirty years had been
part of the Manaus scene. Yet ten years before Governor
Eduardo Ribeiro had created modern Manaus, Araújo had
worked to ensure the city's commercial future, slowly evolving
the giant entrepôt that loaded its rubber directly onto oceangoing
steamers, bypassing the middlemen of Pará on the delta. As
partner in a small trading store, it was J.G. who virtually evolved
the debt system that ensnared both trail owners and tappers,
coaxing local traders to accept more goods than that year's crop
would warrant, keeping the debt alive and fresh in his ledgers.

Even now there was little to show that the 47-year old Portuguese, a teetotaler who shunned tobacco, was feudal overlord of
500,000 acres of land on the upper Negro River. But whenever
J.G. announced, "I am going home"—which meant leaving his
shabby rented house for his beloved office—there was always a
small coterie of men idling on the sidewalk, anxious to keep step
and curry favor. And even Dom Frederico da Costa, Bishop of

---

* Over the years, some colorful legends have grown up around Manaus'
opera house—that not only did Caruso inaugurate the theater, on December
31, 1896, but that at varying times performers of the caliber of Sarah Bernhardt and Pavlova trod its boards. But according to his biographers,
Pierre V. Key and Bruno Zirato, *Enrico Caruso* (Boston: Little, Brown,
1922), during the winter of 1896, the tenor was appearing at the Mercadante
and the Bellini Theatres in Naples; his only Brazilian appearances—in 1903
and again in 1917—took him no nearer the Amazon than Rio de Janeiro.
During my time in Manaus, the theater's historian, Dr. Mario Ypiranga
Monteiro, told me that a scrutiny of every contract from 1896 on had sim-
ilarly revealed no trace of Pavlova or Sarah Bernhardt.

Manaus, humbly sought J.G.'s permission before visiting converts in Negro territory.

Only one man did Araújo fear: Germino Garrido y Otero, self-styled King of the Içana River, whose territory abutted his own. Along 100 miles of riverfront, this Spanish renegade had held sway since 1880 with a 400-strong army, many of them sired by his own loins, foiling all J.G.'s attempts to move into Içana country. Though Otero's countless sons and grandsons were Indian in feature, their manners were those of the hidalgos of old Seville; entering his presence they remained at attention until he gave them leave to speak, and each man kissed his hand before departing. Of like stripe was the Yaquirana River's Encarnación Rojas, a Campa Indian foundling from the forests of Peru, who took his name from the family that adopted him. Even in the sweltering Amazonian heat, Rojas, as absolute ruler of a tribe of four hundred Campas, rigidly observed the conventions. Togged out like a boulevardier, in black derby, black morning coat and mauve spats, he had already put twenty-one children through finishing school in Paris.

Most powerful of all these men was Colonel Nicolás Suárez, whose Bolivian rubber barony embraced 16 million acres. On the Beni River, the freebooting Suárez had built his own townships of Riberalta and Villa Bella; all rubber flowing down the Beni paid formidable tolls to travel a few hundred yards on his miniature railroad. From the eighties on, the seven Suárez brothers had struck boldly into savage Indian country to seek their rubber, prospecting where few traders dared penetrate, quelling the tribes with terrible retribution. Once, when a hail of arrows from hostile Caripúna Indians struck down his brother, Gregorio, Nicolás and his men avenged him with three long punitive expeditions into the forest. By the time they were done they had mowed down three hundred Caripúnas.

Only recently one newsman had estimated, "What Rockefeller is in the world of oil, so is Suárez in rubber." But only a formal Chamber of Commerce meeting could persuade the stocky, taciturn Bolivian, whose huge moustaches jutted from his upper lip like the long horns of a steer, to don collar and tie or go other than barefoot. Hating Manaus' champagne gaiety, he thrived on jerked beef, coarse baked bread and a daily bottle of Guinness stout; his one extravagance in forty-eight years had been the marble monument to his first wife, Constanza, set above the falls of the rapid-ridden Madeira River at Cachuela Esperanza. To drag those mighty blocks round the eighteen portages of the falls had cost months of labor, scores of lives.

So wealthy he controlled 10,000 employees, Suárez was still close-fisted enough to masquerade as one of his own peons, cadging tips from visiting strangers. Yet not long back he had refused a £900,000 offer for his business. Soon, as the boom neared fever-pitch, he would shrug off a £12,000,000 take-over.

But this morning the omnipotent Suárez was scrupulous to treat Arana as an equal. As they stood companionably sipping their demitasses, they chatted of a possible merger on at least one river, the Madre de Dios, where both had trading interests. Manaus' merchants knew Suárez would have crushed a lesser competitor without compunction—but in Arana's case he seemed eager to establish a profitable *modus vivendi*. Even J. G. Araújo, who despised most men present for "squandering a whole year's profit in one night of debauchery," took pains to exchange a word with Arana, discussing the opera house's forthcoming season. "He is a man of quite a different stamp—cultured and serious," was J.G.'s verdict to his cronies, for on the Amazon, Arana's vast library was a legend with men more attuned to balance sheets than bibliography.

It was manifest, too, all through the social get-together that Waldemar Scholz gave Arana the widest possible berth. Though Schloz, rated as a power in the chamber, was expected to be the next vice-president, he still feared Arana's cutting and openly voiced disapproval of his excesses with women.

Though Arana's success in the three years since opening his Manaus office had been phenomenal, it was not only his position as the city's sixth largest taxpayer that so impressed his peers. Nor was it his taste for litigation, though given any incentive the burly, bearded Peruvian instructed his Manaus lawyer, Dr. Solon Pinheiro, to sue at the drop of a hat. Even the corner he was fast building up in residential property, foreclosing on unsecured mortgages, did not rate him such cachet: it was his sudden international status.

Within days he was once more bound for London, a city from which he had returned only five months back, with a project that won the respect of every man present: the formation of a £1,000,-000 company.

As far back as the turn of the century, Julio César Arana had glimpsed this long-sought opportunity. In the year 1899 he had discovered a river so secret, so remote, that he foresaw a time when he could truly call it *"my* river."

This was the winding, tranquil, 1,000-mile-long Putumayo, which flowed into the Amazon almost 600 miles west of Manaus, 200 east of Iquitos. At this meeting point of the waters, the river was 600 yards wide and eight yards deep, and for three-quarters of its length it was navigable at high water by steamers of up to four-feet draught. But what riveted Arana's attention to this fertile forest land was its unique situation. Born as an infant ice-cold stream in the Cordilleras of the Colombian Andes, the Putumayo flowed for much of its length as a natural frontier between Colombia and Peru—a riverfront hotly contested by both nations.

Finally, in May, 1904, the two governments had patched up an agreement—then within three months both deemed it unacceptable. More high-level bickering, before both countries in September, 1905, had submitted their case for arbitration to Pope Pius X. On July 6, 1906, the *modus vivendi* then agreed came into operation.

From this date, pending final settlement of the delineation dispute, Peru and Colombia undertook to withdraw all military authority from Putumayo territory. Overnight, an area of

200,000 square miles became no-man's-land, a land beyond the law.

But in 1899, when Arana's launch *Callâo* first put-putted up the quiet river, only a few Colombians had settled on the contended terrain. Over tall cold drinks on their bungalow verandas, men like Crisostomo Hernandez and Benjamin Larrañaga told Arana they had been exploiting this river's rubber trails unopposed since the early eighties. The Peruvian's offer of trade goods in return for their latex seemed too good to miss. Obtaining supplies across the Andes from Pasto, Colombia, was slow and unreliable and the big rubber markets were, after all, downstream in Iquitos and Manaus. At the time Larrañaga and his brother Rafael, at their rubber depot, La Chorrera, were proud to receive partnerships in the newly established Iquitos business. Though they were slow to realize it, the control of their settlement now virtually passed to Julio Arana.

Neither of the Larrañaga brothers was strong on business acumen, and later lawyers were to apprise them that Arana's purchase of their holdings in 1905 for £25,000 was less than generous. The Calderón brothers at El Encanto, who sold out later, received the same cheerless advice. By December, 1905, Arana had acquired almost 12,000 square miles of Putumayo territory for £116,700. Only four settlers still held out.

In Arana's view, these men were in his way. He now saw the Putumayo's riches as his inalienable right, the key to his future. Given undisputed control of the region he could quit Manaus for good, transport Eleonora and the children to Europe, retire to join them. Day-to-day details could be left to Pablo, now running the Iquitos office, or even, at a pinch, to Lizardo in Manaus. But there were essential preliminaries. To begin with, Peru's President, the militant José Pardo, whose term of office was one long series of frontier wrangles, had called for written proof that Arana—and thus Peru—controlled the Putumayo. To ensure complete control called for more working capital than Arana could command—which made a public company inevitable. Moreover, there were rumors that the famed Percival Farquhar, master builder of South America, whose dream was the unification of all railroads south of Panama, sought Colombian aid to help him exploit the Putumayo.

Thus Arana pondered: Where should he turn for the capital that would worst Farquhar and ensure him his government's support on the Putumayo?

Although years earlier he had formed a New York company, Arana Bergman, he now faced a problem of logistics. No American shipping line operated beyond Pará on the Amazon delta. Wild rubber from the Putumayo, passing through Manaus, must be transshipped at Pará, incurring extra port and freight taxes besides. This would entail setting up a Pará office—another costly overhead. But since the 1890's, the twenty-odd fleet of the British-based Booth Steamship Company had operated a direct Liverpool-Manaus run, even sending lighter craft 1,300 miles on to Iquitos. Finally in 1902, in return for a sixty-year right to work the port, levy tolls and share in the customs revenue, the Booths, through a subsidiary company, began work on an engineering triumph—Manaus' magnificent £1,000,000 harbor. To combat a seasonal fifty-foot rise and fall of tide, towers seventy-two feet high soared from wharves supported by floating steel pontoons, their overhead two-way cables swinging four-ton loads a hundred yards to the shore as effortlessly as a change carrier in an old-fashioned drapery store.

Arana's resolution hardened. Arana Bergman, New York, was soon dissolved. From now on he would ship his rubber direct to the London market, and there form a public company, its ostensible purpose to acquire the assets of Arana Brothers.

Though he reached this decision as early as 1905, two problems still irked him. Four stubborn Colombians in Putumayo territory —David Serrano, Hipólito Perez, Gabriel Martinez and his partner Antonio Ordoñez—would not sell out, their resolve stiffened by Iquitos' Colombian Consul, German Velez, who had dared journey upriver to urge his countrymen to stand fast. Then, too, he needed a yearly increasing output of rubber to tempt prospective shareholders—though this setback was being overcome. By

1905, over one million pounds of rubber had left the Putumayo—
more than double the output for 1903.

For labor, Arana relied, like the Colombians before him, on the
cooperation of the forest Indians who peopled the region—the
Boras, the Andokes, the Ocainas, the Huitotos. But there was no
bond among these tribes to unite them against the rubber men, no
intertribal language—and though the Boras, courageous, firmly
muscled men, with near-Mongolian features, had been prone to
resist, the Huitotos were as tractable as could be. Almost 40,000
strong, they were a mild, inoffensive tribe, clad in beaten-bark
loincloths, who treated their womenfolk with rare respect.

To be sure, the painstaking, semiskilled work of the rubber
tappers would have been beyond them—but all grades of rubber
fetched tempting prices. And Arana's newfound terrain was rich
in unexploited Castilla trees, an inferior grade of wild rubber that
traders called "Peruvian Slab," widely used for scores of household articles: bath mats, garden hoses, children's toys. Even the
simple Huitotos had quickly learned to track down the Castilla—
first scoring V channels in the tree's bark so that the latex drained
into a trench scooped round the bole, next rolling the felled
trunk, ringed with incisions, into a shallow pit, coagulating the
final flow of latex with soap and potassium before packing it into
long, unwieldy, thirty-pound bundles. In time the trees would
become extinct—but the death of each Castilla might yield up to
a hundred pounds of rubber.

A relentless organizer, Arana saw one drawback to the Colombians' system: a lack of hawk-eyed supervisors. Now, along an
invisible grapevine, word spread that Putumayo territory offered
good money to all with urgent reasons to seek a change of air:
men like the Bolivian, Armando Normand, the Colombian,
Rodolfo Rodriguez, and the Peruvians, Abelardo Agüero and
José Fonseca, both anxious to postpone a meeting with the Lima
police. As squads of them set to work training 400 teen-age
Indians handpicked for overseers' duties, in 1904, Arana sent
Normand on a trip to the British island colony of Barbados to
recruit two hundred West Indian wardens.

To put bona fide British subjects under two-year contracts to an ostensible British company was, to Arana, the masterstroke.

At Manaus, on their way upriver, some of the Barbadians heard stories of the region that caused a change of heart; forcing their way ashore, they begged for immediate repatriation. But Arana's name carried weight in Manaus, and the acting British Vice-Consul could find no escape clause in their contracts. Summoning a Brazilian police contingent, he shooed the Barbadians back on board under armed escort.

By 1906, Arana had built up a formidable police force, but he was careful to inform his government in Lima that in the event of Colombia breaking the *modus vivendi* his men were Peruvian patriots first, company employees second. "Have 500 men armed with Winchesters" ran one cable to President Pardo's Chancellory, "Essential you send Mannlichers. Sufficient personnel will await arrival our troops to stage combined operation against Colombian invasion."

And while yet more rubber was ferried down the river—almost 1,400,000 pounds in 1906—few travelers now went either up or down. Except on Arana-owned steamboats, there was no entry to the Putumayo and no means of exit—and passages were never granted without a permit signed by an Arana agent.

For Arana had seen the red light. If ever the time was ripe to clean up and get out, it was now: ahead he saw only the ruin of Manaus and the Amazon, the triumph of the Asian rubber plantations. Over thirty years, as the white city boomed, there had been endless trial and error on the other side of the world. The 70,000 seeds from the Tapajós River were still inch-high seedlings in Kew's hothouses when Henry Wickham sat down in Dr. Joseph Hooker's study to write a nine-page memo to the India office on the vagaries of wild rubber. Amid the technicalities, two points stood out as diamond-clear: rubber trees that grew on low-lying ground yielded only poor-quality latex. Most Amazon travelers, spying them close to the banks, assumed that Heveas thrived under such conditions—never penetrating inland to the high plateaus to find the top-grade trees that Wickham had sought. "From all I have read," mused Wickham, with strange prophecy, "Malaya will most likely have the climatic conditions needed."

Ironically, the pioneer's preaching fell on deaf ears. Barely had the seedlings reached Ceylon's Peradeniya Gardens than forestry budgets were slashed, prompted by the sudden fall of the rupee. Wickham's £700 fee from Kew was quickly swallowed up by ill-starred coffee and tobacco plantations in North Queensland, and his cogent report, no longer an India Office concern, gathered dust for twenty years in a bureaucrat's pigeonhole. The vital factor of altitude remained a mystery. When the Colonial Office asked Kew which colonies might best try rubber, the Royal Botanic Gardens went on record: "In Brazil the tree is found on flat ground contiguous to streams."

Convinced the Amazon Valley was one vast swamp whose plants thrived in semiaquatic conditions, Ceylon's botanists made little headway. Sixteen years after Wickham's seed snatch, the first major site selected for a trial plantation was land recently flooded near the Kaluganga River, where the rainfall touched 170 inches a year. As a result, following three days' flooding, 30,000 young plants were wiped out.

And even though the bulk of Wickham's young plants had thrived in Ceylon's botanical gardens, curators found it hard to give away their seed: the island's planters, oriented to tea, had scant faith in rubber. Malay's coffee-minded planters felt the same. The few who were eager to get rich quick wrought havoc among the trees—working them over with cutlasses, studding them with ten-inch nails, felling every tree that did not fill a bucket after one tapping. And everywhere ignorance of rubber was as profound. One New Guinea planter, pressed to give it a trial, turned the idea down flat: in America, he had heard, at a cost of 1d per pound, they were now mining the stuff. In Borneo, one high official sent some Dyak headhunters swarming up the trunks of some fast-maturing trees to quest for rubber. When they had peered among the topmost leaves and found nothing, he ordered the destruction of a hundred Heveas.

Aptly, it was a 33-year-old Hooker protégé, Kew-trained

The 150-room Grand Hotel Internacional in Manaus (*above*) was locally described as "the finest in Christendom." Among the city's eighteen modistes' and men's outfitting establishments was Old England (*below*). (*Photos: Author's Collection*)

All-night Manaus bars like the High Life dispensed champagne, Scotch and even caviar — at prices four times higher than in London or New York. (*Author's Collection*)

The carnival in Manaus in 1908, when the city went wild.
(*Author's Collection*)

Thirty years after Henry Alexander Wickham (*above*) smuggled 70,000 wild rubber seeds from the Amazon to London's Kew Gardens, Manaus still held tight to its world monopoly. Often 5,000 fortune seekers (*below*) flocked ashore in a single week. (*Upper photo: J. B. Steadman; lower photo: Author's Collection*)

Henry Ridley, who achieved the breakthrough. From 1888, as head of Singapore's botanical gardens, the indefatigible Ridley lived, dreamed and breathed rubber—embarking on a ten-year program of scientific cultivation and tapping, with a hundred virgin trees. Hampered by a meager budget of £100 a year, "Rubber" Ridley, as the planters called him, had first to collect his latex in cigarette tins, coagulating it with acetic acid. But his final evolution of the "herringbone" cut, first used by the wild tribes of Perak for liming birds, changed the fortunes of the rubber industry overnight.

Until this time, botanists had thought that trees could be tapped only at two-year intervals and then only after a long period of growth—up to twenty-five years, some said. But Ridley proved that with care trees from the age of four could be milked daily for latex, and from then on commercial interest grew keen. By November, 1895, his zeal had talked two young coffee planters, Ronald and Douglas Kindersley, into a sample two-acre estate at Inch Kenneth, Selangor, western Malaya. To London the next year, to fetch a price of 2/8d a pound, went blocks of clear, amber-colored rubber from Malaya's first plantation.

As the twentieth century dawned, Dutch planters in Java and Sumatra, profiting by specimen seeds the British had donated them, prepared to follow suit.

Years later, in 1907, all along the Malayan Peninsula, the coffee estates were going down like weeds before a sickle. Savannas of primordial jungle met the same fate, withering for weeks under a hot bright sun until coolies moved in to fire them with oil-filled bamboos, the ten-acre blocks burning like cities in the night. As the charred bitter smell died on the air, the new plantations were rising: 10 million trees spaced in orderly phalanxes over 300,000 acres of Malaya and Ceylon. Through Singapore's immigration depots and coolie brokers, there flowed that year a tide of 387,000 Chinese and Tamil tappers. Their labors, almost doubling Asia's 1906 tonnage, had netted Malaya alone an impressive £785,000.

Arana had acted fast. By January, 1907, following his hasty

visit to London, a London auditor had arrived on the Amazon. Over three months in Manaus and Iquitos, he examined the books and wages sheets of Arana Brothers, but his terms of reference did not take him up the Putumayo. Following the auditor's confirmation of the company's financial status, Arana was soon back in London to see José Medina, company promoter and director of the Cortes Commercial Banking Company, with whom he had done business for ten years past.

Along with Medina, Arana next called on Henry Read, manager of the London Bank of Mexico and South America, in his office on Gracechurch Street in the City sector. To Read, Arana was a stranger but he had known Medina, a shareholder of the bank and fellow club member, for many years. "This," Read later recalled Medina's introduction, "is Mr. Arana, a man with important business who may want facilities."

Read had listened attentively to Arana's request, which he was later to put before his board of directors. For a revolving credit of £60,000—by which Arana could call on the bank for that amount, but undertook to reimburse them within ninety days— the bank, as security, would receive commission on rubber sales up to £75,000. When Read nodded, satisfied, Arana knew he had cleared the first formidable hurdle.

But on August 13, 1907, as that morning's meeting broke up in Manaus' Chamber of Commerce, Arana retired to his office desk preoccupied. There was still work to be done on the draft prospectus before he sailed for London once more to clinch the final details of the company; one false step could wreck the whole intricate plot. At this stage, some items might be better omitted. His pen hovered above the phrase, "The firm has in all this region more than 1,500 civilised employees [whose] occupation reduces itself to that of armed vigilantes . . ." Decisively, he struck it through.

Yet it was essential to show the labor position as satisfactory. Totally absorbed, his pen moved across the paper, "There are at present 30,000 Indians in the company's service . . ."

Arana knew full well that the entire Indian population of the

Putumayo did not number above 50,000 Indians, and only one-fifth of them were in the company's service, but he saw this as no contradiction in terms. In this great gamble he now laid claim to every square yard of earth, every man, woman and child in Putumayo territory.

PART TWO

 The Black Gold

TOWARD 3 P.M. on Monday, December 23, 1907, a canoe was gliding noiselessly toward the southern shore of the Upper Putumayo River, ninety miles from the Colombian frontier town of Güeppí. At first glance, its American pilot and navigator might have passed for river traders, for the 27-foot length of the sturdy cedarwood dugout was jammed with a bewildering variety of merchandise. Bulky 100-pound bundles of food, clothes and medicines were stacked against live turtles and wild fruit, Winchester rifles, revolvers, thirty-inch machetes, and trade goods from harmonicas to handkerchiefs. And there were evident souvenirs, too, of a long river trip: fancy hammocks, blowpipes, quivers of poisoned arrows, pots of Indian paint and poison.

Crouched in the bow over a shallow earthenware cooking pot which served as his galley, the navigator, Walter Ernest Hardenburg, a square-shouldered 21-year-old with dark receding hair, was alert and watchful for the lethal logs and tree stumps studding the yellow water. Astern, in the high narrow poop seat, his friend W. B. Perkins deftly plied his wide-bladed Indian paddle, ears strained for Hardenburg's shouted instructions as the canoe skimmed past hazard after hazard.

"That must be Yaracaya over yonder." On the still air, Hardenburg's resonant musical voice carried clearly to Perkins in the stern. But the bamboo and split-palm house on the southern shore, raised on posts six feet above ground level, seemed deserted. On the northern shore, thin blue smoke from a rubber tapper's fire and a canoe drawing a light scar on the enameled water were the only signs of life.

A few yards from the house, hidden from view by a clump of wild banana plants, a tall bearded man in a white shirt and blue checkered trousers watched them intently, his index finger curled in readiness round the trigger of his Winchester. But in a moment, reassured, he lowered the gun. The strangers were surely harmless enough, for in their curiosity to view the house they had just inexpertly grounded the canoe on the sandbank below. At once he called softly to a peon, and master and servant walked with dignified cordiality to help the newcomers free their craft.

"I am Don Jesús López," the bearded man announced. "You are strangers, but you are welcome to my house."

Walt Hardenburg's face, tanned by long weeks of sun, crinkled in a ready smile. Grasping López' hand, he explained that he and Perkins had had word of Yaracaya Estate from rubber-trail owners farther upriver. Though López nodded non-committally, the canoe's strange freight, piled clumsily beneath the palm-leaf awning amidships, puzzled him, and even for the Amazon Valley the strangers' garb was threadbare. While Hardenburg's torn flannel shirt and trousers and wide-brimmed Stetson hat just passed muster, Perkins wore little more than a sacklike undershirt and a flowing beard.

Hardenburg hastened to explain. He and his partner were engineers from the Cauca Valley Railroad in Colombia, but after fifteen months the lure of the Amazon, the soaring value of rubber, had proved too strong for them. Pooling their savings they had resolved to strike out for Manaus, in the hope of finding work on a railroad newly planned on the Madeira River, 1,000 miles south of the city.

López was bewildered. From where, he asked, had they come? Hardenburg elaborated: "Why, from Buenaventura." Still López' brow was furrowed in perplexity. Buenaventura was on the Pacific Coast. To reach the Putumayo from there, they must have crossed the Andes.

Unconscious of creating any sensation, Hardenburg confirmed that this was exactly what they had done. All summer they had

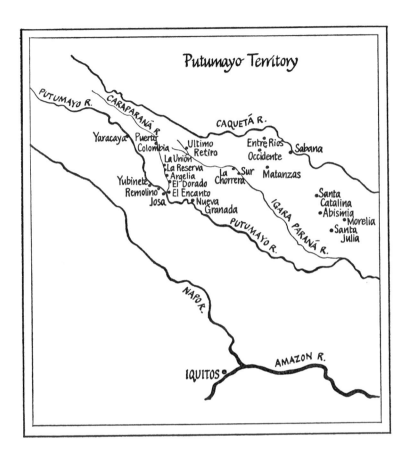

snatched every spare moment to plan their trip in detail: the route they would follow, the necessary gear. Finally on October 1, quitting their jobs, they had set out, hiring teams of porters to ferry their gear through ravines 6,000 feet high, inching their way along trails so precipitous they were often only a toehold away from a fifty-foot plunge onto slippery rocks. Seventeen days after setting out they had struck the Putumayo, then a small, swift-flowing mountain torrent six feet wide, but not until Sunday, December 1, in the back-of-beyond mission station of Puerto Guineo, had they bought their canoe, hired two Cioni Indians as boatmen and set off downriver.

Only the Cionis' consummate skill, Hardenburg said, had brought them unscathed through the tumbling white waters of those first days—but on Saturday, December 7, the boatmen had quit. They would go no farther into unknown country. Assured by friendly Colombians that no falls or rapids lay ahead, Hardenburg and Perkins had opted to steer the boat themselves. Thus far, living off the land had proved no problem, though at each stage of their journey friendly trail owners had furnished extra supplies and introductions to the next man on the route.

Now, as López led them to the cool porch fronting the river, he asked keenly: "Then you had no trouble upstream?"

Hardenburg's lively brown eyes twinkled with amusement. "Trouble?" he responded. "I'll say we had trouble. I've been bitten on the index finger by a vampire bat, chased up a tree by a caiman and for the last six days we've been grounded on another sandbank—it took a detachment of your Colombian police to get us out of that one. Reckoned it was the pearly gates for us more than once, didn't we, Perky?"

Again, López' tension was evident. The police? Then this must have been a detachment under Don Gabriel Martinez, a leading trail owner who was now, since troops had been withdrawn from the region, acting as magistrate in these parts. Hardenburg acknowledged it. On their journey from Buenaventura, many men had spoken of the kindly Don Gabriel, among them his boss,

Octavio Materón, partner in a Pasto, Colombia, rubber company. Now that they owed their lives to Martinez' men, Hardenburg said, they were doubly anxious to meet him.

"Well then," López urged, "he's due here any time now. Why not stay on until he comes?" But Hardenburg, politely yet firmly, declined. Ahead of them lay Manaus and the railroad on the Madeira River, and already their six days on the sandbank had cost them precious time. If they pressed on downriver they would surely meet Martinez on the way.

Walt Hardenburg would have found it hard to explain, but since childhood he had heard the Amazon calling. Born twenty-one years earlier in Galena, Illinois, son of a prosperous agricultural merchant, Hardenburg had no family ties in the Tropics. Yet as far back as he could remember the lure had been there. At twelve, six years after Spencer, his father, had piled up enough cash to switch to hobby farming on a 192-acre estate at Youngsville, New York, under the Catskills, Amazon fever was burning in young Walt's veins.

Already Prescott's famous *Conquest of Peru* and George M. Towle's *Adventures and Conquest of Pizarro* were cherished bedside reading. And at Youngsville's grade school, Walt Hardenburg was long remembered as the twelve-year-old who in geography lesson knew every serpentine curve of the world's greatest river as surely as if he had charted it. This, too, began as an icy Andean stream, then, by degrees became a tawny surging juggernaut of water twelve times greater than the Mississippi, draining an area two-thirds the size of Canada. Even islands crowned with living trees were clawed loose from its banks and swept irresistibly downstream toward the Atlantic, for only land masses like Marajó, on the delta, larger than Switzerland, could withstand its current.

In places, its waters were 150 fathoms deep, teeming with caimans, waterborne anacondas, twenty-six feet long, and savage, razor-toothed piranha fish. In its jungles were fire ants whose sting could paralyze, and bird-eating spiders with hairy obscene bodies seven inches across. Here, too, lurked hostile Indian tribes like the Jivaro, noted for shrinking their enemies' heads, and the cannibal Parintintins.

It was a challenge no youngster as spirited as Walt could resist, and time and again, seizing a pointer, he would swiftly run its tip from Pará, 2,300 miles upriver to Iquitos. "That's where I want to go," the stubborn youngster would reiterate. "I want to get out there."

Now, nine years later, in the heart of the Amazon Valley, within 200 miles of the mighty river itself, Hardenburg could brook no further delay. From October on, he might have known no other existence than this frontier life. At mealtimes, when Walt stood in as cook, he had contrived savory meals from an amazing variety of provender: wild turkey, turtle eggs, fried catfish, even monkey steak, topped off with jiggers of sugarcane rum and the heady maize beer of the Indians.

Reluctantly he explained to López that time was of the essence. They could stay no longer.

López came to a decision. He must warn these youngsters, who had embarked on this venture as lightheartedly as boys at summer camp, of the dangers lying ahead. Downriver, he explained, were Peruvian rubber men who saw the whole Putumayo territory as their own. López himself was one of the few Colombians left, but he feared even his days were numbered.

"There was José Cabrera, at Nueva Granada," he instanced. "He sold out to them—and why? Because they threatened to kill him, they fired at him from ambush, they took away his laborers by force." As it turned out, López stressed, Cabrera had been wise. On the banks of the nearby Caquetá River, the Colombian Cecilio Plata and all his employees had been hacked to pieces when they refused to pull out.

Rapidly filling in the young Americans on the background to the dispute, López confessed his inmost fear: the flash point was at hand. The rubber men, he said, had sent false intelligence to Lima that a hundred Colombian troops intent on a coup had filtered into this territory. As a result, forty Peruvian soldiers from the barracks at Iquitos had been dispatched upriver in the launch *Cosmopolita*.

"They are in the area *now*," said López quietly, "and, señor, this means trouble."

He had barely finished before Hardenburg's mind was made up. No man could question Walt Hardenburg's courage, but he wanted no part of a Latin-American frontier brawl. Already, during their three-month journey, Perkins had twice come down with fever, and the climate and the river navigation were producing problems enough. Only two days back, an unseen log, wrenching their canoe broadside, had hurled him overboard; if Perkins had not struggled to his feet in time to yank him to safety, no power on earth could have plucked him from that current.

Rummaging a sweat-stained chart from their baggage, Hardenburg asked: "Isn't there any way of reaching Manaus without passing through the trouble zone?"

"If you can get as far as Don Gabriel Martinez' house," López conceded, "the rest will be easy. But that's at Remolino—five days' journey downriver. If you miss Martinez, see Señor Ordoñez, his partner." And he elaborated: the two had many Indians in their service and could arrange an overland portage through the jungle to the banks of the Napo River.

Hardenburg's spirits rose. Down the Napo, he remembered, in 1541, Gonzalo Pizarro's lieutenant, Francisco de Orellana, decamping with gold looted from his leader, had sailed until he met "the great fresh-water sea," the world's first intimation of the Amazon's existence.

He rose from his seat on the porch. "We'd better make tracks, señor," he told López, "and we certainly are obliged . . ." But now López cut in sharply. "I don't think," he said grimly, "that your partner will be making any tracks . . ." For Perkins had abruptly slumped forward across the table. Beads of sweat as big as raindrops were rolling down his cheeks and his teeth rattled like castanets.

Walt Hardenburg shook a rueful head. "That's his third attack

of malaria in three months," he lamented. "I guess he won't be
piloting any *montaria* in a hurry." Together he and López helped
the ashen-faced Perkins to a sparsely furnished sleeping chamber,
slung his hammock and wrapped him warmly in blankets until
the shivering fit had abated. As the bearded youngster dropped
into an exhausted sleep, López consoled Hardenburg: the delay
could prove a blessing in disguise. By the time they were ready to
resume their journey, the Peruvian troops might have returned to
Iquitos.

His next remark brought the American upright with a jolt.
"Once the Peruvians were amalgamated into a British company,
we thought the trouble would die down, but since September the
breaches of the peace have daily grown more flagrant."

"A *British* company?" said Hardenburg unbelieving. "What's a
British company doing on the Peruvian Amazon?"

López was somber. The company had indeed been registered in
London two months earlier, on September 25, as the Peruvian
Amazon Rubber Company. "Believe me," he said earnestly,
"these men are fiends. There are thousands in this valley who
bear what they call the *marca de Arana*—the scars of Arana. This
is the name of its founder—Julio César Arana."

Hardenburg never forgot how he first heard the name like
that, dropped casually into the conversation as a stone spreading
deep ripples is cast into a pool.

Next morning, though his fever had passed,
Perkins was still weak and dizzy from quinine. Curbing his
natural impatience, Harbenburg accepted that they must stay on.
He passed the morning chatting with López, absorbing firsthand
details of the region's rubber production, strolling unhurriedly
round the small estate.

To Walt Hardenburg, it was in no way strange that seven
months after his twenty-first birthday he should find himself
stranded on a forgotten Peruvian river, 3,000 miles from the

family farm at Youngsville. As of now, home was where he slung his hammock for the night. Following graduation from nearby Liberty High School, in 1903, 17-year-old Walt had set his heart on becoming an engineer, but his father, inimical to changing trends, just couldn't see the need for a college education. Resentful that the self-made Spencer demanded as much farm work from his sons as from the hired men, Walt found settling down next to impossible—and to keep the peace between the two now called for all the tact his mother, Elizabeth, could muster.

To earn pocket money, Walt for one whole year submitted to the discipline of teaching for $5 a week in grade school at nearby Swiss Hill. Then, following a final showdown with Spencer, he quit home altogether. Already, though christened "Walter Hardenbergh," he had changed the spelling of the surname—ostensibly because it sounded "more Dutch," though friends viewed it as a final rejection of Spencer Hardenbergh's authority.

Moving on to New York, Walt lived first with his Aunt Louisa in the Bronx . . . enlisted briefly in the U.S. Navy but within months, disillusioned, bought himself out . . . finally, hearing South America wanted skilled engineers, shipping out for Panama.

Now Walt Hardenburg's troubles began. On the Canal Zone skilled engineers were as welcome as gold dust, but Hardenburg then had little to offer but muscle and determination. To eat at all he and a giant Negro teamed up to dig a well on contract—living for weeks until the job was paid for on rice stewed, boiled, fried, even raw. For the rest of his life, Hardenburg could not face so much as one mouthful of rice.

But Hardenburg's single-mindedness thrived against such odds. Already, following hours of late-night study, his Spanish was fluent: most laborers on the canal boozed away their earnings in the dives of the Old Town, but Hardenburg, grammar propped on chest, could fight sleep until he had mastered that evening's allotted quota. Finding work as a checker of materials on the canal project, he held down the job until he had funds enough to move on to Cauca, Colombia.

For a youngster fresh from small-town family life, it was a

revelation. Overnight, he became one of the informal fraternity of "tropical tramps" whose know-how belied their nickname: the very antithesis of beachcombers, they earned their money as high-class engineers, grubstaking one another, if cash ran low or adventure called, to jobs as far afield as Panama or Buenos Aires. Their credo was rigid—no job for more than three months, for the one factor uniting Walt with men like "Big Mike" O'Grady, ex-Boston pugilist, or "Bolshevik," an Australian self-educated on Nietzsche and Elinor Glyn, was wanderlust. Yet seeing the chance to improve his prospects, Hardenburg resolved to block the impulse and stay put. Signing up with a survey crew prospecting a forty-mile stretch of track through the Cauca Valley, from Buenaventura to Cali, he next prevailed on the friendly crew boss, César Castro, to give him after-hours instruction.

Fifteen months later, with the lure of the Amazon now as potent as wild geese calling, Hardenburg was running his own survey crew at a salary of $175 a month, gold, plus board and lodging. Drawing on savings from home he had even armed himself with a full-scale surveyor's kit, everything from sextant to theodolites. He and his old friend Perkins, an amiable young-ster from Mississippi, were now ready to move.

In Colombia, even as far away as torrid Panama, Hardenburg had heard men talk of the legendary white city, Manaus, and the spendthrift bonanza river life: one favorite story was of a rubber baron who had shipped an iron house built by Alexandre Eiffel for a Paris exhibition all the way to the Amazon, then, finding its oven heat unbearable, had never passed one night within its walls. Hardenburg, like any youngster on the brink of manhood, was curious to view this modern Babylon, but what most seized his imagination was a strange saga-in-the-making: the creation of the Madeira-Mamoré Railroad.

As far back as the 1870's, Colonel George Church, a veteran of the Army of the Potomac, had dreamed of a railroad that would run from the Madeira River, 1,000 miles southwest of Manaus, to the Mamoré River on Bolivia's border at Guajará Mirim. Between these points, nineteen lethal rapids—some with a sheer 500-foot drop—made the ferrying of Bolivian rubber to the Amazon a perilous, time-consuming progress involving 600-yard portages: often a quarter of all shipments were lost. But any engineer who sought to bypass the rapids faced instead 226 miles of hostile Indian country, where disease and violent death abounded. Forced to abandon the job when two miles of permanent main track cost over 200 lives, Church reluctantly endorsed the verdict of British contractors who had earlier given up: "The country is a charnel house . . . with . . . all the capital in the world and half its population it would be impossible to build the road."

But by 1907 rubber-boom optimism demanded the impossible: a treaty had pledged Brazil to give Bolivia access to the Atlantic, and the contract had passed to Percival Farquhar, the laconic 42-year-old Quaker from York, Pennsylvania, whose dapper insouciance earned him the nickname, "Sir Percival." Already the pioneer of streetcars in Rio de Janeiro, railroads in Cuba and Guatemala, Farquhar's organizing genius and the courage of his hard-bitten "tropical tramps" seemed likely to transform the Madeira-Mamoré from blueprint to reality.

A hundred-carat idealist who could never resist a challenge, Walt Hardenburg saw the Madeira-Mamoré as fulfilling two dreams at one and the same time. At long last he would see the Amazon Valley, and in working to tame its forbidding interior he would work for the ultimate benefit of mankind.

As always, the easygoing Perkins had followed his partner's lead as philosophically as he accepted defeat in their nightly chess game—but as the afternoon of their second day at Yaracaya wore on, Hardenburg grew worried. Once they reached Manaus and pushed on to the railroad, he thought, Perkins would need every ounce of stamina to survive—yet these recurrent bouts of fever were slowly sapping his strength.

Relaxed in a rocking chair on the porch, lost in thought, he heard a sudden hail from López. "Señor Hardenburg—here comes Don Gabriel now."

At once, vaulting nimbly from the porch, Hardenburg ran to join his host. Eyes shielded against the afternoon glare, they watched in silence three canoes laboring upstream, making slow progress against the fast-flowing current. Abruptly, López' lips tightened.

"Wait a moment, there's something wrong. Don Gabriel is not with them."

Squatting on the shelving bank, Hardenburg craned closer. Now he saw clearly why López was perturbed. Huddled in the canoes were eight men wearing the regulation dark blue of Colombian police constables, but their uniforms hung in shreds, stained with sweat and yellow daubs of river mud. Their unshaven faces were wolfish and pinched with hunger, and several shivered convulsively in the first stages of malaria. As the canoes edged into the shore, Hardenburg, following López and his peons, was scrambling down the bank to meet them. Plainly the men were so weak that, though their Cioni boatmen could moor the craft, they needed help even to stumble ashore.

"What has happened?" López demanded when they had shakily disembarked. "Where is Don Gabriel?"

In the aching silence, the corporal in charge of the party blurted out a disquieting story. Five days downriver, near the deserted trading post of Yubinete, a launch manned by forty armed employees of the Peruvian Amazon Rubber Company had barred their passage. Curtly their ringleader gave Don Gabriel Martinez no option; he was to accompany them to their headquarters at El Encanto. When the magistrate indignantly refused, forty rifle barrels swung into unerring focus.

"You can come of your own free will," the ringleader declared, "or you can be taken by force. We are arresting you in the name of the Peruvian Amazon Rubber Company."

Martinez had seen that it was useless to resist. Unwilling to endanger his men, he agreed to board the launch, giving them hasty last-minute instructions. Pending his return they should wait there for three days—then, if no word came, proceed on upriver.

"From that day," the corporal ended, "no word of Don Gabriel has reached us. We were powerless against the devils and we can only fear the worst." Their stock of food and medicine had soon given out, and once the fever struck them they were too weak to live off the land.

"They can have the best part of our quinine," Hardenburg volunteered. "They look more like ghosts than men."

López nodded. "I'll have the quarters under the house made over to them," he said, "and they can stay on for the festivities. You may have forgotten, but today is Christmas Eve."

For Hardenburg, the days that followed had a strange, dreamlike quality. By nature a skeptic, who challenged any fact not proved to the hilt, the innuendos against the sinister, British-based company troubled him. But thus far the only tangible evidence was the mysterious arrest of Don Gabriel—and even on this Hardenburg reserved judgment. In a frontier dispute passions were swiftly inflamed—and who knew what right the Peruvians had on their side?

Yet fear was in the air. As he later recalled it, Christmas Day was "more or less of a jag, which lasted all day." Every man under López' roof—the sick policemen, the Cioni boatmen, Perkins and himself—drank immoderately from a barrel of surgarcane rum, using the liquor clinically to numb their fear. Yet as the hours passed and they turned from rum to turtle steaks and plantain dessert, then back again to rum, nothing moved on the river's surface.

"As if it was likely to," Hardenburg scoffed inwardly. "They've gotten so worked up they're jumping at shadows."

It was still quiet at 8 A.M. on December 26, when the policemen and their Cionis, now in better physical shape and loaded with supplies, set off again upriver to Güeppí. Now that his fever was spent, Perkins confessed he was anxious to move. After a last lunch with the kindly López, he and Hardenburg once more launched their canoe.

After this, time blurred. There were days, navigating shallow, stifling creeks, when the sand flies and mosquitoes tormented them to the breaking point: one clap of the hands, Hardenburg noted, and his palms were damp with the blood of a thousand gnats. To dispel them he piled the shallow earthenware cooking pot in the bow with damp driftwood and lit a smudge fire, but soon the choking, acrid fumes forced him to douse it. On other days rain replaced the insects, falling in gray torrential curtains that blotted out the forest, hissing on the river's surface, drenching them to the skin. The trip, both men decided, was losing much of its charm.

Yet there were unforgettable moments when the Amazon Valley did not disappoint, and all that Hardenburg had read and tried to picture became vivid and third-dimensional. There were the wasps' nests clamped to high branches, just as the books had said, looking like huge tarred lobster pots dripping with black pitch. With a sudden glittering cascade of spray, pink-bellied dolphins broke the surface, diving and cavorting astern of them. Electric-blue morpho butterflies flitted erratically from leaf to leaf. Sometimes a single mauve orchid blossom stood out in breathtaking contrast against a rubber tree's silvery bark. And always, for hour after hour, the river wound in restless curves from oxbow to oxbow and the eternal soundproofed silence.

At Remolino, on December 30, an old peon guarding the deserted trading depot of Ordoñez and Martinez, confirmed glumly that there was still no news of the missing magistrate. Worse, Ordoñez, too, was now operating from the company's main depot at La Unión, on the Caraparaná tributary, four hours' march distant overland. And only Ordoñez, the peon said, had authority to arrange the portage to the Napo River that López had suggested.

"All right," said Hardenburg decisively, "we'll bed down here overnight and in the morning we'll go look for him."

Readily Perkins agreed. Though Hardenburg's senior by several years, he accepted his leadership as naturally as the youngsters back in Liberty High School had done in Walt's schooldays. And on this issue Hardenburg's mind was made up: somehow they would locate Ordoñez, they would persist until they got their portage to the Napo, above all, they would steer clear of any frontier disputes.

Early on the morning of New Year's Eve, along with a group of friendly half-breeds who had arrived to pick up stores, Hardenburg splashed for four hours along a trail of sticky yellow clay, teetering perilously over chasms fifty feet wide, bridged by a single slippery tree trunk. Perkins meanwhile remained at Remolino to guard their gear. At 10 A.M. rain came again from a black sky, a single unbroken sheet of water soaking them within minutes. Knuckling raindrops from his eyes, Hardenburg saw at last the leaden gleam of a river ahead, a huddle of split-palm houses. They had arrived at La Unión, on the northern bank of the Caraparaná tributary.

From the company's canoe, Hardenburg scaled a precarious stairway of tree trunks embedded in rust-colored mud to the main yard. Beyond the houses stood a wide clearing with fenced-in plantations of maize and yams; horses and zebu cattle were browsing on wet lush grass. Beneath the porch of the main building, a score of half-breeds were stacking long, sausage-shaped bundles of rubber. Now further disappointment awaited Walt. A smiling, friendly youngster, introducing himself as Don Fabio Duarte, Ordoñez' assistant manager, shook a regretful head. "Señor Ordoñez is away right now," he apologized, "in the forest getting rubber with his Indians. We don't really expect him back before noon tomorrow."

Then, seeing Hardenburg's crestfallen face, he was solicitous: the American was wet through. Why not dry off by the fire—and, better still, why not stay on until tomorrow to discuss the portage with Ordoñez? Walt accepted. Reluctant though he was to leave Perkins without word, the prospect of a four-hour return trek empty-handed was too awful to contemplate.

Duarte, affable and talkative, explained that La Unión's labor strength was too hundred Huitoto Indians who brought their rubber in return for trade goods. Downriver, at La Reserva, another Colombian, David Serrano, employed forty-five families, though the Peruvians had cornered most of the labor force. He said hotly: "The way they treat their Indians is a disgrace. You know what they say, '*Son animales, señor; no son gentes*'— 'They are animals, sir; they are not people.' "

Hardenburg nodded noncommitally. Foremost in his mind was the belief that all these trail owners were tarred with the same brush. Since leaving Buenaventura he had heard nothing but the Colombian viewpoint. Idly, he inquired, "How about those Peruvian troops we heard about? I guess by now they've all gone back to Iquitos."

But Duarte shook his head. The Peruvian troops showed no sign of moving, though their departure could only be a matter of time. Duped by the rubber men's false reports that Colombian troops were massing, they were duty bound to check their authenticity. Soon, Duarte thought, they would realize their error and order Martinez' release. It was unthinkable they would take part in raids on Colombian settlements.

He ended unemotionally: "If they do, of course, we shall fight to the last man."

Deep inside him, Hardenburg sensed a small core of unease. He had the feeling events were getting beyond control and nothing Duarte had said allayed this fear.

Next morning, Duarte shook him awake with worse news yet. A runner had brought word that Ordoñez and his Indians were still several days' march away. And now Hardenburg, normally ebullient, was so disheartened his mind went blank: a trap seemed to be closing about them and he saw no way out. "Look," Duarte encouraged him, "why not go down and see David Serrano at La Reserva? He'll fix you up with porters, I am certain."

Though another three-hour jungle march lay ahead, Hardenburg assented. Somehow they had to make their getaway from this hostile terrain.

The guide Duarte assigned him was a Huitoto Indian who spoke halting Spanish, a small, stout, broad-shouldered man with coarse black hair. Now, with a brief backward glance at Hardenburg, he plunged assuredly into the green jungle wall. Abruptly, as the youngster followed, the sun went out. Among the giant

forest trees, it was dark and cellar-cool. Branches snapped like
carbine shots and the ground underfoot was as spongy as rubber,
littered with a black paste of rotted sticks. Giant lianas, as stout
and unyielding as electric cables, sent Hardenburg sprawling
headlong, bringing showers of dead leaves in their wake. Sometimes the unbroken roof of trees parted and sunlight shafted
through; a flight of parrakeets winged green and raucous across
the sky. Then the vision was gone and again there was only the
green underwater twilight.

No sooner did the Huitoto speak of rubber gathering than
Hardenburg was on his guard. The Peruvians, the guide told him,
almost as if reciting a lesson, treated his countrymen "very
badly." Skeptical, Hardenburg countered: just what did "very
badly" mean? The Indian grew animated. If they did not bring
enough rubber to satisfy the overseers, indescribable things were
done to them. They were flogged as a matter of course, but there
were worse things than flogging.

Once, at the trading post called Abisinia, when the guard dogs
were hungry, the chief overseer ordered a massacre of Indian
children and had them cut up for dog food. At Matanzas, a
woman wrapped in a kerosene-soaked Peruvian flag had been
burned alive. The head overseer at Ultimo Retiro often blind-
folded young Indian girls for sport, then picked them off from
his veranda with a Mannlicher.

Hardenburg was incredulous. "You've seen these things happen?" he challenged keenly.

The man shook his head. Though all the forest Indians knew
these stories, he had been spared such sights. "But if you don't
bring in enough rubber," Hardenburg queried, "don't the
Colombians flog or shoot you?" The Huitoto denied it: they
were good men, "who treated Indians well." "Just as I thought,"
Hardenburg told himself; "you can take all this with a grain of
kitchen salt."

The rain was driving furiously when they at last broke clear of
the forest into reclaimed land, passing through the head-high
plantations of La Reserva toward a small raised bungalow girdled
by fruit trees. From the porch, three men sipping demitasses

rose to greet them. One, a short, coffee-colored man in his
mid-fifties, cordial and energetic, was David Serrano, who
warmly pumped Hardenburg's hand. His guests, he explained,
were political exiles, banished by Colombia's President Rafael
Reyes, who were now en route to Brazil: General Miguel Acosta
and Don Alfonso Sanchez. Though other exiles had moved on
downriver, Sanchez, prostrate with malaria, had been forced to
rest a few days.

The buoyant Serrano soon convinced Hardenburg his problems were solved. He brushed aside any idea of their undertaking
the portage alone: in five days' time he was following the same
route as far as Iquitos and would gladly take Hardenburg and
Perkins with him. From there they could pick up a steamer
connection to Manaus. "They tell me they're not actually paving
the streets with gold blocks *yet*," he joked. "Still, perhaps by the
time you get there . . ."

And he made further practical suggestions. He would buy the
youngsters' canoe and anything else they wanted to sell. If they
sent a runner to Perkins with instructions to bring the canoe
down from Remolino to Josá, Serrano's trading post on the
Putumayo, they could leave their personal effects there, bringing
overland to La Reserva only what they could dispense with. He
would dispatch porters on foot to rendezvous with Perkins.

"Now if you'll come with me," Serrano wound up, "I'll show
you where you can sling your hammock." For the first time in
days, Hardenburg felt suddenly at peace. Soon, he even dared to
believe, they would be out of harm's way.

Following the fleeting quarter-hour dusk of the
Amazon Valley, night fell upon the river as swiftly as a shutter.
In his bedroom, sluicing himself from an enamel bowl by the
subdued glow of a kerosene lamp, Hardenburg could hear the
eerie symphony of the jungle tuning up for the night: a swelling
crescendo of shrieks, howls, gobblings and sudden startling
guffaws. There was the stealthy rustle of reptiles on the move;

the air was heavy with the smell of death and decaying vegetation, mingled with sweet unexpected stabs of fragrance. Dimly he could distinguish the whiplash crack as a 200-pound Amazon codfish broke the water's surface, the metallic creaking of bullfrogs, the dull deep boom of a falling tree.

The four dined at a table on the main veranda, served by Huitoto girls in simple calico frocks. No other womenfolk appeared, and Hardenburg concluded privately that Serrano was a bachelor. At first conversation was desultory; only beetles and giant moths blundering and banging against the lighted lamp broke the silence. Presently, Serrano, his face softening, began to talk of the valley's first Colombian settlers and the manner in which the Huitotos had received them.

"Those early Colombians," he told them, "were men without hope—sick, penniless. If the Huitotos had resisted them, they wouldn't have had the strength to put up a fight. Yet the Indians welcomed them—they gave them food, women; they even nursed them back to health. Without their cooperation, I don't think even those of us who came later could have survived here."

"They sound like pretty hospitable people," Hardenburg conceded, then his innate honesty forced him to add, "but did they only offer hospitality to the Colombians? Surely all the Peruvians in these parts can't be as black as they're painted?"

Everyone stopped eating. There was a stunned, momentary silence. Coloring, Hardenburg saw Sanchez and General Acosta exchange covert embarrassed glances. With a titanic effort, Serrano controlled himself, though his coffee-colored skin seemed to blanch. "You are young, señor," he said at last, harshly, "and you are also a guest in my house. If it were not for that—"

With natural good manners, Hardenburg hastened to apologize. He by no means wished to offend, but he had heard nothing but ill spoken of the Peruvians since arriving in the territory. Trembling with emotion, Serrano cut him short. Would Hardenburg like to hear how Julio Arana's men from El Encanto, under their head overseer, Miguel Loayza, had collected a small trading debt only a month back?

Now the three guests looked at anything but one another. His voice barely recognizable, Serrano was fighting tears. It had happened one morning in early December, he said, when he and his Indians were busy preparing £1,000 worth of rubber for shipment. Loayza had previously sent word that he was sending a "commission" to collect the debt, but Serrano, well used to threats, paid little heed. The launch full of armed thugs looming suddenly from the river mist took all of them by surprise. Before Serrano could dive for his gun, they had overpowered him, lashing him to a tree. Helpless, he had watched them load every bundle of his hard-won rubber onto their own launch. Then, numb with horror, he had seen a group of them forcing the door of his Indian wife's room, manhandling her onto the porch.

"I could not look but they forced me to look," Serrano cried in torment. "All of them held her down and then Loayza . . ." For an eternity, while Hardenburg sat white-faced, he choked on the words. At length, his voice drained of emotion, Serrano completed the harrowing tale. Following the rape, his wife had been taken aboard the launch along with their small son. Since then he had seen nothing of them. Word had reached him that at El Encanto Loayza held her captive in a house where other concubines were kept. The boy was now Loayza's table servant.

Still Hardenburg sat mute and shamefaced, knowing no words could help. Relieved, he saw Serrano blow his nose violently, summoning up his old energy. After Loayza's raid, he said, his appeal to the Colombian capital, Bogotá, had brought matters to a head. Any day now, Don Jesús Orjuela, a newly appointed government agent, would arrive in the territory, on a special mission from President Reyes. Respecting the *modus vivendi*, he would come unescorted by troops, but his terms of reference were plain: there must be no further molestation of Colombian settlers.

Appalled, Hardenburg burst out: "But this river seems to be a kind of devil's paradise—isn't there any constitution to protect your people against outrages like that?" Serrano's reply, as he raised the Winchester propped beside his chair, was to haunt him all his life. "There is only one constitution on the Amazon, the

Winchester constitution, and only one article that men live by—Article 44."

Dazed and shaken, Hardenburg soon after retired to bed. In his mind's eye was a vivid picture of the map of the Amazon Valley back at Liberty High School, and it struck him that George J. Dann, the headmaster, had omitted some vital facts from their curriculum. The harder he fought to stay clear of this imbroglio, the more deeply was he involved.

Next morning, January 3, Serrano made no mention of the previous night's dispute. Instead, almost shyly, he suggested a stroll round the estate. By degrees, Hardenburg's skepticism diminished, for the Huitotos he saw at work seemed cheerful and contented and many addressed Serrano as "*Mon.*" "It means 'father,' " Serrano confessed diffidently. "Foolish, if you like, but I have done my best to be a father to them."

With the fluency of a man who knew his subject, he pictured for Hardenburg life as the Huitotos knew it. When a man sought a girl in marriage, he saw his prime responsibility as toward her and her family. First he cleared a small plot of land to build their house—then, before claiming his bride, secured a gift of tobacco for her father and cut a stack of kindling for his future mother-in-law. These unions, Serrano stressed, were looked on as binding for life. Not only were the women chaste, it was almost unknown for a man to take more than one woman.

By nature the Huitotos were peaceful people—mild, industrious, humble. Often several families occupied one large, thatch-roofed house, seventy feet in diameter, but quarrels were few. What they treasured above all was freedom to live their simple communal life—making their own bamboo stools and benches, weaving palm-fiber hammocks, hunting fish and forest animals with blowguns and poison arrows.

Their religious beliefs, Serrano explained, were sincere if muddled. Though they worshiped the sun and the moon, they believed also in Husinamui, a superior being who was virtue incarnate, as well as an inferior potentate, Taifeno, the spirit of evil. When the Colombians held the valley, visiting priests from

Pasto found the Huitotos truly receptive to Christian ideas and customs. For this reason alone the Peruvian Amazon Rubber Company had summarily banished priests from the region.

Unmolested, the Huitotos had reveled in dance festivals, skillfully painting their bodies to resemble animals and the branches of trees, girding themselves with feathered ornaments and necklaces of tapir teeth, carrying the dance from house to house to the sonorous throbbing of hardwood drums.

"In those days," said Serrano gravely, "they learned from infancy to say, 'Beside me beauty, below me peace, before me beauty, everywhere peace.' That was before Arana came to the valley."

Stirred by his evident concern, Hardenburg felt involved despite himself. He recalled now his chance phrase of the previous night—"a devil's paradise." From what Serrano had showed him it seemed the Amazon Valley should emerge as a paradise in which all men could live at peace. Sadly he reflected: "It seems that paradise too often attracts the wrong kind of people."

Then he was startled because the kindly, aging Serrano, greatly moved, had seized his arm impulsively. Did Hardenburg really feel like this? Then he had a serious proposition to make to him and his partner, one they must not lightly turn down—a half share in this estate of La Reserva, on terms to be agreed.

"Why go on to Manaus after all?" he urged. "Stay here and help me make this a valley fit for settlers to live in."

Walt Hardenburg had barely had time to grasp the implications of this bolt from the blue when at 2 P.M. a peon's hail sent him and Serrano hastening to the riverbank. The President's agent from Bogotá, Don Jesús Orjuela, with his assistant, Colonel Gustavo Prieto, were already disembarking from their canoe. A handsome, soldierly man of thirty-five, with pale, clean-cut features, Orjuela from the first radiated both optimism and determination. On his journey down from the frontier he had stopped off at La Unión, where Señors Ordoñez and Duarte had told him of the fates of both Martinez and Serrano's wife.

"We can no longer tolerate this kind of treatment," Orjuela told Serrano, "but I think if I have a talk with Señor Loayza, man-to-man, we can reach an amicable agreement."

Serrano was profoundly pessimistic. Orjuela seemed to view what had happened as one man's overstepping the mark. To Serrano, the fate of earlier settlers was proof that Loayza acted under orders, as part of Arana's planned campaign to oust the Colombians from the valley.

"I must be frank," he told Hardenburg at next morning's full-scale conference. "I think if you and your partner came in with me, these molestations would stop. I don't think they would dare play such games with American citizens."

To Hardenburg this seemed simon-pure logic. If Serrano took on American partners, his problems were surely solved. But Walt retained sufficient financial caution to inspect the estate's books minutely before agreeing to consider the offer further.

Events now moved swiftly. Soon after lunch, General Acosta, along with Colonel Prieto, set off with guides toward La Unión to brief Ordoñez and his men on Orjuela's plan: to proceed by canoe down the Caraparaná tributary to El Dorado, the last Colombian trading post, and from there send word inviting Loayza to a conclave. By 6 P.M. when Perkins, along with three of Serrano's Huitoto porters, stumbled half-drowned from a thunderstorm, Hardenburg was beside himself with excitement. Barely had his partner donned dry clothes and settled to turtle stew than he was pouring out details of Serrano's offer.

"I've seen his books and his profits and his offer's a giveaway," Walt insisted. "We'd be crazy to turn it down."

Perkins was staggered—but as always Hardenburg's small still flame of enthusiasm was not easily dimmed. "It's certainly worthy of investigation," he temporized. "At least we ought to stay on with Serrano and look over the estate."

Fired by adventure, both youngsters had momentarily forgotten the earlier lure of Manaus and the Madeira-Mamoré Rail-road—but to be their own bosses with a voice in the running of the estate seemed a greater prize yet. And now, seeing Perkins enthused, Hardenburg reached a characteristic decision.

"I'm going to ask Orjuela if I can't go along with him on that conference," he said. "I'd like to tell this Loayza face to face that as prospective purchasers we'd be obliged if he kept his hands off La Reserva."

On the Cauca Valley Railroad both men had saved the bulk of their pay, and they had other tangible assets—not least their $80 canoe—to trade in. Moreover, Hardenburg well knew how to live lean when the need arose, eschewing luxury and ostentation. Between them, they believed, they could raise the cash.

Two days later, at dawn on Tuesday, January 7, Walt Harden-burg was having disturbing second thoughts. Along with Orjuela, Sanchez, now recovered from fever, three boatmen and a peon they had paddled unharmed downriver; at Argelia, the only Peruvian trading post they had passed, dividing into two ports on either neck of a narrow peninsula, their reception by the chief overseer, Ramiro Pardo, had been civil enough. But at 4:30 P.M. on January 6 they reached El Dorado to find the proprietor gone. He was out seeking new land, his manager said—any land, however remote, where Arana's men couldn't reach him.

Still Orjuela was sanguine; by overland trial he sent an Indian runner speeding to Loayza, proposing a conference at dawn on the seventh.

But this milky-blue dawn had brought not Loayza but a small fleet of canoes pulling rapidly upriver—and Orjuela, watching from the shore, now gave a sudden cry of recognition. To Walt's surprise no sooner had he hailed them than the boats pulled in for the shore. Then he realized they were eight Colombians, along with their women and children and boatmen, and, as Orjuela began a rapid catechism, it was plain that all of them were frightened people.

Soon Hardenburg understood why. The fugitives were former employees from El Encanto—whom Arana had taken on his books when he bought out the Calderón brothers in 1905. Now, oppressed by Loayza's ill will, they had given notice to quit and were heading back for Colombia. And they added a chilling item of news: together with a Peruvian gunboat, another sixty soldiers had just arrived from Iquitos on Julio Arana's launch, the *Liberal*. Their hot though unconfirmed tip: Arana's men, with military support, planned a massed once-for-all raid on La Reserva and La Unión.

When they confirmed that Don Gabriel Martinez was still held prisoner at El Encanto, Hardenburg told Orjuela quietly: "We're for it, sure enough."

Already Hardenburg was wishing devoutly he had never journeyed with this mission. He cursed himself for ever contemplating Serrano's offer. If he had not taken Duarte's advice to trek on to La Reserva, if he had summoned patience to wait a few more days for Ordoñez, Perkins and he and their canoes would be peacefully en route to the Napo River. Meanwhile, the long soggy day wore on, and still, as the hours passed, no word came from Miguel Loayza. But the capable, scrupulous Orjuela insisted: "He may have been detained. We must give him one more day."

But when at 8 A.M. on January 9 there was still no word, Orjuela agreed to give up. They would return to Serrano's post without delay. For the whole of that day, tormented by sand flies, they crouched in the canoe while the boatmen, laboring against the five-knot current, made little progress. And to Hardenburg, normally a sound sleeper, the "veritable night of torture" that followed was worse by far. Unable to locate a convenient sandbank, the boatmen, wrapping themselves in rags, elected to sleep in the brush at the river's edge, leaving Hardenburg, Orjuela and Sanchez to share the cramped canoe. As they tossed and kicked, awakening each other every half hour, Hardenburg found himself praying for dawn.

On January 10, at first light, they struck out again, traveling more rapidly now. Foremost in every mind was the thought of reaching the sanctuary of La Reserva. To be sure, the river was quiet, but unnaturally quiet, the silence broken only by the croaking of frogs that always stole over the forest before a storm.

But the river stayed as quiet all day; by 7 P.M. Walt and the others felt the tension ease. Because the prospect of another night in the canoe was unthinkable, they moored it to an overhanging branch, hacking a clearing in the underbrush on which to bed down. Swathed from head to foot against insects, Hardenburg, exhausted, dropped off to sleep.

At 11 P.M. he came wide awake to blackness. For a moment his mind registered nothing, then he realized Orjuela was tugging urgently at his arm. In the glimmering starlight he saw that the government agent's finger was to his lips, enjoining silence. Wordlessly he pointed.

Hardenburg at first saw only twin pinpoints of light mirrored ahead on the shining water, moving from downriver, the route they had just traversed. Then a red-gold flurry of sparks fanned upward to the night; he heard the deep uneven pulse of wood-burning engines. Without warning, the whole river was bathed in a white uncanny daylight, as two craft, a launch preceded by a gunboat, passed within yards of them. An excited babel of voices came from the lighted decks; a wash of yellow water set their canoe rocking violently.

Then the craft had passed on, the deck lights dying to a faint shimmer like summer lightning. At length the engines' throbbing was indistinguishable from the river wash, the hoarse croaking of frogs.

Orjuela broke silence with a sharp exhalation of breath. "Do you think that the raid has begun?" he asked.

Hardenburg replied grimly: "I wouldn't know—but to use an old American phrase, I think they have the drop on us." Ironically he wondered: though no contract had been signed, was he already Serrano's partner.

From rubber trails like those of Colonel Luis da Silva Gomes on the Itacuaí River, where trappers (*above*) display typical wooden paddles used in the curing process, some £14,000,000 worth of smoked rubber (*below*) went down the Amazon each year. (*Photos: Author's Collection*)

Feudal overlords of the Amazon Valley included Colonel Nicolás Suárez (*above, left*), "Rockefeller of Rubber," ruler of 16 million acres and 10,000 hirelings, and mass executioner of hostile Indians; J. G. Araújo (*above, right*), who controlled the 1,500-mile Negro River; and Germino Garrido y Otero (*left*), King of the Içana River, who sired his own private army to police the waterfront. (*Photos: Author's Collection*)

Walter Ernest Hardenburg (*Courtesy of Mrs. Deborah Bressi*)

On the 1,000-mile-long Putumayo River (*above*), territory disputed by Colombia and Peru, Walt Hardenburg and his friends were shanghaied on the *Liberal* (*below*), one of twenty-three armed launches owned by rubber baron Julio Arana. (*Photos: Author's Collection*)

Rhythmic, persistent, the wide rounded blades of the Indians' canoe paddles sliced the yellow water. On the Caraparaná tributary, toward midmorning on Saturday, January 11, 1908, it was now the only sound that broke total silence. Neither Hardenburg nor Orjuela nor Sanchez volunteered a word, for the good reason that everything had been said a long time ago. Plainly their sole hope of reaching La Reserva was somehow to sneak their canoe past Arana's trading post at Argelia. Doggedly they held on to the thought that on the way down their reception had been friendly.

At 11 A.M. the lower port of the southern neck of the peninsula hove into view. A few peons slumbered in the shade of a rose-wood tree, pariah dogs huddled in the dust near their feet. Vultures roosted as motionless as statues on the rooftrees of the palm huts. Not a soul stirred near the river's edge. Unchallenged, the canoe glided on.

The hours crawled. At 1 P.M. Hardenburg, again standing in as cook, scrambled some turtle eggs for lunch, though they ate with little appetite. By 2 P.M. the river still hugged the southern neck of the peninsula and the upper port remained hidden from view. Another half hour and then they saw it: a large unpainted frame house cresting the hill above the river. "Just keep going," Hardenburg murmured.

But now it was plain that all along unseen eyes had kept track of their progress. Outside the trading post, the agent, Ramiro Pardo, already waited, along with an armed peon. From the corner of his eye, Hardenburg saw him beckon to them summarily, shouting something they could not catch. Again Hardenburg muttered: "Didn't hear a thing, did you? Just keep her going!"

As they swept on, Pardo called again, his voice a harsh echo across the water: "*Alto!*" Then, as they made no move to obey, "*Tiro al blanco!*" The peon's Winchester jerked upward. "It's no good," said Orjuela despairingly. "We'll have to go in."

But Hardenburg's blood was up: he had no intention of yielding without a fight. As the prow nudged in toward the shore and Pardo and the gunman started down the hill toward them, he whispered urgently, "Listen, señores—there are three of us and only two of them. When I give the word, open up and we'll drop them both." For the peon, assured of their surrender, had let his rifle fall, leaning on it as negligently as if it were a shooting stick.

Momentarily, Hardenburg's own counsel took him aback; until now, the biggest game that had ever fallen to his six-shooter were woodchucks in the maple woods behind the Youngsville farmhouse. In this land beyond the law, he thought, you swiftly learned to count life cheaply when kill-or-be-killed situations arose. "Let's give it to them," he urged again.

But Orjuela, fatally, hung back. His instructions from President Reyes were to come in peace; he could not willfully disobey the order. "What is the trouble?" he called to Pardo, feigning nonchalance.

His voice shorn of emphasis, Pardo answered: "No trouble—you are my prisoner."

Now the peon's rifle was trained, rock-steady, on Orjuela's heart. Without further argument, all of them came ashore.

Inside the trading post, Hardenburg tried every trick to reverse Pardo's decision. Acting as spokesman for the courteous, aloof Orjuela, he denounced their detention as "high-handed"—an insult to a Colombian Government envoy, and to the United States. "But you," Pardo told him wearily, "are free to go, señor. And so is this gentleman"—indicating Sanchez. His orders from above were explicit: to detain Orjuela and his Indian servants. Despite all Walt's objections, he would elaborate no further.

Still the youngster argued heatedly until Pardo cut him short. The American should make no trouble and leave without delay.

Sadly Hardenburg recognized that it was useless. They must go ahead without Orjuela.

Minus two boatmen, their progress was now painfully slow. Long after darkness had fallen they paddled stubbornly on, palms blistered and bleeding, plunged deep in gloomy silence. As Hardenburg later recalled it, they were "completely at the mercy of these latter-day pirates, who seemed to stop at nothing in their greedy ambition."

They were making as little headway at 9 A.M. on Sunday, January 12, when Hardenburg abruptly raised his hand, commanding silence. All of them craned forward, listening. From upriver, in the direction of La Reserva, came a sudden fusillade of rifle shots.

The firing went on for an hour. Hardenburg wondered if it would ever stop.

Down the darkened length of the river, a whistle sounded, shrill, challenging, peremptory. As if in reflex, the nerves of the three men in the canoe jumped painfully. At 8 P.M. on this sultry Sunday it was fully eleven hours since that ominous barrage of rifle fire had erupted. Since then they had heard no sound at all—until now, when the whistle of this unseen launch seemed to split the night.

At once as a safety precaution Hardenburg ordered: "Pull over to the right bank—the propeller wash will sink us otherwise."

But to Hardenburg's dismay, no sooner was the craft secured than the Huitoto boatman, with a cry of "Peruvians very wicked men," sprang ashore. Momentarily, lianas and underbrush whipped and swayed, as the Indian clawed his frantic way into deeper jungle. Poised on the gunwale, Hardenburg said quizzically, "We could do worse than follow that aborigine's example."

But Sanchez wavered. Arana's men hadn't harmed an exile and a foreigner at Argelia, he argued. Was it likely they would do so now? But if they saw the canoe abandoned and took it in tow,

what hope was there of reaching La Reserva? For precious
seconds, fighting his better judgment, Hardenburg hung back.
Then, with a blaze of light, two craft rounded the bend and were
upon them.

For Hardenburg the next moments held a nightmare unreality.
Across the floodlit water whiplashed a staccato volley of orders—
"Fire! Fire! Sink that canoe!" Her bow wave almost swamping
them, the first boat, the 148-ton launch *Liberal*, overshot the
canoe—but from the river gunboat, the *Iquitos*, a solid sheet of
carbine fire blasted them. With a hornet whine, one bullet passed
clean between Hardenburg and Sanchez; there was a threshing
sound like rain on the river as other bullets fell short. Outraged,
Hardenburg was roaring: "Hold it, hold it, will you?"

As abruptly as it had begun, the firing ceased. Through a
bullhorn, a voice speaking harsh Spanish interlarded with ob-
scenities ordered Hardenburg and Sanchez to approach the gunboat. "And don't try any funny business," it warned, cautioning
the soldiers. "Keep those men covered! If they try anything
smart, drill them between the eyes." As Hardenburg and Sanchez
hesitated, bemused by this onslaught, the officer shouted savagely,
"Row you———! Do you think we've got all night?"

Paddles clamped between blistered fingers, the two men did
their best—but pulling crabwise across the current without a
skilled boatman was well-nigh impossible. As he labored, Hardenburg felt a prickle of horror, for again he heard the shouted
order, "Fire!"—this time from the deck of the *Liberal*.

Then, to his eternal relief, an angry officer on the *Iquitos*
bawled, "You will disobey that order! *I* am in command here."
At once a furious slanging match broke out, snarled insults and
profanities winging from deck to deck, while Hardenburg and
Sanchez, conscious of a reprieve, paddled for dear life. Once,
dashing the sweat from his eyes, Hardenburg looked up to see a
blur of green-clad soldiers, thirty at least, glued to the *Iquitos'*
rails. Unmoved by the wrangle, they were following every move
he made, and there was not a carbine that did not hold him in its
sights.

It seemed an eternity before the canoe jarred against the *Liberal*'s side. At once rough hands clutched down at them, jerking them breathtakingly aboard. Abruptly Hardenburg saw the deck lights arc upward as a fist like an iron glove crashed against his jaw. Now the lights loomed through a red mist as chopping blows landed brutally, methodically, snapping back his head. A rifle butt drove against his kidneys; a heavy boot jarred his shins. Not only Captain Arce Benavides, of the Peruvian Army and Benito Lores, the *Iquitos*' commander, but also a motley horde of employees were jostling to work him over.

Braced against a bulkhead, Hardenburg tore free, swinging wildly, feeling his fists connect with bone-jarring force. As the thugs, startled, crowded back, he found his voice in spluttering fury. Had all of them gone crazy? How dared they open fire on an American citizen and shanghai him aboard a Peruvian Government launch? "I demand that you set us free now," he told Captain Benavides wrathfully, "and let us continue our journey."

Though his impassioned tirade soon spent itself, still the men held back. Hardenburg's keen brown eyes, blazing now with youthful indignation, suggested a man to be reckoned with. Subdued jeers and taunts followed his outburst, but no man doubted he was in earnest. "Search him," Captain Benavides ordered. "Search them both and search that canoe. We'll see how much truth there is in this."

Still protesting bitterly, Walt and Sanchez offered no resistance. They saw their hammock and other gear hauled from the canoe, which was then cast adrift. Their money belts and personal papers were confiscated. His face thrust close to Hardenburg's, Benavides now launched into a dramatic account of the victory he had that morning achieved "against great odds" at La Unión. The American heard him out in silence, his jaw jutting mutinously. Tiring of this, Benavides set a sentinel to guard them.

For three hours launch and gunboat throbbed on downstream. Toward midnight they jarred alongside, making fast, and Hardenburg, recognizing the dim outline of Argelia depot, where they had argued with Pardo ten hours back, wondered about

Orjuela. Still under armed guard he and Sanchez were hustled aboard the *Liberal* for the night. A familiar bearded face loomed suddenly from the darkness.

"When I heard an American voice upriver cursing a blue streak," said Perkins thankfully, "I guessed it was you."

Huddled on the *Liberal*'s deck, Hardenburg, Perkins, Sanchez and one of Serrano's employees, a slender handsome lad named Gabriel Valderrama, exchanged hastily whispered news. At La Unión, Perkins had learned, Arana's men were piling ashore with the troops when the angry Señor Ordoñez ordered them from his land. Then, as Colonel Prieto unfurled the Colombian flag, the uneven battle began. Against the massed might of 140 men, some manning a machine gun on the *Iquitos*' deck, the twenty-odd settlers stood no chance. After half an hour, Ordoñez, General Acosta and other survivors fled for the forest. Young Fabio Duarte and two peons were already dead. Prieto and another peon, severely wounded, had been cut to pieces with machetes.

At La Reserva, it had been much the same story. Following a pitched battle, Serrano, mortally wounded, had retreated with his men to the jungle, but Perkins and Valderrama, less fleet, found themselves cut off. Just as at La Unión, Arana's men had sacked and burned the dwelling house, carrying away prisoners and eleven tons of looted rubber.

Though it seemed prudent to feign sleep, Hardenburg and the others were certain that by dawn they would be dead. Arana's men were drunk that night and in a bloodthirsty mood.

Early next morning Hardenburg awoke with a start. A short, slim, copper-colored young man with a luxuriant moustache and restless untrustworthy eyes was staring down at him. "I am Miguel Loayza," he said flamboyantly. As Walt struggled to his feet, protesting, Loayza listened politely, smiling with faint condescension. Then in halting pidgin English, he explained: "We do this for your own good, you see—take you safe place. Or else Colombians, they kill."

"Are you out of your mind?" Hardenburg demanded, beside himself. "We don't have any fear of the Colombians—we've been their houseguests. And what we've seen of the Peruvian Amazon Rubber Company hasn't given us the idea it's any kind of life-saving syndicate."

For reply, Loayza, he later recalled, gave him "a peculiar snake-like smile." "I'll look after you all right," he repeated, then turned abruptly on his heel.

At 9 A.M., Hardenburg's heart sank to see Orjuela booted aboard under a heavy guard, his handsome face chalk-white, his immaculate linen stained with grime and cobwebs. Along with seven others he was thrust below deck into a cage no bigger than a chicken run, so cramped that no man could stand upright. But the American's attempt to parley with them was in vain; a sentry jammed a rifle against his rib cage and drove him back. Half an hour before sailing, Pardo came aboard to shake him formally by the hand.

"I tried to intercede with Loayza on your behalf," he said, "but I can do nothing for you."

At 6 P.M., as dusk was falling, the wharf at El Encanto loomed ahead—a strange place, Hardenburg thought grimly, to christen "Enchantment." From the rails he could see the station head-quarters, an ugly two-story building roofed in galvanized iron, sited high above the shelving riverbank and set amid land re-claimed for garden plots, with laborers' huts, washhouses and storehouses clustered beyond. But no sooner had the *Liberal* nudged against the wharf than a troop of gunmen raced for the water's edge, screaming execrations as they brandished their Winchesters.

Still closely guarded, Hardenburg, Perkins and the two Colom-bians were herded ashore. The gibing gunmen at their heels, they were marched up the dirt slope to the depot's wide compound, into a small stifling hut smelling of dust and mold. Behind them, they heard a bolt rammed home. Striking matches they found no furniture, no beds, not even a candle; it was plain their captors denied their prisoners even food or water. In the darkness each man heard eerie rustling sounds as his neighbor undressed for the night.

Crouched on the bare boards in one corner, Perkins and Hardenburg held a muttered colloquy. To Perkins, the situation was frankly desperate: they could expect no grain of mercy from "these human beasts." Striving to sound more cheerful than he felt, Hardenburg consoled him: "Maybe things'll work out by morning—these hounds snarl louder than they bite, I guess." But as he lay down, knowing sleep would not come, one thought excluded all others from his mind: If I don't think of something this is our last night on earth.

Back and forth across El Encanto's wide, sun-splashed compound, the noise resounded. Overseers trooping to the dining hall, others emerging from the bathhouses with soap and towel, stopped and stared. In his quarters behind the main kitchen, the Barbadian Armando King, who was both depot cook and chief flagellator, was alert with anticipation. Someone would be due for the whipping post before the hour was out. From the hut where the Americans and their friends had been confined the previous night, the steady drumming of fists and feet grew louder every minute, mingling with cries of "*Hola! Abierto!*" (Hullo! Open up!)

Cursing, his Winchester at the trail, a half-breed carabineer was already doubling toward the hut, convinced the prisoners had gone berserk. As he struggled to free the bolt he could not know that through the gloom the captives were eyeing Hardenburg, their leader, with both hope and apprehension. Perkins, for one, knew that the audacious plan Walt had conceived overnight was their one chance of getting out alive.

"You take me to Señor Loayza right away," was Hardenburg's immediate demand as the door swung back; "I want him to read this, get it?" In the strong sunlight, the guard saw that Hardenburg was flourishing an imposing-looking document, bearing an official seal.

Beset by indecision, the guard stood grumbling—then, when Hardenburg let loose a torrent of Spanish profanities, gave in hastily. Besides his thorough groundwork in grammar and syntax, Walt had studied the salty argot used by his survey crews—it was rarely, those who knew him conceded, that a gringo could swear so fluently in Spanish.

On the main building's second story, beyond the airy dining hall floored in polished cedarwood, were Miguel Loayza's combined office and living quarters. At this hour, the room was a tangle of rumpled bed sheets and half-read novels: after a long night of the insomnia that afflicted him Loayza looked at breaking point, dark smudges rimming his eyes. Every day in this forgotten pesthole seemed like a week, enlivened only by Florida-water baths, liberal tots of whiskey and frequent visits from his concubines.

As he stared at Hardenburg and his escort, barely able to focus them, the young American came at once to the point. "I know just what you have in mind for us," he told Loayza bluntly, "murder."

The agent dissented weakly: this was ridiculous, the prisoners had been confined for their own safety. But Hardenburg swept his protest aside. "You needn't try to deny it, that's the way the Peruvian Amazon Rubber Company operates," he asserted, "but let me warn you, if you murder us you'll sign your own death warrant. Shall I tell you why?"

Until this moment, deliberately, Hardenburg had spoken in English: vividly he recalled Loayza's uncertain pidgin aboard the *Liberal*. Now, seeing Loayza's face wrinkle with incomprehension, he switched to Spanish—at the same time thrusting the document he carried, which was worded in English, into Loayza's hands. "This," he claimed, "will tell you who I am, and who Señor Perkins is."

It was as he had hoped. Plainly, though the Peruvian made a brave show of scanning it critically, it might have been written in Greek. Hardenburg seized his chance. "You've heard of the Brazil

Railway Company?" he asked. "You've heard of Señor Farquhar?"

And one glance told him that Loayza had; the fame of Percival
Farquhar had penetrated even as far as El Encanto. The railroad
pioneer of South America, whose motto was "Think in conti-
nents," was to Arana's men more than the creator of the Madeira-
Mamoré Railroad, who was currently, backed by French capital,
constructing a magnificent $52 million port at Pará, on the delta.
The rumor that Farquhar's eyes were turned toward the
Putumayo had sent Arana speeding to London to form his
company and establish prior rights.

Aware that he had Loayza's attention, Hardenburg forged
ahead. As Farquhar's personal representative, he said, he had been
sent ahead to prospect the region. Already he was overdue in
Iquitos, where he was scheduled to open the biggest mercantile
establishment the Amazon had ever seen. If he and Perkins disappeared, a manhunt unparalleled in history would ensue to find
the culprits. The United States would certainly send a battleship
to Iquitos and beyond, as they had done nine years earlier—in
fact, a goodwill visit by the U.S.S. *Wilmington*, which Brazil and
Peru had misinterpreted as an invasion of their territorial waters.

Thumping the table, Hardenburg wound up: "I'm not asking
for—I'm *demanding*—our immediate release and a passage back
to Josá to recover our baggage."

Unnerved, Loayza made no attempt to examine the document
further. Instead he stressed how responsible he felt for the
Americans' safe conduct, so much so that he could not risk their
going to Josá, Serrano's port on the Putumayo. The Colombians
were still causing trouble. But in a few days' time the *Liberal* was
leaving for Iquitos; he would grant Hardenburg and his friends
free passage on that. Meanwhile, he would visit Josá and pick up
their baggage.

"You are now, of course, at liberty," added Loayza magnifi-
cently.

Back at the prisoners' hut, his partner's quietly triumphant air
told Perkins all he needed to know. But not until they were

strolling in the sunshine, out of earshot of the guards, did Hardenburg explain to the bewildered Sanchez and Valderrama the ruse he had employed.

One of Perkins' relatives was John Sharp Williams, Democratic Congressman from the Yazoo district of Mississippi, lawyer, free trader and personal friend of the noted lawyer William Jennings Bryan. At Perkins' request, he had furnished the two young men with impressive-looking travel credentials in case they fell foul of authority. It was these documents Hardenburg had brandished to bluff Loayza that he was Farquhar's right-hand man.

Emboldened by liberty, the two Americans mapped out a plan of campaign. Within the hour they again sought out Loayza. In view of past events, Hardenburg said sternly, they could not rely on his word beyond a point. Thus one of them intended staying on at El Encanto to ensure that the baggage was recovered, while the other went ahead on the *Liberal*.

Later Hardenburg recalled with pain his anxiety to draw lots— and how strenuously Perkins resisted. Their talk the previous night had revealed that Walt did not intend to take this treatment lying down—and that his plans for Iquitos included protests to the United States Consul and to Arana, as head of the company.

So Perkins hung back. All through their trip it was Hardenburg's resource and ingenuity that had seen them through: constructing sleeping shelters of palm leaves and wild cane, siting their cooking pot in the bows to save time grounding the canoe, even winning every chess game except when urgent decisions arose to distract him. If it came to official protests, Perkins decided, Hardenburg was the man to go to Iquitos. He would stay on at El Encanto.

And there were other more urgent reasons for Hardenburg to go ahead. Until now their own sufferings had taken pride of place—but now he and the others could roam El Encanto at will. Though a gunman loitered close at hand, ready to fire if they strayed too far, what Hardenburg saw within the stockade was enough to appall him. For the first time the horror of El Encanto struck home.

On the waterfront, aboard the *Liberal* and other craft, more than fifty Huitotos were busy piling the ships' holds with rubber, unloading supplies. Women worked alongside their menfolk, and all, regardless of sex, were as gaunt as famine victims. Their bodies were like skeletons thinly layered with flesh, on which the scars from past floggings stood out in huge raised weals. Nearby a watchful Barbadian overseer nursed a terrible tapir hide whip, five feet long and as thick as a man's thumb. Now Hardenburg recalled how Jesús López, only three weeks back at Yaracaya, had spoken of the *marca de Arana.*

Young and idealistic, Hardenburg's first thought was for Arana. Obviously the Peruvian, a man of honor, founder of a reputable British company, would be shocked to learn that on the Putumayo his name was a symbol of cruelty and oppression. It was now paramount to contact him and report these facts.

At noon, when the dinner triangle sounded, Hardenburg held the others back. They had been allotted a separate table in the overseers' mess hall but his first thought was for the Huitotos. How did they fare for rations? Incredulous, they watched carabineers marshal the Indians into fours, doling out a breakfast cup of farina from a copper caldron and a small tin of sardines to each group. Spotting one hireling as a Colombian, Valderrama engaged him in conversation then reported back.

"That's their one meal of the day," he said, "and they work for sixteen in every twenty-four."

On jungle treks in search of rubber, he added, supplies ran low and the Indians fared worse still. Sometimes the trails were choked with branches and creepers that they tore down and gnawed to stay their hunger, as if a herd of wild animals had passed through.

In the dining hall, conscious of the overseers' probing glances, Hardenburg found every mouthful a penance. Not only did his knowledge of the Indians' hunger torture him; he was eager also to witness more of Loayza's system so that Arana might know the worst.

Strolling with the others, like a man who craved the boon of sunshine, he learned many things. Close to the laborers' quarters stood a palm-slatted hut with a plank ceiling—it was called "the convent," a friendly guard told them with unwitting irony. The fifteen Indian girls who lived there, aged between nine and thirteen, worked as laundresses and swept the patio—yet their tawdry, Paris-style gowns seemed in strange contrast to their duties.

Soon Hardenburg unearthed the truth. These girls, captured on raids among the forest tribes, were unwilling prostitutes in the service of Loayza and his men. Forced to do menial work by day, they were divided among the crew of the *Liberal* when the company boat arrived every three months from Iquitos; on other nights they were securely locked in at 6 P.M. But any overseer, on applying to Loayza for the key, could summarily order a chosen girl to his quarters.

All afternoon the skyline was black with slow-moving silhouettes: in steady defile, the Indians were returning from their labors in the forest, staggering under 100-pound bales of rubber. Tiny children struggled desperately to tote bundles heavier than themselves. Often men fell headlong until kicks and oaths from the carabineers goaded them to their feet. At the section house Loayza stood, impassive, as the foremen weighed each bale, the Indians watching fearfully as the needle of the balance quivered. When it hovered on the full amount, some cried out for joy and leaped in the air, capering with pleasure. If it fell short, they flung themselves prostrate on the ground, like animals awaiting a blow.

Though Hardenburg saw no one flogged, he guessed shrewdly that only his presence as eyewitness saved the Indians that day.

Next morning, while Loayza was preparing his monthly report for the Iquitos office, Hardenburg and Perkins chanced on the worst sight of all. In the woods on the encampment's perimeter, groups of Indians were stretched helpless on the dew-soaked grass like survivors on a battlefield. All were sick and many were dying, without medicaments, or even food. The odor of putrefaction spread like a gas attack, but a Barbadian guard, seeing their horror, called out:

"This is nothing—there are days you can't eat your food on

account of the Indians lying around." Several times that morning they saw men die, and watched a silent procession of mourners commit the bodies to the wide river.

Vainly, Hardenburg tried to confer with the magistrate Martinez, confined with his men in a dirty eight-by-ten-foot room under the main building. But the two soldiers on guard duty drove them off; by Loayza's orders, visitors were forbidden. Nor could he make contact with Orjuela; the agent had all along remained in his cage aboard the *Liberal*. From both men, Hardenburg sought an answer: how much was known of these conditions outside the Putumayo?

Late on Thursday, January 16, he and Sanchez had word from Loayza: the *Liberal* would sail at first light and they must hasten aboard. "The sooner I get on to Iquitos and see our Consul, the better," Hardenburg decided, meanwhile briefing Perkins to keep a sharp eye open.

"Find out everything you can about how these characters operate, how many other posts there are, the names of the chiefs, things like that," he suggested. Perkins, puzzled, promised to do his best, though he wanted nothing more than to secure their baggage and rejoin his partner in Iquitos. He could not truly see the object of collecting data on a place so remote.

Now a final blow awaited Hardenburg. At the *Liberal*'s gangplank, his passage was blocked by Carlos Zubiabur, the commandant, a burly ex-army sergeant, long wanted by the police for the murder of thirty political prisoners. Whirling a huge billet of firewood around Walt's head, Zubiabur refused point-blank to honor Loayza's promise of a free passage.

"Nobody travels on my ship for free," he grated. "The passage money is £17 apiece."

Hardenburg protested violently: this was almost all the cash remaining in his money belt. Their canoe and everything else of value he possessed still awaited recovery from Josá. Sick at heart, he and Sanchez were forced to pay up—and he saw that unless some miracle transpired he would reach Iquitos penniless.

And once aboard the *Liberal* the frustrations mounted. Sullenly, Zubiabur told them that every cabin was occupied; they would have to sleep on deck. No, they could not have dinner; the last service was over. His anger mounting quietly, Hardenburg had just slung his hammock in a secluded alleyway when Zubiabur again strode up. Still twirling his billet he said that both men had sited their hammocks in an inconvenient place. They would have to move.

Now Perkins, who had come aboard to say good-bye, and Sanchez, were electrified. Over the days they had assessed Hardenburg as unfailingly cheerful and resourceful, a youngster whose gentle teasing was never tinged with spite. Neither had suspected the pent-up force within him if he was pushed too far. Already secure in his hammock, he refused to budge. "Quit henpecking us," he told Zubiabur finally.

Zubiabur was adamant. If the two did not shift this instant he would summon men to move them by force.

It was the snapping point. With one lithe bound, his eyes blazing like a cornered animal's, Hardenburg sprang from his hammock. Heedless of both Zubiabur's physique or his reputation as a killer, he slammed him violently against the bulkhead.

"Now look, Commandante," he said, his voice strangled in his throat, "I give you fair warning. If you molest us just once again during this trip, the second we get to Iquitos I'll drag you off this launch and so help me I'll club your brains out on the dockside."

For fully a minute Zubiabur stood there, staring, his face dangerously impassive. Then, slowly, he turned on his heel and lurched away. Perkins, impressed, drew breath sharply, but now Walt seemed sorry to have made so much of it. "He just got me wild," was all he would say. But Sanchez noted that throughout the voyage even at mealtimes, when only hunger enabled them to stomach the stale codfish, watery tea and rancid butter, Captain Zubiabur kept well out of Hardenburg's way.

Hardenburg, too, was quiet, fighting a battle within. As a railroad engineer seeking work on the Madeira-Mamoré, he did not want to become involved in a battle with an obscure upriver rubber company. Yet he knew that he could not move on from

Iquitos until he made these facts public. The drawn, somber faces of the Indians at El Encanto haunted his sleep. And the plight of Gabriel Martinez, who had been brought aboard to join Orjuela and seven others in their cage, assailed by a day-long barrage of gibes and taunts, cried out for action.

        On Saturday, February 1, 1908, Walt Hardenburg walked ashore at Iquitos, a mongrel Peruvian town perched on a bluff a hundred feet above the tawny waters of the Amazon. A rubber-rich community of about 12,000 people, it sought to follow the pattern of Manaus—though for one house faced with gay *azulejo* tiles, twenty were built of flattened paraffin tins. It was a town of bizarre contrasts, still lit on moonless nights by flaring kerosene lamps, its sidewalks thronged with bejeweled Indians, hoop-skirted belles and dudes in cashmere trousers, scented handkerchiefs pressed to their faces to block the aroma from the open sewers coursing down the streets.

    Inquiry now took Hardenburg to where the wide, sun-baked main street, Prospero Street, was cut by Morona Street. On the ground floor of the corner site, a house faced in black, red and green lozenge tiles with graceful silver-painted balconies, was Martin Norden's A la Ville de Paris, a dressmaker's gay with corseted waists and osprey-feather hats. But to the upper story was affixed a sign which read "Dr. Guy T. King, American Dentist. Consular Service of the United States of America, Peru." Up the stairs, on fire with crusading zeal, Hardenburg now strode.

    But here he received as rude a shock as any he had known to date. A tall, thin, indecisive man, recently appointed Acting Consul, Dr. King heard him out in worried silence, before commenting: "You may expect me to commiserate with you, young man, but I think congratulations are in order." Then, seeing Walt's blank astonishment, he supplemented, "Any man who escapes death at the hands of Arana's assassins deserves congratulations."

Hardenburg was flabbergasted. Hadn't King taken in his story of the raids on Serrano and the abduction of his wife? What would happen to Martinez and Orjuela who were even now caged aboard the *Liberal?* Didn't the treatment of the Huitotos upriver demand that something should be done?

But to King it was a twice-told tale. As recently as December, 1907, the then Consul, Charles C. Eberhardt, had reported in detail to Secretary of State Elihu Root, in Washington, on the harsh "rule of the rifle" that subdued the Putumayo. American investors would be wise to steer clear of this troubled terrain; in twenty years, Eberhardt estimated, "the wild Indian of the Upper Amazon will have disappeared almost entirely." A Harvard anthropologist visiting the region, William Curtis Farabee, backed this to the hilt: "The condition of the Indians is in reality nothing else then slavery."

But Washington, King pointed out, could do little but take note of the facts. As disputed terrain, the Putumayo was not even the responsibility of Colombia or Peru. "I don't have either the powers to interfere or the finance," he told Hardenburg, "and I've got my business as a dentist."

Hardenburg was blunt. King also had the duty which his post as Consul conferred on him. "Are you saying," he asked, "that Julio Arana knows what goes on up those rivers?"

But King would not be drawn. How could he postulate what Arana knew or did not know? "I make it my business *not* to know," he admitted. "On the Amazon a man lives longer and stays healthier that way."

"In that case," said Hardenburg doggedly, "the only way to find out is for me to ask Arana personally."

Now King showed an almost paternal concern. "Son, don't do that," he begged. "Steer clear of Julio César Arana. This man is a medieval despot. They don't run things on the Amazon the way they do back in New York State. Up here it's frontier law, the way Dodge City was sixty years back."

Anxious to pacify this prickly youngster, he proposed a compromise. As Consul, he would submit a claim for the baggage, if it was not forthcoming, to Leslie Combs, the U.S. Minister in

Lima. But he warned Hardenburg to expect no speedy reply. Iquitos and the Putumayo were as cut off as any region in the world—which did much to explain "Winchester law." The only routes to Lima were over the Andes, by way of the Pichis or the Cajamarca trails, little more than mule tracks; for mail to travel just one way sometimes took seventy-five days. "A man can get from here to New York City quicker than he can get to Lima," King explained.

Meanwhile, he asked Hardenburg, how was he fixed for money and clothing? When Walt confessed his poverty, King's solution was characteristic: for the time being, the young man had better lodge with him. They could reach a settlement on terms later, after he had written home. A widower, King confessed that at times he was lonely; there was little fun apart from musical evenings he organized for the town's teen-agers. He stayed on in Iquitos only because his son was joining him as a partner, but as yet the boy had still to graduate from dental college.

Despite his severe reservations regarding King's moral fiber, Hardenburg saw that the dentist was a kindly man who meant well. Penniless as he was, he was grateful to accept his offer.

His first step was to wire New York, through the Booth Steamship Company, for an immediate remittance of $300—some of the money saved from his fifteen months on the Cauca Valley Railroad. An introduction from King next took him to Dr. Serafín Filomeno Peña, director of the newly built Iquitos Departmental Secondary College on Pastaza Street, and Peña found his Spanish fluent enough to offer him a twice-weekly job teaching English for £10 a month. Calling on the Prefect, Carlos Zapata, Walt struck it richer still; the town badly needed public buildings, and if Hardenburg cared to design a new hospital, the job was his for £30 a month. At nights, he often sat in on Dr. King's guitar sessions with the town's young men, though the evenings were not complete until he had taught them to render his own favorite, "Over the Waves."

For the moment, biding his time and still awaiting news of Perkins, he did nothing about Arana. In any case, he learned, the

Peruvian was rarely in Iquitos; for more than a year now his house had stood empty. No one even knew for certain whether he was in Manaus or London. To Hardenburg, this only confirmed his theory. The cruelties were of recent origin and Arana himself knew nothing of them.

One afternoon, a few weeks after the Colombian Consul had secured the repatriation of Orjuela and Martinez, the commotion of a mob sent Hardenburg hastening to the second-floor balcony of King's living room. Across the way, on Morona Street, close to the waterfront, a crowd was boiling angrily round a flat-roofed, one-story building. Speeding downstairs to find the cause of the trouble, Walt saw that the police were raiding No. 49, a small printing shop. Already the street was littered with mounds of gray type, compositors' sticks and smashed fonts, and smudged galley proofs fluttered everywhere.

As he watched, a tall, thin, dark-skinned man with gray, close-cropped hair was hustled from the building by a squad of green-uniformed police. His collar was askew and there was an angry swelling below his right eye, but despite this, Hardenburg was impressed by his dignified bearing. Soberly, impervious to the hooting of the mob, he was frog-marched toward the waterfront, followed by two small Indian boys carrying his meager belongings.

At dinner that night, he found that King knew all about it. The man's name was Benjamin Saldaña Rocca; it had long been rumored that the police were going to run him out of Iquitos. Both journalist and printer, he was in truth a small-town scandal-sheet proprietor, who, since July, 1907, had been waging a one-man grudge war against Arana's firm. His attacks took the form of random newssheets, called either *La Felpa* or *La Sanción*, printing testimonies from former employees up the Putumayo. "Some say he was a Colombian agent," King said indifferently. "Whatever he was, the company no sooner fired somebody than he'd go to Rocca who rushed into print with a story."

Hardenburg was intrigued. If Arana was no longer in town, why should the police bestir themselves on his behalf? King was

vehement. Whether in or out of Iquitos, Arana effectively con-
trolled it, for most of its prosperity was due to his concerns.
Arana had been Mayor in 1902, President of the Chamber of
Commerce one year earlier, twice President of the Departmental
Assembly. "It's like I warned you," he stressed again, "Arana's a
man to be reckoned with."

Hardenburg persisted. What kind of allegations had the newssheets made? Was there truth in them? But King didn't know.
Consul Eberhardt had reported to Washington that they were
"more or less accurate," but even he had been relying on hearsay.
King himself had seen only one example—an amateurish affair
printed on bright yellow paper, illustrated by crude cartoons.
"What I do know," he stressed, "is that these things are best kept
quiet. In Manaus there was a man who went round hawking these
papers. Later they found him stone-cold in an alley—someone
had sewn up his eyes with cobbler's thread and blocked his ears
with hot beeswax."

Hardenburg was afire was curiosity. Where could he see
copies of these papers? In vain King tried to divert him. They
had been merely rags, overnight sensations—Rocca had been too
smalltime to maintain a filing department. "Could Arana have
seen them?" Walt pressed the dentist.

King, rising abruptly from the table, thought it unlikely. The
newssheets had only circulated in the last seven months, during
Arana's absence. The man most likely to have seen them was
Pablo Zumaeta, Arana's brother-in-law, who ran the Iquitos
office, but the dentist neither knew nor cared whether they had
been brought to his attention.

Hardenburg was not giving up. Now, along the waterfront, in
poolrooms, in small dark bars with palm-trunk floors, he began
his cautious inquiries—making each glass of beer last a long time,
for Iquitos, like Manaus, imported its beer from Germany at a
cost of four shillings a bottle. Who had seen the papers? What
had they contained? But strangely, all the people who had ever
glimpsed them had since left town. Hardenburg got no closer

than meeting men who had known men who had seen a copy—once.

Toward April's end he was striding along the Malecón, the fine balustraded promenade which the citizens had built to command the waterfront, when a loafer blocked his path. His bearded face was hollow-cheeked and waxen and the clothes hung on his skeletal frame in rags. For a second Hardenburg stared, uncomprehending, then a chill of recognition ran through him.

"It's me all right," Perkins whimpered. "You'd better have it straight from the shoulder, Walt; we've lost everything—everything in the world."

Hardenburg was stunned. It seemed that he was looking not at his old partner but at what was left of a man. Gently he led Perkins to a waterfront eating house and ordered a meal to set him up—shrimp soup, wild duck with rice, tamales and Indian maize beer. At first his friend was so incoherent he had difficulty piecing the story together, but little by little it emerged.

No sooner had Hardenburg left El Encanto, than Miguel Loayza, as good as his word, went by launch to Josá to recover their baggage. His suspicions aroused by the bulky instrument cases, Loayza ransacked their trunks—to find not only surveyor's kits but papers identifying both men, not as Percival Farquhar's agents, but as humble railroad engineers. Returning to El Encanto in a frenzy at the trick, he had Perkins dragged before him, threatening to murder him on the spot.

For days he was confined to the stifling hut from which Hardenburg had freed him. Soon he was again racked by malaria, but even at the height of the fever he had been denied quinine, blankets, even water to slake his thirst. Daily he was beaten and abused by Loayza's men. Only his American citizenship and the fear of ultimate reprisals had finally induced Loayza to ship him downriver on the *Liberal*.

"But," Perkins cried out, his eyes brimming with tears, "I did better than any other prisoner there, because I was the only one who wasn't murdered after I came there."

Hardenburg was incredulous, but Perkins, close to hysteria, gave him horrified chapter and verse. Three weeks after Walt had left, twenty-nine Colombians had been cornered in the jungle, tricked into laying down their arms and brought to El Encanto. Ordering them to be bound hand and foot, Loayza had appointed an execution squad to dispatch them with pistols and machetes.

"They didn't only murder them," Perkins related, "when they were dead they mutilated them, even decapitated them, and Loayza stood by and let it happen."

And this had been only the beginning. Perkins could not condemn the whole Peruvian race, but these men, he said, were "mongrels, cowardly murderers and thieves." Though briefed to keep his eyes open, he would have had to be deaf and blind not to see what was going on, for no sooner had Hardenburg sailed on the *Liberal* than all pretenses were abandoned. One morning he had seen a party of Huitoto porters, laden with provisions, set out for a camp in the woods. Most were so far gone in starvation that one man had been too weak to carry his seventy-pound load.

"They warned him not to fall down anymore," Perkins said, appalled, "but the poor devil began staggering as if he was going to fall. A carabineer just shot him in the back and he died."

To extract the rest of the narrative took all Hardenburg's time and patience. Often, overcome by memories, Perkins cried like a child. Time and again he had seen Huitotos, tied hand and foot to stakes driven in the ground, flogged by the Barbadian Armando King until they died. Others had been jammed in the stocks for weeks on end until their legs gave out and they could never walk again. Once, as punishment, Loayza's men had penned some Huitotos in a straw-thatched hut, firing it with a torch and shooting down every man who broke and ran. Each raid into the jungle brought more young girls as inmates of "the convent," and every company boat leaving El Encanto took others down for sale in Iquitos.

At length, recovering himself, Perkins put aside past problems for present. What he had seen, he confessed, had turned their adventure sour. Never again would he set foot in the Amazon Valley. His one desire was to board the next freighter to America —but with their canoe and all their baggage stolen, how could they raise the fare?

Hardenburg reassured him. His $300 had long since arrived from New York. Some of it he had spent on clothes and personal accessories, but enough remained for him to stake Perkins to his passage money: he owed his old friend no less. Now that the fate of their gear was known, King could submit a claim to the Peruvian Government through the Minister in Lima. He himself would visit the company's office to see about compensation. Meantime he was working, and with £40 a month he could even save as well as cover board and lodging.

Perkins was uncomprehending. What did Walt mean? A job? Board and lodging? "You're not planning to stay in this hell-hole?" he gasped.

Gently, but firmly, Hardenburg explained: he saw no other way. It was right that Perkins should return to the United States, for plainly he needed hospital treatment, but he must stay.

"How could any man who'd seen what we've seen rest easy in his conscience without trying to do something for these poor devils of Indians?" he said. "I plan to stay and see that something *is* done."

Perkins shook a despondent head. He did not see what Hardenburg or any one man could do. Men like Loayza were a law unto themselves, and in that farflung territory there was not even a constitutional authority to keep them in check. "I don't think anyone would credit us in the first place," he said shrewdly, "especially if we told the *whole* truth."

But Hardenburg, quietly indignant, shook his head: he would persist until people not only listened to him but believed him also. And he told Perkins firmly: when he reached the United States he must not only take up their claim in Washington, but he must also write Hardenburg a letter setting out every item of the story he had related—the dates, the names, details of the atrocities.

"Meanwhile," he added, "I'm going to make inquiries here and, as soon as I can save passage money, in Manaus, too, and in time I think I'll find a whole lot of people willing to write me letters."

He summed up somberly: all over the world people saw the Amazon's "black gold" as something essential to an automobile. To millions more, it was a sticky substance put to such comfortable domestic uses as tobacco pouches, fountain-pen fillers, babies' comforters and door silencers. Now he could not rest until those untold millions realized at what cost much of this black gold was won.

Still Perkins was unconvinced. "I admire your spirit right enough," he said, "and as long as I live I'll be proud to have known you. But I don't think that you've one chance in a million of pulling it off."

Though Perkins could not know it, back in Youngsville, New York, in the small farm at the foot of the Catskill Mountains, Walt's mother often illustrated his patience and persistence by relating how, as a boy, he would spend hours at a time balancing a row of corncobs on a wall, setting them up as a target for his Harrington .32.

"Walt never minded how long it took to balance those cobs," she told neighbors. "He just went on until he'd got them set up right. He was like that about everything."

Now, for the first time, Walt Hardenburg had picked himself a moving target: the most powerful and ruthless man in the whole valley of the Amazon.

PART THREE

 The White City

BY EARLY May, when Perkins departed for New York, Walt Hardenburg was already a familiar figure on the streets of Iquitos. His lithe, square-shouldered figure, swinging easily across the Plaza de Armas en route to his twice-weekly lesson at the college, or heading for Elías Aguirre Street, site of the newly planned hospital, had become part of the life of the town. Familiar, too, was his weekly advertisement in *La Occidente* announcing his services as a private English tutor. Before summer was far advanced he had signed up fourteen pupils.

In a lawless town, Hardenburg was notable as a strangely law-abiding figure. On the side streets a brimming chamber pot full in the face at daybreak was the mildest threat a man might encounter—and *La Occidente*'s columns featured more advertisements for "companion dictionaries" (pretty señoritas to act as interpreter and common-law wife) than for sober English tutors. Walt, the quiet industrious chess player, might have seemed out of place but for his canny knack of blending in with his surroundings, of hearing more than he ever said.

And Hardenburg had cause to watch his step. On the Amazon, he had learned, life was counted so cheap that only the presence of a corpse could prove murder. Failing this, the charge was dismissed as "gossip that can't be checked." If his vendetta against Arana's company became public knowledge, he would wind up dead or disabled in a side street, and the townsfolk wouldn't even blink. As one old-timer told him: "When a young fellow goes to confession here, we get to asking ourselves just who it was he murdered."

Later, one man was to testify: "There was nothing to prevent the Arana brothers, who were all-powerful in Iquitos, taking Hardenburg and throwing him into jail. That he was an American citizen was undoubtedly his protection."

An extrovert with a rare sense of humor, Walt Hardenburg was no smug do-gooder. His anger and disgust at what he had seen up the Putumayo stemmed from one simple mainspring: his own untroubled childhood. As far back as he could remember, life around the Youngsville farm, with its simple Methodist faith, had been serene and tranquil. Even financial pressures had been absent, for heavily built Spencer Hardenbergh had long since made his pile; the sheep he raised, the corn and buckwheat he grew, were pleasure, not grinding necessity. From early on, life for Walt had been a joyous round of making hay in their thirty-acre field, The Big Meadow . . . cavorting in the swimming hole of Stump Pond with his brothers, William and Wesley . . . hunting rabbits, gray squirrels and ruffed grouse through dense woods of maple and beech and chestnut . . . chewing the fat with the hired men, John Hollenbeck and Doc Conklin, who were independent enough to run their own small farms and only "worked out" at seedtime, or harvest, or cutting stove wood in the fall.

To Walt and his brothers it was a never-ending source of mystery why both men, oblivious to the seasons, wore three pairs of threadbare pants, not one—though Walt suspected it was quicker to pull on one more pair than to patch the holes.

Sturdy and self-reliant, Walt still knew little of the world beyond: his own world was a Currier and Ives print come to life. Even the nearest village was four miles away, close to an hour by horse and buggy over rutted roads—and there was little call to venture that far, save for a twice-weekly jaunt to collect mail. In summer, a boy could jog pleasurably for hours astride the nags that were hacks, buggy horses and plow horses all in one, and there were spirited games of baseball and "one old cat." In the fall, there were chestnuts to gather before the snapping winter days brought new delights—sleigh riding, skating on Stump Pond, fishing for pickerel through the ice.

From youth, Walt, like his father, was a prodigious reader; it was Spencer's pride that he subscribed to forty periodicals and read them from cover to cover. Most often on winter evenings, tiring of games of euchre and pinochle, or hilarious sessions with toy boats in the attic, Walt turned back to chosen favorites, not only *Youth's Companion*, which his brothers read, but significantly, tales of great crusades and wrongs righted—*Two Years Before the Mast*, *Uncle Tom's Cabin*, and everything that Richard Harding Davis ever wrote.

In his teens, his difficulties with Spencer grew keener, but home was still a haven of love and peace. His mother saw to that. Always pin-neat in her trim shirtwaist blouses, her hands never idle, she preserved the balance of power unruffled; even when Walt, at twenty, decided to change the spelling of his surname, she made no move to interfere. To Walt, the kitchen which was the center of family life remained what it had always been: a sanctuary fragrant with his favorite clam chowder, sweet-and-sour green beans, pot roast and apple cake.

Fired by the precepts of that home, he had reached the Putumayo with his ideals wholly untarnished: with the simple Christian standards of Youngsville as his yardstick, nothing in life had stirred him like this cruelty and oppression. Quietly but persistently indignant, he was setting out to right the wrong— and the realization that he was in mortal danger in no way deterred him.

Late one afternoon, he had news that galvanized him into action: Julio César Arana had returned to his Iquitos home. That evening, without hesitation, Hardenburg set out to see him.

Dusk had already fallen as he strode from the dentist's surgery toward the big sprawling family house on the corner of Prospero and Magua Streets. From the Plaza de Armas, the strident music of a merry-go-round's calliope drowned even the cries of the street vendors, but passing through Arana's iron gates, standing open to the sidewalk as always in Amazon houses, he entered a world of total silence. At the end of a passageway, he glimpsed a wide courtyard, its red stone walls sprouting ferns, a family laundry tank sited beneath the shade of a giant mamarosa tree. Clapping his hands loudly, he called *"Permiso."* A servant appeared, then departed hastily. The American was left standing alone.

It was some moments, as he later recalled, before he realized that Julio Arana already stood before him, framed almost theatrically against the half-light of the courtyard, studying him intently, smoke wreathing from his long Havana cigar.

"That you enter with God," Arana said, voicing the automatic welcome of the Amazon, "my house is yours." Impassively, he ushered Hardenburg into the parlor on the passage's right-hand side, sparsely furnished with a sofa, rows of wicker chairs formally ranged to face one another, and the piano on which Angelica had so often played for her father. Lowering himself into a chair, Arana made a steeple of his fingertips, inclined his head suavely and waited for his visitor to begin.

But Walt, as he was later to confess, was none too certain of the best way to handle things. On the Putumayo, he had been all along convinced that no blame could attach to Arana personally —but was the rubber baron's return to Iquitos so soon after the railroading of the journalist Rocca a shade too coincidental? For the moment, at least, he decided to play it safe. He and Perkins, as casual travelers, had been subjected to imprisonment and bodily harm, and had lost their baggage and "valuable scientific instruments." What, he asked Arana point-blank, did he propose to do about it?

"But what were you doing in this territory?" countered Arana. "How did these trunks of yours come to be lost?"

Now a small but significant thing happened. A shade flustered, Hardenburg was replying in English, when Arana at once shook a positive head. "English, no," he declared, holding up the fingers of his right hand. "One, two, three, four, five—that is my English."

As Hardenburg, apologizing, switched back to Spanish, he could not know that Arana's grasp of English was prodigious. And though he had an equal command of Portuguese and French, he would rarely admit to any language but his own. Convinced of his ignorance, people lowered their guards, often letting fall facts he could use against them.

Haltingly, the American went on. Though he had formed no prior impression of Arana, he had not in truth expected a man so worldly and self-possessed. There had been *cosas malas* at La Reserva and La Unión, he explained, and Arana nodded, imperturbable. These he had heard about—what then?

In fact, Arana, preoccupied, was only half-listening: in the past nine months his plans had suffered bitter setbacks. Only two months after the Peruvian Amazon Rubber Company became a registered London concern, the world demand for latex had dwindled alarmingly. Following a crisis in America, which closed several factories, prices had plummeted, with almost every grade on the market showing falls up to 1/3d for the year. Worse, as world supplies increased, stocks were piling up unconsumed, and three months earlier, in February, had come yet more disquieting news. The price of top-grade wild rubber, the market's yardstick, 5/3d a pound in 1907, had slumped to 2/9d, the lowest since 1894.

Now the London promoters counseled a six-months' delay before the company went public, giving the panic time to die down—and at the very moment Arana had maneuvered the situation to his own advantage. Of the whole corporate structure, nominally capitalized at £1,000,000, 700,000 £1 shares would be held, as part of the purchase price, by Arana, Pablo, Lizardo and Abel Alarco, another brother-in-law, securing them the true control of the company. Even the expenses of indemnity and promotion—£30,000—would be borne not by them as vendors but by the new corporation.

Meantime, the promoters, busily seeking "front-pagers"— names that would look imposing on a company prospectus—had come up with two likely men. First to join the board was Henry Read, manager of the London Bank of Mexico and South America, anxious to see that shipments of rubber kept pace with

Arana's £60,000 revolving credit. Soon Read's old friend, John Russell Gubbins, a merchant with thirty-eight years' experience of Peru, would join him.

On the face of it, Arana still needed a steady rise in production and profit to tempt investors—though here again he had hit on a master stroke. The final prospectus the public saw no longer placed the accent on rubber. Rechristened "The Peruvian Amazon Company," its main assets, as security for the preference shares, were now shown as the trading houses at Manaus and Iquitos. Almost as an afterthought, Arana's Putumayo holdings were listed as "in addition to the above assets."

Thus, on this May evening, Arana had much to preoccupy him: only with an effort did he force his attention back to Hardenburg's hesitant narrative. Yet the young man stood his ground gamely, again pressing the Peruvian: "What are you going to do about our baggage, señor?"

"I will certainly see about it," Arana promised, summoning up a benevolence he did not feel. "I am on my way up there at the moment."

Then, seeing Hardenburg's surprise, he explained. The Peruvian Government had summarily instructed the Prefect, Carlos Zapata, and Carlos Rey de Castro, Manaus' Peruvian Consul, to secure the district against the "raids of the Colombians, which were being constantly made." They were en route with a force of two hundred men and Arana was ordered to accompany them.

Prior to this he said, "I have only during the whole course of my life spent a few days in the Putumayo district." Plausibly, he enumerated them: in December, 1901, to settle a dispute on a debt; in 1903, to check on the credit status of some debtors; again in 1905, to buy some Colombian properties.

"Even then," said Arana vehemently, "fighting was taking place between the Colombians. I decided to buy the properties as the best way of saving money which I had invested." But now, glancing at his watch, he pleaded another engagement. "It may be that we can find out something about this baggage of yours," he assured Hardenburg. "At any rate I'll do what I can."

Agents like Miguel Loayza (*upper left*), captor of Hardenburg and Perkins, whom Hardenburg tricked into releasing him, received no salaries, only commissions on the dead weight of rubber (*above*) that their depots handled. Barbadian witnesses like 32-year-old John Brown (*lower left*) helped to unmask the killers. (*Photos: Author's Collection*)

The above panorama shows El Encanto, one of Arana's forty-five Putumayo rubber depots. Held prisoner in a shed on its main compound (*below*), Hardenburg vowed to expose the system. (*Photos: Author's Collection*)

Above: Huitoto Indians lined up at La Chorrera depot; in twelve years, Hardenburg revealed, Arana's men had slain 30,000. *Below:* The Huitotos' overseers included 400 teen-age Indians, taught from infancy to kill. (*Photos: Author's Collection*)

Above: Hell's Cauldron on the Madeira River. To bypass nineteen rapids as lethal as these, and bring Bolivia's rubber to the Atlantic, Percival Farquhar, master builder from York, Pennsylvania, pioneered the 226-mile Madeira-Mamoré Railroad. *Below:* So dense was the jungle along the line of the future Madeira-Mamoré Railroad that earlier contractors even abandoned their locomotives. (*Photos: Author's Collection*)

As the youngster muttered his thanks, Arana glanced at him keenly. "May I now ask you something, señor?" he said. "During your journeys in this region, what impression did *you* form of conditions up there?"

Hardenburg looked the Peruvian squarely in the eye. Despite the half-light, for the oil lamp remained unlit, Arana's eyes, black and glowing, seemed to bore into him, though his face, as always, was expressionless—as blank as Hardenburg's own, when he answered, after only a second's pause, "If you are on your way up there, señor, I think you'll best be able to judge conditions for yourself."

In this way, as he afterward reasoned it, he had given nothing away. If Arana knew nothing of the system at El Encanto, he could not fail on his arrival there to espy the plight of the Indians and to act. If he was privy to Loayza's methods, then he was a man who would stop at nothing—and it would be tantamount to suicide, here on the Amazon, to disclose such perilous knowledge.

Hardenburg could not then foresee how Arana would one day contrive to turn his reticence against him. As the Peruvian rose to conclude the interview, he was conscious only of Arana's feral power: the burly shoulders and the massive unrelenting jaw contrasting oddly with the beautifully shaped almost feminine hands. As he made his exit, Arana was staring after him, brooding, inscrutable, not a muscle moving in his face. On the street, the blare of the calliope again shattered the silence, and Walt felt relief to be back in the smoky, charcoal-smelling twilight, alive and free.

Following this interchange of frigid courtesies, Hardenburg was baffled as to his next move. As a chess player who saw situations in terms of Fianchetto defenses and Petroff counter-attacks, he felt it was now stalemate. Arana could pin nothing on him but a natural anxiety to recover his missing baggage. But he equally lacked any valid evidence of Arana's complicity.

One night, three weeks after Walt's twenty-second birthday, King retired to his surgery after dinner to browse through some Dental Association magazines newly arrived from America. In the living room Walt was settling to correct some of his pupils' English lessons when the servant announced a visitor. Halfway up the stairs, hovering just within range of the lamplight, he saw a slender lad with a proud sensitive face, aged about seventeen. He recognized him as an occasional visitor to King's musical evenings.

"I guess the servant made a mistake," he told the lad. "Isn't it Dr. King you've come to see?" But the boy shook his head. "No, Señor Hardenburg, it is you."

Then, seeing the American's mystification, he explained: "My name is Miguel Galvez. I am the natural son of Benjamin Saldaña Rocca."

Hardenburg, though quietly excited, was wary, too. He sensed he was on the verge of a breakthrough, but Galvez' appearance out of the blue was disturbing. Inviting the boy into the parlor, he asked how he could help. Now, with quiet sincerity, Miguel outlined his mission. At last, word had come from his father who had only recently reached Lima when his letter was dispatched. As yet, he had secured no more profitable work than as a legman on *La Prensa*, a daily hotly opposed to the government's land-grabbing policies.

But Rocca's heart, Miguel said, lay in the work he had left undone in Iquitos. Hours before the police put him aboard the steamboat that took him, by way of Yurimaguas to the Peruvian capital, a friendly source had tipped him off that a raid was imminent. Losing no time, Rocca had gathered together all the evidence he had so far amassed and hastened with it to his long-standing woman friend, Doña Amelia, who kept a pension for Spanish laborers on the waterfront. Over the years she had borne him several children, of whom Miguel was the eldest, giving them her name as was Amazon custom.

"He has been a good father to us," Miguel avowed, and Hardenburg knew enough of the river's domestic vagaries not to dispute it. "This is why I have come on his behalf." Rocca, he said, was brokenhearted that no one was left to carry on his work. That his earlier efforts should not be in vain, he had given Miguel full permission to pass on the documents to anyone who could make incisive use of them. "So," the boy ended simply, "I came to you."

The American was uneasy, sensing a trap. For all his open-handed manner, the boy might be in Arana's pay. But, supposing he was in earnest? If Hardenburg was cast as Arana's adversary before even mapping out a campaign, his camouflage must be wholly inadequate. "What kind of documents are these?" he asked, playing for time.

Miguel explained: they were letters his father had solicited from former employees of Arana. Some Saldaña Rocca had contrived to print, but many arrived too late for publication. At first Hardenburg was equivocal. If some had already been printed, what good use could he make of those?

The boy's reply was disingenuous: did this mean that Hardenburg had been able to locate the back numbers he sought? He asked because some weeks back he had been fetching beer from a waterfront bar for a guest of his mother's. By chance he had overheard Walt inquire for anyone stocking old copies of *La Felpa* and *La Sanción*.

"These are not all back numbers," Miguel admitted, "but I think perhaps they are better—the original statements, published and unpublished." Seeing Hardenburg still hesitant, he tried to reassure him: he didn't question why the American wanted the papers. But if he could make use of them, they were his for the asking.

Hardenburg decided to trust him. The story of the bar encounter rang true; he prayed that his casual inquiries had not been widely voiced abroad. But he did want to see the documents and right away. Had Miguel brought them along?

His casual approach seemed to shock Galvez. Doña Amelia's pension was at the far end of the waterfront. Only a foolhardy man would walk that distance thrugh the town with incriminating papers. Now that Don Julio was back in the region, his spies were always on the lookout. He had risked coming here tonight only because his connections with King's musical evenings were known.

Hardenburg was abashed. Beside this lad, five years his junior but already skilled in the tricks of survival, he felt like a naïve amateur. "Then," he asked humbly, "it's best if I never come near your mother's pension?" Miguel agreed: they must not compromise Doña Amelia. Better to meet on neutral ground—say tomorrow night at 8 P.M. at Juan Wu's.

This, Hardenburg learned, was not a bar; bars were dangerous meeting grounds, for many bartenders, as well as barflies, were in Arana's pay. It was one of many waterfront grocery stores, kept by Chinese who, along with the Moroccan Jews, made up most of the town's small traders.

"We shall meet casually," Miguel instructed the American, "and I shall carry the documents wrapped in a musical score which I am taking to Dr. King. Then when we meet, you will offer to save me the trouble and take the score from me."

For the first time since reaching Iquitos, Hardenburg felt he was on the track of something tangible.

Next night, loitering near the dimly lit grocery store, its rafters festooned with hidelike strips of dried salt codfish, he saw Miguel enter to make a purchase and followed him in. The meeting went without a hitch, and shortly Hardenburg, the bulky score tucked beneath his arm, was hastening back through the streets to the lamp-lit privacy of his roon and his first mental encounter with Benjamin Saldaña Rocca.

There were fully a dozen testimonies, all of them handwritten, together with typewritten facsimiles. Sorting them into piles on his bed, he noted that Rocca's first informant had contacted him as far back as July 16, 1907, though refusing to disclose his name. Perhaps in the hope of tracing the man, Rocca had withheld publication until the following January, though on August 7 he had struck luckier. A man named Anacleto Portocarrera, "an eye-witness of many tragedies" had not only furnished a graphic account but also had sworn it before a notary public. On August 29, Rocca had splashed it across the front page of the newssheet *La Sanción.*

Other testimonies followed, though by December, 1907, Rocca, still precariously in business, had changed his masthead to *La*

Felpa. In his final issue on January 5, 1908, three weeks before Hardenburg reached Iquitos, he featured the testimony of his first anonymous correspondent.

But now for the first time since embarking on his crusade, Hardenburg realized how widespread was Arana's infiltration of the Putumayo. For example, though he leafed through the papers more than once, he found only passing mention of Miguel Loayza or the cruelties of El Encanto. In this, an eyewitness named Juan Vela, onetime first cook on the *Liberal*, charged that Hardenburg's old enemy, Captain Carlos Zubiabur, had so mutilated one of his deckhands the man had been driven to suicide. But Loayza, the statement said, had meted out no punishment.

And while the other witnesses' indictments stoutly named names and detailed charges, all of them denounced men unknown to Hardenburg, in locations that were foreign to him.

Testimony after testimony told the same appalling story. On Easter Saturday, 1906, avowed witness Portocarrera, José Fonseca, head agent at the station Ultimo Retiro, saw several Aifugas Indians fetching water from the well. "Look," he boasted to a group of underlings, "this is how we celebrate Easter Saturday here." Opening fire with revolver and carbine he cut down a man and a girl aged fifteen. At times, the witness said, they came back from punitive raids with the heads of Indians wrapped in banana leaves as sickening proof they had followed orders.

Another witness, Juan Castaños, confirmed the story—and related how, after refusing to kill three Bora Indian women held as hostage against nondelivery of rubber, he had defied Fonseca and taken his case to Victor Macedo, section chief at the trading post La Chorrera. To his chagrin Macedo, upholding Fonseca, had fired him on the spot. "Here," Macedo had insisted, "no employee is exempted from doing what is ordered. Here it is necessary to kill."

Appalled, Walt read on—though in truth the testimony of the last anonymous witness most vividly summarized the extent of the evil. Fully nine other section chiefs and head agents were charged with crimes as black—among them Andrés O'Donnell, who had ordered the killing of 500 Indians, and Armando Normand of Matanzas, a crazed 22-year-old sadist who would award a man fifty lashes for trying to steal a piece of bread.

As late as December 29, 1907, Benjamin Saldaña Rocca had issued a last vain clarion call: "Come to No. 49 Morona Street, and I will give you details . . . see me before going to the Putumayo. I do this for the sake of humanity and to save many from crime . . . the Putumayo is a school of the most refined and barbarous crimes. Honest men! Avoid the Putumayo!"

Everything his Huitoto guide had told him on the jungle trek to Serrano's estate, Hardenburg saw now, had been true. Arana controlled a slave empire—and only a penurious 22-year-old American engineer existed to challenge him.

With typical caution, Hardenburg told King nothing of his windfall. Instead, painstakingly, he set himself the task of translating these testimonies into English. On many nights his lamp burned late in the small back room on Prospero Street, less than a block away from Arana's own house, though Don Julio, it was said, had already left for the Putumayo. But as he labored, he became aware of two salient deficiencies in Rocca's material.

Only two of the witnesses could legally be counted as deponents—that is, had sworn their statements before a notary public. Worse, not one of them had ever faced Arana with a direct accusation.

And though he broached the point with Miguel Galvez, the boy held out little hope. Only a very brave man or one tired of life, he said, would have dared risk such a confrontation with Don Julio. Most had been too scared to appear before a notary; they had only filed their testimonies on the eve of leaving the Amazon forever.

Now Hardenburg made what he later saw as his first crucial mistake. To keep Rocca's originals by him was a burdensome responsibility; he could build up his dossier only at night and for much of the day he was absent from his room. Supposing one of

King's servants was in Arana's pay? His plan now was to return the originals to Miguel for safekeeping and to work from photocopies. Calling on a Prospero Street photographer, Rodrigues Lira, he asked him to process the documents.

Lira retired to his darkroom but, within minutes, his face thunderous, he swept back through the velvet curtains. "These are statements for use against the Peruvian Amazon Company," he accused.

"Just don't concern yourself with what they are," replied Hardenburg evenly. "You're a photographer, go ahead and photograph them." But Lira, tight-lipped, shook his head. "I won't have any part in it," he avowed, "and don't come back to my shop again, señor—you won't be welcome."

A few nights later, Hardenburg again had cause to wonder. One of his most recently acquired English pupils was Dr. Julio Egoaguirre, a noted lawyer and Senator for the Loreto district of Peru, in which Iquitos stood. But though he made twice-weekly visits to the Senator's fine town house on Pastaza Street, the American was scrupulous to keep his professional and private activities separate. Not with the handsome silver-haired Senator or with any of his pupils did he ever discuss his one-man war against Arana.

But on this night, to his surprise, Egoaguirre began to draw him out. The whole town, he said, was intrigued that their American guest should have chosen to stay on in Iquitos so long. Hardenburg's reply held a grain of truth. He had arrived penniless, and only by working could he earn enough to pay his passage back to the United States.

The Senator appeared politely skeptical. Was this really the reason? he asked. Persistent rumor said that Hardenburg was hard at work on a book about his experiences up the Putumayo. It even charged that he had stayed on to gather additional background material. Surely this was nearer the truth?

But Walt, as he later affirmed, was stubbornly noncommittal. Never at any time did he admit to the Senator that he was writing a book, although it was just then that this project began to take shape in his mind. Idly he wondered why Egoaguirre should be so curious.

At his second lesson that evening he apologized for his un-punctuality. He explained that he had walked from the Senator's house and hadn't realized that it was such a distance. "My congratulations," enthused his host, Manuel Mattos, the town's Portuguese bandmaster. "You are really collecting some distin-guished pupils now. Pretty soon you will be instructing Julio César Arana."

Hardenburg was puzzled. Arana—why Arana? "Well, what more natural?" asked Mattos. "Dr. Egoaguirre is Julio Arana's lawyer."

At the rail of the stern-wheeler *Yavarí*, Walt Hardenburg caught his breath. Through the dancing heat haze, he had his first glimpse of the fabled city of Manaus: the blue-gray cathedral spire, soaring above the opera house's glittering dome, made an unrivaled backdrop to the serried fleet of ocean liners and steamboats jammed alongside the floating wharves. Already he could distinguish Brazil's green and yellow flag . . . the red St. Andrew's cross of the Booth Steamship Company . . . the black-topped, white-starred funnels of the Italian Liguria Brasiliana . . . ships of the Hamburg Amerika Line, yellow shield and blue anchor vivid against the white and blue of the company's flag.

On the wharfside, white-jacketed porters from the city's hotels jostled for custom among the melee of passengers now dis-embarking from the open-decked "birdcages" . . . salesmen with gold teeth and fiber attaché cases . . . country boys taking their first view of the big city . . . trail owners down for a spending spree . . . wrinkled old women seeking miracle healers . . . the ever-present riverboat prostitutes, their teeth, following fashion, filed as sharp as a shark's, conspicuous by their green-

starred red skirts and elegant French slippers. Framing the panorama, the galvanized iron roofs of the rubber warehouses loomed
for fully a mile, topped with the white lettering that spelled out
M.H.L. (Manaus Harbour Ltd.).

It was late afternoon on June 24, 1908, the eve of the long-
awaited Feast of St. John, that marked the end of the rainy
season. But it was in no festive mood that Walt Hardenburg had
at last reached Manaus. He was here to search for one man,
known to him only by name.

Days earlier, young Miguel Galvez had contacted him with a
highly promising lead, a name that Doña Amelia had recalled
from the past. One man whom Benjamin Saldaña Rocca had
sought as a witness had migrated downstream to Manaus before
the journalist could reach him: the carpenter, Aurelio Blanco, a
former Arana employee.

Blanco, said Miguel, was believed to be the one man who had
taxed both Arana and his brother Lizardo with their crimes and
lived to talk about it.

Dipping into his savings, Hardenburg had promptly booked
passage on the *Yavari* for the 1,000-mile journey downstream, but
now, following his first glimpse of Manaus, he wondered if
impulse had not for once triumphed over native caution. How
would he set about finding one carpenter in this brawling, fancy-
free city, whose population had now passed the 38,000 mark?

After months of jungle silence, he found the noise deafening,
the crowds bewildering. Beggars plucked peremptorily at his
sleeve, Brazilian style, making plain that the world's wealth was
something to be shared. Carriages, mounted by liveried flunkies,
rattled by, their high-stepping Spanish horses almost annihilating
the vultures that hopped as stiff-gaited as marionettes between
the wheels. Streetcars whined and banged along the cobbled
stretch by the fish market, and every corner café had its head-
tossing resident violinist.

And on this eve of St. John, as a porter guided him to the
Grand Hotel Internacional on Municipal Street, Manaus' boulevards were more than ever like a stage. The air shivered with the

steady throb of drums borne from the side streets, and fire balloons soared, to burst like rockets against the paling sky. Bonfires built from huge balks of timber were ablaze in every street; sparks and blown smoke drifted with the smell of incense. Already the city was warming up for the time-honored procession of the Bull, when mummers disguised as white bulls, capering on their hind legs, were followed by long defiles of "Indians" in tall flowered headdresses, and "Portuguese" in scarlet satin tunics and cocked hats. Behind the weird and complex pageantry lay a spirit of primordial thanksgiving: the rains had passed, summer had come, and rubber tapping could begin again, the black gold once more flowing down to the white city.

In the Grand Hotel's lobby, ornate with its rose-marble pillars and string orchestra, Hardenburg checked in, then made prompt inquiries. A hotel, he thought, standing in constant need of maintenance, might have a reliable carpenter on its books. But the reception clerk, foxed, sought the aid of the proprietor, Antonio Borsa, a plump, swarthy Italian who despite the heat affected a black cutaway, stiped trousers and cravat.

It seemed to Walt even then that Borsa eyed him strangely, though perhaps with reason. Manaus must have scores of carpenters, the hotelier said. Why did he seek this man Blanco in particular?

The American had his explanation pat. On Eduardo Ribeiro Avenue, en route to the hotel, he had spotted the newly opened offices of the Madeira-Mamoré Railroad Company. Again, invoking Percival Farquhar's protection, he now cast himself as a recruiting agent in search of labor. The carpenter Aurelio Blanco was said to be a skilled tradesman, and the railroad paid big money for men like that.

His face stony, Borsa shook his head. But no sooner had Hardenburg left the hotel than the Italian, after checking his signature in the hotel register, set out for the Marshal Deodoro Street offices of the Peruvian Amazon Company.

Two hours later Hardenburg was ready to give up. Behind him lay a despairing progress from bar to bar and street to street, a mission impeded at all points by the sluggish progress of Manaus in carnival mood. Now bonfires crackled merrily outside every house, and his way was blocked by the family groups thronging round them, cheerfully munching on roasted sweet potatoes and tapioca cakes. Youngsters circled the fires in solemn procession, crying, "May St. John live long!"; some, more daring, swooped to seize brands from the embers, for this was a night when long-standing rituals reaffirmed family ties. But Hardenburg, at his wit's end, drew nothing but a blank. No bartender within blocks had ever heard of Aurelio Blanco. And on Eduardo Ribeiro Avenue, the furniture store salesmen were positively pained at the suggestion they employed local talent. Surely the American could see their wares were all imported from Rio de Janeiro or London?

Sunk in gloom at a pavement café, the American sipped iced beer and watched the maelstrom of humanity surge past. If he had to return to Iquitos empty-handed, over £30 of his hard-earned savings would be gone for nothing. Then suddenly he sat bolt upright and alert, for on Eduardo Ribeiro Avenue four sturdy black horses clip-clopped through the dusk, capped with black nodding plumes: a hearse returning empty from St. John's Cemetery.

Not even Manaus, Hardenburg thought, would be likely to import its coffins from Europe. So could this be the trade that Aurelio Blanco now followed?

Not until 9 P.M., he learned, did the stores close their doors for the night. Now, though his Spanish was not readily understood, Hardenburg began his inquiries from funeral parlor to funeral parlor. On this sultry night the air was so close that the sweat ran from him in rivulets; the ashes of bonfires, still glowing, threw back an animal heat from the warm cobbles. But his pertinacity triumphed at last. As the municipal clock on Eduardo Ribeiro Avenue chimed 8 P.M., he was approaching a small stifling shed redolent of cedarwood, west of the dockyard gates, across from the streetcar depot on Commercial Square.

By the glow of a palm-oil night-light, the carpenter was

working late, his plane chasing long ruffles of cedarwood shavings from the bench, sweat coursing down his bare hirsute arms. Grizzled, proud, suspicious-seeming, his eyes met Hardenburg's fearlessly: yes, he was Aurelio Blanco. What did the gringo want? The American did not mince words. In Iquitos, it was said, Blanco could have supplied testimony Saldaña Rocca wanted. Instead he had vanished to Manaus. He had come in search of that testimony.

Blanco, a sharp-spoken, stooping man in his late fifties, shrugged impatiently. He was booked aboard the steamboat by the time he had word of Rocca's quest—should he have traded in his ticket merely to talk with a journalist? In any case, the events he had witnessed had taken place two years back. He added grudgingly: "I could have told him plenty if I wanted to. But what good would it have done?"

Hardenburg demurred. It might have done incalculable good, for he himself had seen that such things were still happening today.

"It was two years back," Blanco repeated, "and I left Iquitos to forget it all, not because I was afraid. What good can you do, raking over the bones of dead men? You won't bring them back to life."

Hardenburg saw that Blanco was a thorny man, so fiercely proud that he always spoke the truth and damned the consequences. He said nonchalantly that he had wanted to meet Blanco because rumor—doubtless exaggerated—claimed he was the one man who had ever faced up to Julio Arana.

He could have chosen no better gambit. Soon Blanco was more than willing to recount what was doubtless a thrice-told tale: how he alone had had courage to stand up to the great Arana. Hardenburg was enthralled. Not only had he found his first eyewitness but the story, as it emerged, made plain Arana's knowledge of the conditions—a strange story to hear on this warm dripping night, the mango leaves glistening waxlike under the streetlamps, fire balloons whooshing and bursting against the sky, to light the long row of polished coffins stacked against the wall.

"I remember it as if it were yesterday," Blanco said. "I shan't easily forget the date—January 15, 1906." A native-born Peruvian, he had drifted downriver to Iquitos, seeking work, at the time when good jobs were advertised in Putumayo territory. The contract Arana Brothers had offered for his services seemed fair: £15 a month, plus laundry, board and lodging. One clause in particular seemed commendably businesslike. If either party broke the contract, they would compensate the other for damage or inconvenience suffered.

Next day, January 17, Blanco left Iquitos for Argelia on the Caraparaná, then still a Colombian trading depot in which Arana held a share. It was here, Hardenburg recalled vividly, that the agent Ramiro Pardo had taken Don Jesús Orjuela into custody. But Blanco had been destined for another post, still farther up the Caraparaná tributary. After six days at Argelia, he transferred from the streamer to the launch *Junín*. At last, on February 10, he reported to Paulino Solíz, agent in charge of Puerto Colombia.

Solíz now explained there had been some delay. Blanco had been hired to construct storehouses and additional barracks, but as yet no lumber had arrived. "You can get busy on some furniture meanwhile," Solíz suggested; "we don't even have chairs and tables enough for the buildings we've got."

At the time Blanco had thought nothing of this. Improvising a bench, he set to work. Then, two weeks later, Arana's trading representative Patrocinio Cuellar, a supercilious young Colombian, arrived on a visit. Was Blanco settling in all right? he wanted to know. Had Solíz treated him fairly? Finding the carpenter entirely content, Cuellar further reassured him. By the time the furniture was done, lumber would be *in situ* to set up barracks.

But on March 17, the furniture completed, there was still no sign of the lumber. And now Blanco, chafing at the enforced idleness, sought out Cuellar again. "How should I occupy myself?" he asked. Cuellar's reply flabbergasted him. "Some of the Indian rubber gatherers have run away," he said. "I'm sending you and a few others to go out and round them up."

Angrily, Blanco refused to have any part in it. He said he had signed on as a carpenter not to hunt down Indians. Cuellar only laughed scornfully. "We hadn't realized you were a coward," he sneered.

Manfully, Blanco kept his temper in check. Instead he answered with iron dignity: "I am not a coward—but hunting down Indians is not my business. Above all, I do not want to stain my hands or my name with the blood of innocent human beings."

Just about two weeks later, the pressure began to step up. On March 30, Blanco recalled, he sauntered into the company's store for a roll of tobacco. But the storeman, coloring, shook an embarrassed head. He was sorry, but definite orders had come through. From now on Blanco was not permitted to buy so much as a toothbrush.

Shrugging, the carpenter persuaded his friend, Augusto Salcedo, the bookkeeper, to make what purchases he needed, but Arana's agents were in an implacable mood. On April 6, around 6 P.M. Blanco, at the riverside, was taking his daily dip from a canoe secured to the shore. Suddenly, the hard brittle crack of a rifle bullet shattered the stillness. A second bullet, then a third, slammed into the canoe below the gunwale. For the first time since reaching Puerto Colombia, Blanco knew stark fear. Dressing hastily, he bolted for his quarters to impart the news to his roommates.

The bookkeeper, Salcedo, had already feared the worst. Just prior to the first report, he and the others had seen Cuellar and an Indian, both armed with carbines, sneak into the underbrush fringing the riverbank. That night, to guard against surprise attacks, Blanco and his roommates slept in shifts, each man taking turns to do lookout duty.

Next day, according to plan, the carpenter went to Salcedo's office to ask for his current account. When the bookkeeper obliged, Blanco, armed with positive proof that he owed Arana nothing, felt free to quit. Soon enough he found he would have company on his journey. When Cuellar found what Salcedo had done, he was so incensed that he fired the bookkeeper on the spot.

In truth, both men were glad to leave; already they had seen enough to haunt them all their lives. Within weeks the commission which Blanco had refused to accompany returned exulting from the forest, claiming the massacre of forty tribesmen. On several occasions, the depot's Indians, punished "worse than in the Spanish Inquisition," had died after inhuman sentences of 600 lashes.

"If we don't leave this place," Blanco agreed with Salcedo, "they will surely murder us."

But for those Colombians then still in business on the river, the carpenter might never have lived to tell his tale. By great good fortune, a trading canoe owned by Ordoñez and Martinez was just then passing down the river, bound for La Unión, and Blanco and the bookkeeper were able to hitch a ride. "You should have left much sooner," Cuellar shouted after them. A spatter of carbine fire followed up his words.

En route to La Unión, Blanco and the bookkeeper again narrowly escaped with their lives—this time when the canoe turned turtle in the whirling waters of the rapids. With the help of the boatmen they struggled free and righted the craft, but everything else—including Blanco's £60 tool chest—was lost.

From La Unión, the carpenter had moved back downriver to Argelia. The Colombian Hipólito Perez, though he had virtually surrendered control of his business to Arana, found him work. Then six months later, to Blanco's deep relief, the *Liberal*, putting into port, disembarked the dapper jaunty figure of Lizardo Arana. Here was his chance not only to lay his claim before the company but also to reveal the true state of affairs to the men who should know. He told him the full story of the bloodbath at Puerto Colombia.

But Lizardo, as always, fought shy of making a decision.

"You'll have to see Don Julio about it," was all he would say, making no comment on the darker revelations. But Perez, like many of the Colombians whom Arana was slowly stifling, had implicit faith in the Peruvian as a man of honor. "Of course you have permission to go to Iquitos," he said; "you will get nothing but justice from Don Julio."

But even then Blanco wondered. Though all his baggage had gone, he had retained his precious contract, but on producing it to Captain Carlos Zubiabur he, like Hardenburg after him, ran up against a stone wall. No contract in the world gave an employee the right to travel gratis on the *Liberal*, Zubiabur snarled; the fare was £ 14. When Lizardo, already fogged with drink, refused to intervene, Blanco paid up.

On October 3, back in Iquitos, the carpenter marched into Arana's office to state his case. At first the rubber baron brushed it impatiently aside. "I know nothing about you," he told Blanco flatly. "Your claims are useless." But Blanco, standing foursquare on his rights, now produced a statement signed by no fewer than eight witnesses—among them the bookkeeper Salcedo and Hipólito Perez. Together they constituted cast-iron proof that Blanco, contrary to the provisions of his contract, had been ordered to hunt Indians and that he had lost the tools of his trade in the company's service.

Surprised by the carpenter's tenacity, Arana played for time. Just what, he asked, did Blanco want? Blanco was uncompromising: six months' pay, plus compensation for his tool chest and baggage. "Perhaps I may ask a small favor from you?" said Arana reasonably. "As a matter of routine I must hear Cuellar's version. He is due on the *Cosmopolita* any day."

But two months later Cuellar had still not reached Iquitos, and shortly, from another employee who had quit the company, Aurelio Blanco discovered why. Soon after his interview with Arana, a note had reached Cuellar upriver, instructing him to delay his visit at all costs.

Blanco wasted no more words. Armed with his contract and the witnesses' statements, he consulted Dr. Lanetta, a local lawyer, offering him a half share in whatever he could recover from the company. Though Lanetta agreed to handle the claim, within days he had changed his tone. "Drop the case and take whatever Arana offers you," he advised flatly. "You'll gain nothing by fighting."

Dissatisfied, Blanco demanded the return of his papers, but the lawyer was now so evasive he suspected the worst. Returning the contract, he admitted that Arana had "retained" the witnesses' statements for further study. Later the carpenter learned that for £20 cash the shark had sold Arana these documents.

No man to take such treatment lying down, Blanco stormed back to see Arana. His face disdainful, the rubber baron opened a cashbox to count out £15 in Peruvian *soles*. "Now understand clearly," he said with cutting contempt, "I give you this not because I *have* to but because I choose to—as a gift. I have looked into your contract closely, and I find it was never signed before a notary public. Therefore, it is invalid in law."

Even eighteen months later, reliving this moment, Blanco's eyes were ablaze with indignation. With deliberation, he said, he had picked up the money and checked it as correct. Then, trading insult for insult, he had tossed the thick bundles of notes at Arana's feet. "I don't need this," was his crushing verdict. "You are welcome to it. Keep it to add to the filthy millions you've piled up making poor naked Indians work to the tune of the lash."

Throughout Blanco's narrative, Hardenburg had sat as still as a statue, craned intently forward in the night-light's glow, not even intervening to prompt an answer. Now he relaxed as the carpenter concluded quietly: "This is the truth, as though I were before a tribunal."

"What use may I make of your statement?" Hardenburg asked him.

The carpenter shrugged almost indifferently. It was all one to him what use the American made of it. He had merely told him the facts as they occurred.

It was now, in the workshop's flickering half-light, that Hardenburg had an inspiration. Why had Senator Egoaguirre, in Iquitos, been so anxious to learn if he was writing a book? Was it because the one thing Arana feared most was the publication of such facts in a free world beyond his control? Then and there he decided to take his cue from the enemy. Blanco was now the first to hear the outline of his plan: from testimonies like these he would compile a book and publish it so that the public might learn the truth. But to do this called for a complete documentary record. Would Blanco accompany him before a notary public and swear to the facts?

But Blanco shook an emphatic head. So far as the law was concerned, his experience with Dr. Lanetta had soured him forever. If the notary sold the statement to Arana, his life would be worth nothing. "All the lawyers as well as the authorities here sell themselves miserably," he said bitterly.

And try as Hardenburg might, he could not budge the carpenter. At last he decided on a compromise: having seen and heard Blanco, he could vouch for his sincerity. If the man wrote him a letter it would suffice.

"Well," said Blanco finally, with moving simplicity, "one day my eyes must close forever, so I will write you such a letter— though I can relate to you only what these eyes have seen."

Hardenburg assured him he asked nothing more—but to his dismay Blanco would set no time limit as to when the letter should be written. He was no literary man; he needed time to assemble his thoughts before putting pen to paper. The letter would be sent on to Iquitos, but meanwhile he must have time.

At length, frustrated, Hardenburg took his leave. Fireworks and rockets, red, green and gold, spangled the night sky as he strode back toward the Grand Hotel, and the bonfires of St. John's Eve still flickered in the side streets, but he paid little heed to them. If this first eyewitness slipped through his fingers, months of endeavor would have yielded him little more evidence than the translation of Rocca's testimonies.

Days later he arrived back in Iquitos, determined from now on to spend every waking moment pressuring for information. But with the impatience of youth he had momentarily overreached himself.

It would be eight long months before he persuaded another witness to talk—and through all this time, he afterward realized, every move that he made, night and day, had been spied on and reported.

By the late spring of 1909, Walt Hardenburg's plan was formulated as painstakingly as a chess-player's opening gambit. He was ready for action. All through the rainy season, when the horizon trembled with blue-white lightning and the heat lay like a thick quilt over the Amazon, he scribbled and amended a narrative of his travels in Arana's territory and polished up his translations of Rocca's material. Other testimonies were slow to come, but Blanco's letter arrived finally and Perkins filed his promised account from America.

Meanwhile, the savings in Walt's bank account grew steadily. After paying his passage money to England, he calculated he would still have £40 in hand.

For Hardenburg had at length reached this drastic decision: realizing there was no chance of arousing the public conscience against Arana on the Amazon, he had decided his one hope was to reach London and lay the facts before the British directors of the Peruvian Amazon Company.

Around January, young Miguel Galvez brought him word of another man who had aided Benjamin Saldaña Rocca: Julio Muriedas, an Iquitos accountant, briefly an Arana employee, who had an office on Ucayali Street. Though some townsfolk looked down on him as a drunkard who rarely bestirred himself, Hardenburg found the fat jovial Spaniard one of his most amusing and responsive witnesses. Once he traveled with him to his small rubber estate upriver, and there Muriedas repeated willingly the substance of what he had told Rocca as far back as July, 1907. Three enforced months at El Encanto, where his servant had been stricken with smallpox, and three more under Victor Macedo at La Chorrera had enabled him to study the system at firsthand.

At both depots, Muriedas said, it was common to torture Indian children to force them to reveal where their fathers were hiding in the forest. One of the worst offenders, he swore, was the agent Bartolomé Zumaeta, Arana's brother-in-law, a hard-drinking syphilitic whom the Indians had sworn to kill.

Walt did not realize that Muriedas was under constant police surveillance or that his friendship with the accountant had promptly been reported to the Prefect, Carlos Zapata.

In fact, Hardenburg had no reason to anticipate trouble. At last, after a long hiatus, his campaign was going well. For months he had known that every potential witness he approached who had refused to testify was now a potential informer: how soon would the news filter back downriver to Arana in Manaus? But by the spring of 1909, word had spread that the American was a man to be trusted, a campaign in which both Muriedas and young Gabriel Valderrama, Serrano's former employee, now working at the Colombian Consulate, had played an important part. To Dr. King's undisguised alarm, a steady trickle of witnesses now made inquiries at the Prospero Street surgery—and often returned bringing others in their wake.

Some men, like the illiterate Genaro Caporo, could never have set their stories down unaided—yet their faltering words were as damning an indictment as any Hardenburg had heard to date. Employed at Matanzas in 1907, under the insane Bolivian, Armando Normand, Caporo had time and again seen scouting parties twenty-five strong return with captive Indians in chains. As a warning to others to bend the knee, Normand had killed many, the witness said, with his Mauser or machete.

"It is enough to walk around Matanzas to discover the truth," Caporo swore. "On all sides you see the ground sown with skulls and human bones."

Others, like the overseer Celestino López, just refused to believe that conditions were as bad all over; stubbornly he had requested transfers from post after post. From El Encanto, in April, 1908, shaken by the same sights Perkins had witnessed before his release, he had opted to work at Abisinia—assured by the chief, Abelardo Agüero, that his Indians were well-nourished and floggings, forbidden. Though López was glad to accept his word, the first spectacle he witnessed on arriving was three Indians being cut to pieces. At last, irked by his constant complaints, Agüero transferred him to Santa Julia—where laborers fared worse than Roman galley slaves. Soon, feigning sickness, López engineered a transfer to Iquitos.

To López' knowledge, Arana had established forty-five such centers in Putumayo territory, and at all of them the same conditions prevailed.

Almost every witness stressed this same factor: to a man, Arana's overseers were bloodthirsty psychopaths with police records, killers who had to kill. Typical was the stocky, curly-haired Rafael Calderón, a Colombian mule-driver-turned-bandit who had fled his country to duck a murder rap. To underlings like Aquileo Erazo, who sought out Hardenburg in mid-May, Calderón had told long boastful stories of how he, Agüero and other chiefs, had diverted themselves with target practice on tethered Indians, with the forehead counting as bull's-eye.

"It was interesting to see them jump about," Calderón had related, "when the bullets didn't kill them right away. As for women, I had as many as I could handle. Our motto was, Kill the fathers first, enjoy the virgins afterward."

Peruvians who would not conform suffered as much as Indians —though few had endured the system as long as Daniel Collantes. A onetime fireman on the Arana launch *Mazán*, he had spent seven stark years in the territory—often as a captive himself for refusing to hunt down Indians. Chained in a damp cell at La Chorrera, under Victor Macedo's orders, he protested bitterly. For answer, Macedo awarded him a hundred lashes—a sentence that left him prostrate for seven months.

On carnival days, Collantes swore, section chiefs from all over the region flocked to La Chorrera to toast in champagne the man who could claim the greatest number of murders in the year past. Almost always the palm went to José Fonseca of Ultimo Retiro, who before Collantes' eyes had convened a gathering of hundreds of Indians—Chontaduras, Ocainas, Utiguenes—whose rubber deliveries had fallen short. Then, aided by six overseers armed with carbines and machetes, Fonseca had cut a bloody and unbelievable swathe through 150 men, women and children. The carnage ended, he had railed at the survivors: "I will exterminate every Indian who doesn't obey my orders about the rubber that I require them to bring in."

To this, another witness, M. F. Camacho, added a grim footnote: by no means all these infamies were the work of adults. At Abisinia and elsewhere, the dispatch of the wounded was normally carried out by *cholitos*—teen-age Indians captured in infancy and brought up to wield rifle and machete against their fellows from that time on.

The senseless slaughter baffled Hardenburg—at first. Many overseers were undoubtedly natural-born killers, but this did not explain the relentless insistence on more and yet more rubber. The one agent he had encountered, Miguel Loayza, had struck him as indolent to a fault. So why, he asked, should men in receipt of adequate salary, board and lodging exert themselves so zealously to step up rubber production on Arana's behalf?

Now more than one witness laid bare the ingenious infamy of Arana's scheme: *most section chiefs received no salary whatsoever.* Their sole remuneration was commission, varying from section to section, on the rubber passing through their depot. Thus, Armando Normand, at Matanzas, received a flat 20 percent on the value of each year's tonnage. Others, like the murderous Fonseca, claimed eight shillings on every thirty pounds of rubber brought in. At La Chorrera, chief agent Victor Macedo drew a nominal salary—£30 a month—but was guaranteed 6 percent of the profits of every section under his command. It was by no means uncommon, Hardenburg learned, for a ruthless section chief to bank £1,000 a year—with his atrocities serving as a grim warning to all Indians who delivered below their quota.

To obtain these statements, Walt's methods never varied. If a man was disposed to talk he became friendly with him, put him at his ease and heard his story through. Then he persuaded him to write a letter, stressing any points that needed elaboration; in the case of the illiterate Caporo, a friend, José Antonio, penned a letter on his behalf. Then, along with letter and witness, Walt called on Frederico M. Pizarro, an Iquitos notary public, and had the statement sworn.

A lawyer who had fallen foul of the Arana brothers and had taken the statements of two of Rocca's witnesses, Pizarro was impressed, and with reason. In one three-day period, May 15–18, Walt had hustled five people in and out of his office.

"If these statements aren't true, you realize Arana will have a legal case against you," Hardenburg was careful to warn each man, though the reply of witness Daniel Collantes spoke for all. "I am ready to swear if called before a court of justice."

By May 21, with eighteen sworn depositions in his possession, Hardenburg made one last appeal to Dr. King: was he prepared to forward them to the United States Minister in Lima? When King declined, Hardenburg was final: "Then I am going to the British people."

One June 1, Dr. Serafin Filomena Peña, headmaster of the Iquitos Departmental Secondary College, where Walt had given English lessons, recalling instructions he had received some weeks back from the Prefect, Carlos Zapata, sent a pupil hastening with a note to police headquarters.

One hour earlier, he said, Hardenburg had come to him and formally resigned his job. The American was leaving for London.

To Walt Hardenburg's surprise, two days before leaving for Manaus aboard the *Yavarí*, the first stage of his journey to England, he found that Julio Muriedas, the jovial accountant, was traveling with him. "I've done it at last," the Spaniard exulted, in the course of a casual encounter on Prospero

Street. "I've sold my rubber estate, lock, stock and barrel. Now we'll be able to travel together. After all these years I'm going to have another look at Spain."

Insisting that the deal rated a celebration, Muriedas coaxed him to a nearby bar, calling for drinks. The sale had been providential, he confessed, for the estate had not yielded well; it was sheer luck that another Spaniard, seeking a foothold in the Amazon Valley, had faith that he could make it prosper and was backing that hunch to the extent of £830. He was a merchant named Estanislão Bazan, only recently arrived in town, but the name meant nothing to Hardenburg.

"There's just one small point," Muriedas said diffidently, after Hardenburg, for politeness' sake, had ordered a second round, "Bazan has paid me with a bill of exchange. Are you familiar with them?"

Hardenburg had only a hazy notion of the procedure involved, so Muriedas explained: a bill of exchange was a written order requiring the person to whom it was addressed to pay a certain sum of money at a fixed date. It was at this point, as he later recalled it, that Muriedas first offered him a sight of the bill, by way of clarification. Issued by the Iquitos branch of the German house of Wesche and Co., it bore that day's date, June 6.

"But I don't want to present it here in Iquitos," the accountant confided; "the discounting charges are a scandal. I can get a far better rate in Manaus. The trouble is, until we get there I'm going to be a bit short of cash."

Sensing that Hardenburg, as always, was sympathetic to a hard-luck story, Muriedas soon confessed that the problem was more acute still. He lacked even the cash in hand to pay his fare downriver.

For a brief moment Hardenburg wavered. Years of paring his costs to the bone had made him cautious in the matter of loans—but one of his foremost attributes was loyalty. Had it not been for the accountant, he recognized, his work in obtaining the statements would have been doubly difficult; if ever he was under an obligation to a man, it was Muriedas. Readily he told the Spaniard to set his mind at rest. Not only would he pay his passage as far as Manaus, where they would transship to a steamboat for Pará, but also, until Muriedas could get his bill discounted, he would advance him £20 out of the £40 he had saved.

"You're a true friend," the Spaniard said, brightening perceptibly. "You wait until we reach Manaus—*hombre*, I'll really show you that town."

And one week later, on June 13, as the *Yavarí* nudged toward Manaus' floating wharves, Muriedas was once more promising to be as good as his word: never had there been such a cosmopolis, Hardenburg would see. But Walt, though eager to see more of Manaus, was already glad he and Perkins had bypassed the rubber boom. In truth, the latex barons had built their wealthy wicked city on the bones of Indians—and the people's frenzied way of life hinted that they knew it. It was as if they sought to stifle their consciences in a nonstop round of free spending, high living and liquor.

Soon he wondered whether Muriedas, too, felt this way. Not once in six months, despite his reputation as a drinker, had Walt seen the accountant tipsy—yet now the prospect of Manaus seemed to be his undoing. As the city loomed ahead, Muriedas, at the rails, was drinking deeply from a quart of sugarcane rum, and by the time the steamboat docked he had become difficult and perverse. On the wharfside, a noisy inconclusive wrangle broke out when Hardenburg checked porters from the Grand Hotel Internacional from trying to commandeer their baggage. Following his previous encounter with the Italian proprietor, Antonio Borsa, he had found the hotel haughty and impersonal. He opted for the well-known Casino Hotel, near the Governor's Palace.

But Muriedas, sulky and argumentative, raised every obstruction possible. There just wasn't, he insisted, better value for money than the Grand. In vain, Hardenburg pointed out that both hotels charged the same rates: £4 a day full board, exclusive of wine. Finally, to avert an open quarrel, he gave in—though no sooner had they arrived at the Grand than he regretted it. Again Borsa manned the reception desk—to announce with scant civility that only single rooms were left. The two would have to share a bed.

When Walt forcibly demurred, urging that they move on elsewhere, the Italian merely shrugged. They were welcome to try, but his 150 rooms were packed out and every hotel in the town could tell the same story. Already the porters were manhandling their baggage toward the service stairway. Again, Hardenburg assented.

But he rejected the Spaniard's proposal to repair to the bar for a party then and there. His campaign against Arana still had first priority. Leaving Muriedas in unsteady search of drinking companions, he set off for the Colombian Consulate on Joaquim Nabuco Street.

Weeks earlier, in Iquitos, young Gabriel Valderrama had given him an introduction to a Colombian named Justinio Espinoza, said to have firsthand knowledge of the plight of the Indians upriver. Valderrama explained that his fellow countryman, having pulled out of the Putumayo, was at present in Manaus exploring business prospects, as house guest of the Consul, General José Torralba.

Espinoza, a slim elegant man, welcomed Hardenburg warmly. The files of the consulate, he said, contained a telling exposé of conditions on the Putumayo from a 38-year-old Brazilian, João Baptista Braga, who had escaped downriver to Manaus with a Colombian confederate after almost four years' incarceration. Over scalding-hot demitasses of coffee, Hardenburg digested what by now was a too-familiar story: how Braga, signing on as an overseer at Morelia in December, 1904, had been appalled to see his chiefs Abelardo Agüero and Augusto Jiménez split a bottle of cognac between them as the prelude to massacring eight securely trussed Indians.

Held prisoner, despite all protests, Braga had seen scores of Indians massacred until the night in July, 1908, when he and the Colombian overseer, Felipe Cabrera, had stolen a canoe and escaped under cover of darkness. Both the governments of Brazil and Colombia, Espinoza said, had repeatedly pressed Lima for an explanation, but so far in vain.

Promising Hardenburg a copy of the statement, Espinoza added: "From what Valderrama says, you are interested in evidence that Julio Arana knew about these crimes. Then while you are in Manaus, you should call on the *Jornal do Comercio*."

Back in the autumn of 1907, he explained, this newspaper had accused Arana's company of specific outrages on the Indians—and there was proof positive the Peruvian had been aware of it. At the insistence of Arana Brothers, the journal had later published their denial.

A do-it-today man, Hardenburg was eager to visit the newspaper offices without delay, but his innate sense of responsibility first sent him back to the Grand Hotel's bar in search of Muriedas. Within minutes he regretted it. Flushed and perspiring, already the center of a group of boon companions, the accountant still had his heart set on showing Walt the city—and faced with the urgent pressure of the others, the American good-naturedly gave way.

Afterward, Walt had only the dimmest recollections of the monumental spree that followed—or of the tortuous route the revelers pursued. It began, in relatively minor key, on the terrace of the Garden Chalet on Republic Square; already the tables were packed with white-clad "colonels" quietly sipping champagne and awaiting the nightly arrival of the demimondaine in their carriages. But once Anita Lopes, the reigning cabaret star, launched into her first huskily provocative number, the atmosphere grew clamorous. Fists, tumblers and gold-mounted canes pounded the marble-topped tables; three times the girl delayed her exit to scoop up the whirling blizzard of banknotes thrown by her fans. Watching Muriedas pound the table as loudly as any, Hardenburg thought he had rarely seen a man drink with such abandon. It was almost as if he was trying to incapacitate himself.

But to the Spaniard and his cronies the night was still young. Chartering one of the new taxis from the garage of the Restaurant Degas, they whirled through the sultry, airless streets to the Pim-Pam Bar on Epaminondas Avenue. As Walt discovered to his cost, the fake try-your-strength machine, ranged alongside the genuine article and rigged to give the tenderfoot an electric shock, was always good for a laugh. From the Pim-Pam, the taxi now swept them to the Happy Future Bar at Flores on the jungle's edge, where Muriedas and some of the party, clustered round the pianola, sang chorus after mellow chorus from *The Merry Widow* and *Carnival in Venice*. Others, pumping coins into the newly installed perfume atomizer, took turns spraying each other with violet and jasmine essence. Nursing his drink, the American saw Muriedas switch from sugarcane rum to beer and then champagne and wondered what he was trying to forget.

But around midnight even the resilient Hardenburg lost track of time and place. At one unremembered bar there was a long argument about hiring horses to ride up the steps of the Hotel Europa, because it drove the proprietor wild. In the small hours, jammed at a table in the throbbing twilight of The Terrible Ones, the more prudent drinkers in the party, Walt included, settled for beer and chicken soup. But Muriedas, his soup almost untasted, called loudly for whiskey.

The municipal clock had told 4 A.M. when the taxi deposited them at the Grand Hotel in a boisterous volley of good-nights; by now the Spaniard was in terrible shape. Though Hardenburg finally settled him in the bed, he had no fancy to share it with him; he settled for a shakedown on the day couch.

After a few hours' restless sleep, he was, though feeling the worse for wear, ready to shower and dress. At twenty-three, aided by black coffee, he could quickly shake off the effects of unaccustomed liquor. But Muriedas, he was perturbed to find, seemed worse than ever. All morning, gray-faced and vomiting, he waved away both food and coffee, steadfastly refusing to call in a doctor.

Walt did what he could for him, then decided he had best leave the accountant to sleep it off. Soon after midmorning, threading through hot narrow streets smelling of fruit and charcoal where clamorous youngsters flew paper kites, he was heading for the Eduardo Ribeiro Avenue office of the *Jornal do Comercio*.

To the best of his belief, as he was later to swear on oath, this was Manaus' sole existing daily. The existence of another newspaper, *Amazonas*, on Itamaraca Street, was unknown to him.

In the cool twilight of the journal's filing room, the clerks heard his request casually then handed him a weighty bale of back numbers. "Take what you want if you can find it," one suggested as Hardenburg settled to browse at a trestle table. He found the story finally in the issue of Saturday, September 14, 1907, bannered across the top right-hand columns of the front page:

BEASTS IN HUMAN SHAPE

In Colombian Territory—Atrocities—Men, Women and Children tortured by a Horde of Beasts—A Victim's Story.

The victim, a 21-year-old Colombian, Roso España, described as "of low stature and agreeable features," told a story much like Hardenburg's own. One of a party of rubber gatherers taking trade goods to the Andoke Indians on the Lower Caquetá River, he had been ambushed by a force of twenty Peruvians under Armando Normand. For daring to do business with España's men, more than a score of Indians had been massacred, and the traders, first imprisoned aboard the *Liberal*, had finally been cast adrift in a small canoe. Once inside Brazilian territory, some of the party elected to stay put, but España, hitching a ride on a Brazilian naval launch, had come to Manaus to tell his story.

But what intrigued Hardenburg was the paper's Monday issue which featured a prompt refutation from Arana's Manaus office. "Our commercial house," ran their rejoinder in part, "has no affiliation in Colombian territory . . . it seems strange that Roso España should seek to involve us. Certainly we have a branch in Peruvian territory, adjoining the contested area, but conflict there is provoked by Colombian citizens who are, however, always soundly repelled . . . we request you to publish our letter in order to vindicate us of any charge of unseemly conduct."

The American was more than satisfied. This was proof in black and white that the outrages had continued even after the facts had been brought to Arana's personal attention. Leaving the journal's office, the back numbers tucked beneath his arm, he now made tracks for the Colombian consulate, again to seek out Espinoza.

Later that day, armed with the promised copy of Braga's statement, he and Espinoza were returning to the Grand Hotel. As they crossed Eduardo Ribeiro Avenue, the Colombian gently restrained him. "Perhaps we will take coffee at the Casino Hotel instead," he suggested. "There is a gentleman you probably have no wish to encounter."

Following his gaze, Hardenburg saw a burly, vaguely familiar figure vanish into the Grand. But only when Espinoza had prompted him did he now recognize Julio Arana. His meeting with the Peruvian over a year earlier had lasted barely fifteen minutes. Though he had spared no effort to bring him to justice, he could not, he realized, have identified him at a distance. Another factor surprised him, too; he had not even known that Arana was in Manaus.

Hardenburg had no suspicion that Antonio Borsa, slipping from the hotel, had paid yet another visit to the Peruvian Amazon Company's office. And had he realized that only an hour back he had been the pincipal subject of discussion at a meeting between Arana, Lyonel Garnier, editor of *Amazonas*, and his deputy, Sénhor Bahia, he would have been shocked and incredulous. His main preoccupation was now with Muriedas; in three days the steamboat would sail from Pará, but still the Spaniard, ashen-faced and near delirium, refused to budge from his bed or allow a doctor to examine him.

As events transpired Hardenburg's innate compassion almost cost him severe financial hardship. Only twenty-four hours before sailing did he reluctantly climb the stairs to their room and tiptoe to the Spaniard's bedside to raise the question of the loan. "Muriedas," he said apologetically, "I should like to have the £20 I advanced you." His face a dew of perspiration, the Spaniard groaned softly, though his eyes remained closed. "Well," he muttered at last, "I will do what I can for you. Give me until noon."

A few hours later Hardenburg returned. Beckoning him closer,

Muriedas groped beneath his pillow and for the second time produced the bill of exchange Walt had seen in Iquitos. It had been endorsed in blank, he saw now, by "E. Bazan," in payment for the rubber estate. On the back of the bill Muriedas had written, "Pay to the order of Señor W. E. Hardenburg, for value received." Hardenburg did not think to question why he had dated it, Iquitos, 8th June, 1909.

"This is what I have decided," said the Spaniard painfully, "to trust you to cash this. You get it cashed and come back and I will give you your £20. So if I am not able to go tomorrow, you can go ahead anyway."

Hardenburg hesitated. On the Amazon, even more then elsewhere, to trust a man with more than £800 was to confer great honor on him—but would a bank place such credit in a stranger? "Well," Muriedas granted him, "I suppose you will need an introduction, but couldn't your Colombian friend arrange it? See if he's known to the Bank of Brazil—they give the fairest rates hereabouts."

It was then Hardenburg realized with near-panic that time was running out. Within an hour the banks would close for the day— and the steamboat to Pará sailed on next morning's tide. Hastening downstairs he hailed a carriage and set off once more for the Colombian consulate, praying that Espinoza would not have left. But luck was with him. The Colombian agreed to drive back to the hotel and meet Muriedas; the problem, he told them, was virtually solved. As a long-standing customer of the Bank of Brazil, he would gladly introduce Walt to the manager, Dr. Alvaro de Mello. But he cautioned him in advance against disappointment. Business was so brisk that at the close of the day's trading banks often ran short of funds. For a sum so large they might require prior notice.

With Espinoza, Hardenburg hastened feverishly through the sunlit cathedral gardens to the bank's handsome new central office on the western side of Commercial Square. Once inside, Hardenburg was too worried to take in the scene in detail: he had a swift impression of clerks in clean frayed shirts gabbling into telephones and customers lined on hard wooden benches clutching the numbered brass tallies they presented in turn at the cashier's grille.

But Espinoza's introduction disposed of all problems. Dr. Mello had funds to cover the draft and was glad to help. All told, Hardenburg thought the bill of exchange was in his possession for no more than fifteen minutes. He had time to note that the bill was divided into three parts; this, the manager explained, was to safeguard against one section being detached and lost. Any man, he added, for Hardenburg's future reference, could obtain such a bill from a bank.

Carefully Hardenburg endorsed the bill "Pay to the order of Agencia de Banco do Brasil, Manaus, value received," then signed it. Ten minutes later, after thanking Espinoza, he was back in the Grand Hotel and Muriedas, after checking off £830 in bundles, had repaid him his £20.

Now to Walt's surprise the accountant was sitting up in bed, a healthier glow in his cheeks. "Suddenly I feel much better," he confessed. "I have ordered them to send up some chicken soup. I think with luck I may be able to travel with you on the steamer tomorrow after all."

Still Hardenburg felt no cause for alarm. At dawn on Thursday, June 17, he and Muriedas boarded the steamboat in Manaus harbor without incident. At Pará they had arranged to take passage on the Booth liner, *Ambrose*, Muriedas disembarking at Lisbon, Hardenburg en route for Liverpool. The American's sole aim was still to bring the truth home to Arana's British co-directors in London. He did not know that a trusted British representative of the company, having conferred with Arana in Manaus, was at this moment up the Putumayo River with orders to toothcomb the whole system.

The door swung open so violently that the Reverend John Harris came bolt upright in his chair. On this dusty, sweltering August afternoon the windows of his third-floor office were flung wide to catch every breath of air—and the rattle of carriages on Vauxhall Bridge Road, South London, had drowned the staccato rapping on the outer office door. At this hour, his clerk was absent on an errand; there had been no one to check the progress of the earnest young man in his sober double-breasted suit of black broadcloth who now entered so unceremoniously, two thick bundles of manuscript clamped beneath his arm.

As an official of the recently formed Anti-Slavery and Aborigines Protection Society, whose concern was the global welfare of native races, the 35-year-old Harris was used to men who did not mince matters—but rarely had he encountered anyone who came as directly to the point as the newcomer. Thrusting forward a visiting card inscribed "W. E. Hardenburg," the stranger in the same moment dumped the weightier manuscript preemptorily on his desk. "Read that," he told Harris brusquely, "and I'll come back in two days."

Then, brandishing the second dossier, he added forcibly: "Here is supporting evidence—but I'm not going to part with these documents." With this, before Harris found time to utter a word, the visitor departed as unceremoniously as he had arrived.

Hardenburg had reason for his seeming discourtesy; the past two months had brought him only bewilderment and black frustration. From the moment he left Manaus on the riverboat, he had found Muriedas' behavior as strangely unaccountable as his violent sickness and inexplicable recovery. No longer the warm-hearted companion of Iquitos days or the dissolute barfly of Manaus, he became increasingly morose and withdrawn—

shunning both liquor and Hardenburg's company. On arrival at Pará, the two had no sooner checked into the Central Hotel than the accountant departed to call on friends. Within hours he returned and began repacking.

"One of my friends has offered me a job as an accountant in Mato Grosso territory," he said briefly, cramming shirts into a suitcase. "It's my job, after all, so I'd be a fool not to accept."

Hardenburg was puzzled. Until now Muriedas had set his heart on passing the rest of his life in Spain. But the accountant merely shrugged. "It was an idea, of course," he said indifferently, "but a man's entitled to change his mind." At this moment Hardenburg had the feeling he was bidding farewell to a total stranger.

Not that the accountant's inconsistency troubled him for long: the great adventure of his English journey loomed too large in his mind. On July 17, when the liner *Ambrose* steamed through the heat haze of the Mersey into Queen's Dock, Liverpool, the belief that his long crusade was nearing its end was paramount above all other thoughts.

But soon, to the young American's fury, he found himself balked by a blank wall of suspicion and indifference. Settling into lodgings on Sandwich Street, near London's Euston Station, he set out on the dogged daily round that never varied—to the publishers on Paternoster Row by St. Paul's Cathedral, on to the news editors of Fleet Street. At first he had sought nothing more than an introduction to the Peruvian Amazon Company's directors, none of whom were known to him by name, but now it struck him that they might conspire to suppress his facts. His surest course of action was to publish the evidence verbatim—and let public opinion force the directors' hand.

But it was a bitter uphill task; on all sides he met only coldness and distrust. To most publishers, the whole incredible story had the ring of melodrama. Nor did the news editors prove readier listeners. As one explained angrily: "The Peruvian Amazon Company has English offices and English directors—and that means libel. Can you imagine the cost of fighting an action where most of the witnesses would have to be brought from some inaccessible forest in Peru?"

Night after night Hardenburg returned to his lodgings numb with despair. "I imagined every Englishman would jump at the opportunity to set things right," he said incredulously to Mr. and Mrs. Graham who owned the boardinghouse, "but they just don't seem to want to listen."

One friend he made at this time tried her best to understand and console him: Mary Feeney, a slender 24-year-old brunette with melting blue eyes, who had worked as both nurse and governess. A family friend of the Grahams, Mary divined something of what Walt was suffering, for she was no stranger to loneliness. Born of Irish parents, who had died when she was young, she had passed all her childhood in a convent. As often as she could the lively petite colleen coaxed Walt away from the feverish revision of his manuscript into the gay, gaslit streets of Edwardian London.

But though the girl's sympathy warmed his heart, Hardenburg was nursing a sense of black injustice. By degrees, his youthful ardor changed to sullen resentment at the total apathy of the British. Though he took up a news editor's suggestion to call on the Reverend John Harris, already noted as a reformer, he had prejudged the equable, good-looking young minister as a weak reed. Disgusted with the lack of interest on all sides, he was fast making plans to return to America.

In fact, Hardenburg could have enlisted no doughtier ally in his battle with Arana. A cheerfully resolute man, of magnetic personal charm, later knighted for his work, Harris was never happier than when pottering round the beehives and flower beds of his Sussex garden—but if the need arose he was a crusader after Walt's own heart. Eight years earlier, as a missionary on the Belgian Congo, he and his wife Alice had combined with a young British Consul, Roger Casement, to unmask the infamous rubber empire of King Leopold, whose £40,000 Anglo-Belgian India Rubber Company had netted a £5 million profit in fifteen years.

It was left to the Harrises and Casement to bring home to the shareholders the bloody cost of rubber. Appropriating 800,000 square miles of territory with the aid of armed mercenaries, Leopold's reign of terror had, in many regions, wiped out 60 percent of the native population.

Though his life had been in constant danger, Harris, like Casement, had defied the slavers in order to turn the spotlight on these facts—and thus Walt's narrative struck an answering chord from the first. Then, too, as he was later to testify, Harris was influenced profoundly by "Hardenburg's personality . . . his intense desire to do something to save the remnant of the Indians." Within hours of his return to Vauxhall Bridge Road, two days later, Walt, for the first time since reaching the Putumayo, found a powerful alignment of friends. No sooner had he met the society's treasurer, E. Wright Brooks, than the energetic Harris hustled him off for a meeting with the vice-chairman, Francis William Fox, another pioneer reformer, at the Union Club, Trafalgar Square.

As Hardenburg later recalled it, Harris never at any time suggested his laying the facts before the British Foreign Office. Privately, the minister thought the Foreign Office more likely to act once the press took up the cudgels. For this reason he urged Walt, "I advise you very strongly to go to *Truth* and take this material with you. I think you'll probably get publicity in *Truth* more quickly than in any other periodical."

For more than thirty years, he explained, this hard-hitting weekly periodical had been the nation's militant and unofficial conscience, always ready to publish-and-be-damned if a wrong needed righting.

At No. 10 Carteret Street, in the shadow of Big Ben, Walt found that *Truth*'s newly appointed editor, Robert Bennett, was holidaying in Switzerland, but Harris's name proved a ready passport to the office of assistant editor, Sydney Paternoster. Paternoster never forgot his first meeting with "this quiet reserved young man, burning with zeal," who brushed aside the news that *Truth* did not pay for exposé material.

"It isn't me that needs to benefit from the story," he said, "it's those forest Indians. I'm convinced these crimes are of so terrible a nature no exaggeration is possible. I'm determined to do all that a man can to put a stop to them."

"The United States have every reason to be proud of you," Paternoster applauded him.

That evening Hardenburg returned to the Grahams' three-story house on Sandwich Street glowing with happiness. At last, he told Mary, he had found allies who would fight with him shoulder to shoulder.

Events now moved swiftly. By mid-September, editor Robert Bennett returned to find his deputy had already completed the groundwork for one of the most astounding campaigns the paper had ever undertaken. A call on the Colombian Consul General, Francisco Becerra, proved especially fruitful. In Becerra's Kensington office in West London, Paternoster had soon filled a notebook with the testimonies of expatriate Colombians who knew too well the cost of rubber on the Putumayo.

Moving on to the Foreign Office, Paternoster struck luckier still. The British Consul for Iquitos, David Cazes, had recently returned on leave and was just then enjoying a seaside holiday at Llandudno, North Wales. A hasty note secured Paternoster an appointment with him on his return to London.

A lanky, red-haired native of Gibraltar, Cazes, as Paternoster later confessed, was "naturally reticent"—but as head of the Iquitos Trading Company and Consul for seven years, he had heard enough to convince the journalist he was on the right track. "Personally," he explained, "I'm not in a position to know anything. But similar charges have been made in Iquitos by old employees of Arana Brothers—though generally they're attributed to malice by discharged servants."

To some, Benjamin Saldaña Rocca's publications fell into this category. As the story went, Arana had refused him a loan to set up a printing press and, as a result, the editor bore him a grudge. The Consul had studied early issues of *La Sanción* but the charges struck him as "rather fantastic in the horrors they depicted."

Shortly after, observing that they deeply distressed his wife, he had tossed them into his wastebasket.

Though Cazes had always found Arana "courteous . . . very honorable," he recalled that he had twice protested at the employment of Barbadians along the Putumayo. One agent, Ramon Sanchez, had been accused in 1905 of brutally beating women and West Indians who refused to work. At once Cazes had warned Arana: "My government will take this matter up very seriously." The Peruvian, he said, was plainly horrified and struck Sanchez off the payroll. Then, in November, 1906, a fugitive Barbadian, invading the consulate, claimed that he and his fellows were forced against their will to go out and hunt Indians. Again Cazes bearded Arana and Pablo Zumaeta, though both spiritedly denied the allegation.

"Well," Cazes sidestepped diplomatically, "you *are* employing Barbadians to police your territory. I think they are being put to illegal uses, and I must insist on the whole of these Barbadians coming back to Iquitos." Once again, Arana had proved reasonable. He said Cazes' belief that the men were ill-treated or illegally employed did not hold water. Nevertheless, he would respect his views and bring back downriver any man who elected to come.

As Cazes recalled it, upward of forty West Indians who were anxious to leave the region came down to Iquitos and were repatriated at his insistence direct to Barbados. More than this, Cazes said, he was powerless to do. Though he had twice routed reports to the Foreign Office in London, he had been given little guidance. Since Arana controlled the river, it was not feasible to make a personal investigation, and his sole official funds were an annual £21 office allowance—to defray overall expenses of £150.

It was now, as Paternoster completed his investigations, that Hardenburg received what seemed a final vindication. Writing from the American Legation, Lima, on July 3, 1909, Minister Leslie Combs announced that the Peruvian Government, after weighing the claim, had awarded the two engineers £500 compensation. To editor Robert Bennett and the staffers of *Truth*, it was a tacit admission that Walt's allegations were proved to the hilt.

Grouped in Bennett's office as the long shadows of an autumn evening barred St. James's Park, Hardenburg and the two editors held a final eve-of-publication conference. A onetime barrister who had been called by the Inner Temple and later served as a law reporter on *The Times*, the 54-year-old Bennett had no illusions as to what lay ahead. "If these facts aren't correct," he told Walt soberly, "we can expect a writ by tomorrow afternoon's post. It could be a very costly case—and you may have to go into the witness box."

"Believe me," Walt assured him, "there's nothing I want more in the world than to give evidence on oath against Julio Arana."

Satisfied, Bennett nodded. The smudged page proof on his desk, headed, "THE DEVIL'S PARADISE: A BRITISH-OWNED CONGO," was already passed for press. Within hours, Hardenburg's simple declaration of faith would be blazoned across the newsstands: "In making these exposures, I have obeyed only the dictates of my conscience and my own sense of outraged justice; and now that I have made them, and the civilised world is aware of what occurs in the vast and tragic forests of the Putumayo River, I feel that, as an honest man, I have done my duty before God and before society. . . ."

Four miles east, in Room 532, Salisbury House, London Wall, the offices of the Peruvian Amazon Company, the clerks were filing two letters which forty-eight hours earlier had been placed before the British directors. The first, from Lyonel Garnier, editor of Manaus' leading daily *Amazonas*, described in detail how in June, 1909, Hardenburg had demanded sums ranging from £5,000 to £100 for material calculated to blacken Arana's character.

The second, also from Manaus, was briefer, and came from Julio Arana himself. Hardenburg, it said, having failed to extract money from *Amazonas* had coolly forged a £10 bill of exchange, converting it to £830, and escaped scot-free to London.

Reporter Horace Thorogood, of *The Morning Leader*'s news staff, fidgeted uneasily, tugging once more at his watch chain. It was as he had feared. The time by his battered Waterbury was now 5 P.M. on Friday, September 25, and the deadline for the story he had yet to secure was fast approaching. To Thorogood, it seemed that the lead he had stolen on his rivals in Fleet Street would count for nothing after all. For two days now he had been almost a fixture in the dingy third-floor outer office of the Peruvian Amazon Company.

What galled Thorogood most was that the assignment had begun so promisingly. At midafternoon on the Tuesday, the news editor, summoning him to his desk, had tossed over a copy of that day's issue of *Truth*—already the focus of excited discussions among the reporting staff. "Read over these charges," he was instructed, "and then slip down to London Wall and get their official reply. Don't let them fob you off with the secretary —we want the directors' viewpoint."

Secretly, Thorogood felt he needed luck. The news value of Walter Hardenburg's astounding charges seemed incalculable— stories of a primeval forest that had become a slave empire, of crucifixions and child murders, harems of concubines and men fed to the guard dogs. If the directors were willing to release any statement, he was sure *The Times* or *The Morning Post* would have beaten him to it.

Thorogood, in fact, was wholly unprepared for the warm welcome accorded him at the company's office—or for the grave countercharges that were forthcoming. Few other papers had made even a routine inquiry, he was told cordially by three men, all of them Spanish, who were grouped round the polished board-room table. One he was later to identify as the managing direc-tor, Abel Alarco, Arana's brother-in-law, a flamboyant mous-tachioed man with receding hair and black restless eyes. The second was introduced as Alarco's brother, German, former Mayor of Iquitos, and an authority on the region. The third, a burly, black-bearded man whose name he never knew, acted as spokesman for the group. Later Thorogood was almost certain he had been face to face with Julio Arana.

Here a mystery arises. No British director was present at the interview, but Arana's whereabouts, they later swore, was at this time unknown to them. Though he was known to have left Manaus, some believed he was still aboard a Booth liner or had broken his journey at Le Havre—to do business in Paris, or to visit his family, now in Geneva. Not one of the Britons was aware that Arana, if it was Arana, had paid a fleeting visit to London.

Whoever the spokesman, the exclusive story he now gave Thorogood was a reporter's dream. For twenty minutes, while the journalist, propped against the marble mantelpiece, scribbled busily, he unfolded a graphic account in halting but comprehensible English of Walt Hardenburg's brazen attempt to blackmail the company. In Iquitos, he said, the American had sought out the company's legal adviser, Dr. Julio Egoaguirre, to stress the book he was writing need never see the light of day—for a consideration of £7,000.

A seasoned reporter, Thorogood knew a libel when he saw one. His story, featured in Wednesday's *Morning Leader*, was discreetly ambiguous: "Recently a man called upon the company's legal adviser threatening to publish a book about the Company unless he was paid a sum of £7,000 to keep quiet." In any case, the directors had promised a detailed refutation of every charge if he called again on Thursday. His appetite whetted, Thorogood had hastened back—to meet with his first setback. As yet, he learned, the directors were still debating the issue. Would he call again at 4 P.M. on the Friday?

Now, though Friday had dawned, Thorogood was cooling his heels in the outer office for the second time that day. At 4 P.M. he had been told that the managing director had still not returned from lunch. Could he conveniently return in an hour?

Undaunted, Thorogood complied, but already time had

dragged on; only two employees remained in the office. One, who looked like a senior clerk, was, he later found, the company's secretary, A. Vernon Smith. The other was an office boy. Finally, glancing up, the journalist saw Smith approaching him.

"Would you mind," he asked Thorogood, "coming in here for a moment?" Leading the way into a small inner office, he carefully closed the door.

Apologizing, Smith now explained that the managing director would not be returning that day. But the board, in any case, had come to the conclusion that they wanted nothing more written on the matter. Accepting defeat, Thorogood rose to go. "But," Smith added hesitantly, "they are much obliged for what you did before for them. They ask you to accept *this*." Across the desk he passed a plain business envelope, unaddressed, unsealed. Turning it over and raising the flap, the journalist saw that it contained a banknote—for what amount he never knew.

At once, indignantly, he thrust the envelope back. "What is this for?" he asked. Smith, he later recalled, was too confused to reply. "What is this for?" Thorogood repeated. "Well," said Smith wretchedly, "we are much obliged to you for the trouble you took on Tuesday."

Thorogood was at first incredulous. "But you surely know that it is very improper to offer a reporter money?" The secretary, floundering, now made matters worse. "Oh, it is not a bribe," was his naïve assurance. "It's in recognition for the trouble you took on Tuesday." "I repeat," said Thorogood tartly, taking his leave, "it is a very improper thing to do."

Outside, on London Wall, he summarily hailed a hansom cab. Clattering back through the mellow evening light to seek a personal interview with his managing editor, Thorogood was reaching the same conclusion that had already dawned on the staff of *Truth:* he was on to the biggest scoop of his journalistic career.

Around 6:30 P.M., the offices of *The Morning Leader* on Stonecutter Street, below Holborn Viaduct, hummed, as always at this hour, with urgent life. But though the night's work of preparing Saturday's issue for press had already begun, only a handful of men so far knew of Horace Thorogood's astonishing interview. Those who did know were still puzzled how best to handle it.

Among those few was George Bernard Tickton, private secretary to the managing editor. Though Thorogood had reported the attempted bribery, an engagement out of town and the explosive nature of the story had momentarily led the editor to defer his decision. But it seemed hard to quarrel with Thorogood's own interpretation. Some at least of the Peruvian Amazon Company's directors were anxious to silence the one London newspaper that had followed up the story. So how did their charges against Hardenburg stand up now?

Tickton, standing in for the editor, was tidying his papers prior to the weekend and still pondering these details when an office boy brought in a visiting card. The secretary had to examine it twice before the full implications sank in. Mr. A. Vernon Smith, of the Peruvian Amazon Company, was in the front hall, soliciting an interview.

And as Smith entered, it was evident he had come to put a bold face on things. "I called in," he explained, "because of the enquiries you've been good enough to make. The directors are sending a letter to *Truth* replying to that article, so it seemed only fair that we should supply you with a copy."

Tickton eyed him unmoved. Wasn't it Smith who had seen the paper's representative only that afternoon? When Smith admitted it, Tickton challenged him: "The incident which took place at that interview was rather extraordinary, wasn't it?"

Smith hastily agreed. It was extraordinary, but it had been an unfortunate mistake. "It was my fault," he confessed, "entirely my fault. I alone was responsible." Then, as Tickton made no comment, he stumbled on. His managing director, he said, was Spanish, speaking the most imperfect English. "Because of this," Smith ended lamely, "I completely misunderstood his instructions. That was at the root of it—it was my fault entirely."

Tickton waited until the company secretary had stammered to a conclusion and bowed his way out. Then, pressing a bell he summoned a copyboy. "Find Mr. Thorogood," he instructed. "He may be in the newsroom, he may be in The Black Dog, but I want him back right away.

On Monday, September 27, *The Morning Leader*'s front page carried this item:

OUR CONGO

STRANGE STORY OF A BANKNOTE

PERUVIAN AMAZON COMPANY

AND THE MORNING LEADER

The grave allegations against the Peruvian Amazon Company of Salisbury House, London Wall, have been the subject of further enquiry by *The Morning Leader* with remarkable results . . . on Friday afternoon, when our representative called at the appointed hour, five o'clock, a clerk and a junior were the sole occupants of the office . . . the clerk immediately invited our representative into a private room, where an extraordinary scene occurred . . .

In the offices of the Peruvian Amazon Company, there was consternation. All morning the acting chairman, John Russell Gubbins, had sat alone in the boardroom, chin cupped in his hands, staring with growing apprehension—first at *The Morning Leader*'s front page, then at the private note which his codirector, Henry Read, had rushed by hand from the London Bank of Mexico. "Gubbins, what on earth is this?" Read had scribbled. "What on earth are we to do?" But on this September Monday morning, Gubbins and the other British directors simply did not know.

In truth, Thorogood's damning report was Gubbins' first intimation that the press had ever visited the company's office—and his fellow directors were none the wiser. None of them doubted that Hardenburg's allegations were false, for Arana had furnished what they saw as genuine evidence that the American was a forger and a blackmailer: the editor Garnier's letter from Manaus, plus the fraudulent bill of exchange, on loan from the Bank of Brazil. But why, when their cause was just, had Alarco now gone to ground, chosen such a dangerously incriminating way to hush up the story?

At 63, John Russell Gubbins prided himself on knowing his way about the world. Though his memory was faulty, and lately he had grown deaf, his tall slim figure, clad in an elegant silk-faced frock coat, was still imposing. To one contemporary, his pointed white beard and silver mane of hair only strengthened his impression of being "a gentleman with a real nose for business." As recently as July, 1908, he had accepted a position as alternate director with his boyhood friend, Henry Read—then, just prior to the company going public, had taken his seat full time on the board.

As acting chairman for the past nine months, Gubbins had seemed admirably fitted for the job; during thirty-eight years' residence in Peru he had been on intimate terms with every President. Yet now he had to confess it: faced with this disastrous story of the bribe, he was as nonplussed as any junior clerk in the outer office.

The first British director to join the board, Henry Read, felt the same perplexity. He, too, had spent most of his life in Peru, but only the gentle pressure of company promoter, José Medina, had persuaded him to accept a directorship. "I am such a busy man," Read had pleaded, but Medina had assured him, "There won't be much to do." Finally, in December, 1907, Read had acceded; since the London Bank of Mexico had granted the company that £60,000 revolving credit, it seemed his duty to sit in and ensure that rubber shipments arrived in time to meet the bills. But Read had never relished the post; three times in 1909 he had told his codirectors: "Things are going well now—I should like to put my resignation in your hands." But each time they had dissuaded him; following a major surgical operation, Medina was just then on the point of resigning. If Read, too, quit the board, the British would at once be in a minority. On Monday, September 27, in his Gracechurch Street office, Read had bitter occasion to remember this.

By a strange chance, Read, one month earlier, had been the only one among them to light on two copies of Benjamin Saldaña Rocca's *La Felpa*, lying in the company's office. He found its cartoons "disgusting," but thought it right to raise the matter with both Medina and Abel Alarco. Their explanations were identical.

"This is one of these regular lampoons," Alarco assured him. "The moment the man was tackled he ran away. Don't trouble your head about it."

Tearing the papers up, Read confessed himself entirely satisfied —so much so that even Hardenburg's first article in no way disturbed him. "They've got hold of a mare's nest here," he chuckled grimly to his chief clerk. Neither then nor later did he inform Gubbins or the third British director, Sir John Lister-Kaye, that he had ever glimpsed Rocca's articles.

They would in any case have meant little to Sir John. A handsome, soldierly 55-year-old, a product of Eton and the Royal Horse Guards, Sir John, too, was a man of the world. As Groom-in-Waiting to King Edward VII, he and his beautiful Cuban wife, Natica, were popular figures in London society. But although in his business career he had employed labor as diverse as Blackfeet Indians in Canada, Chinese coolies and Hungarian peasants, he had never set foot in Peru—nor could he speak or read Spanish.

Along with the others, Sir John had accepted implicitly the wording of the prospectus that had launched the company on the market on December 7, 1908: as a subsidiary to his trading houses in Manaus and Iquitos, Arana had developed a "civilising agency" on the Putumayo, whose "legal rights" would be in no way affected by ultimate boundary arbitration. Over £500,000, the prospectus claimed, had been expended in the region where "a population of about 40,000 Indians . . . are being taught to improve the crude methods, which were previously used, of treating the rubber. . . ."

All three men had envisaged bright prospects for the company, though in the panic year of 1908 the issue to the public had failed disastrously. Fewer than 130 investors had taken the plunge; the city's silk-hatted underwriters had been forced to cover the bulk of the shares. But Arana and his covendors had scored an unqualified triumph. Not only did they control £700,000 of ordinary shares and £50,000 worth of preference shares, they now enjoyed the status of a British public company with British directors.

Within hours of the *Leader*'s disquieting headlines, these three directors held a hasty meeting at the company's office. Despite their faith in Arana, they must hit back at *Truth* without delay. Accordingly, the letter Vernon Smith dispatched to the editor made plain: "The directors have no reason to believe that the atrocities referred to have, in fact, taken place, and indeed have grounds for considering that they have been purposefully misstated for indirect objects."

This was their one oblique reference to Hardenburg's tainted motives—but now the same thought struck all of them. Hardenburg might be a forger and a blackmailer—but supposing the conditions he depicted *had* prevailed on the Putumayo early in 1908? To absolve themselves from blame, they added this rider: "Whatever the facts, however, may be, the Board are under no responsibility for them, as they were not in office at the time of the alleged occurrences."

Only two weeks later did they make belated reply to *The*

Morning Leader: "I beg to inform you that the Board has no knowledge of either of the occurrences which are stated to have taken place until they read them in the newspapers." This time the letter was signed, as managing director, by Alarco, who returned to the office refusing any explanation for his conduct.

Nonetheless, the position was, as Gubbins put it, "very disagreeable," and all three men anxiously looked ahead to the promised arrival in London on October 10 of the one man they trusted could put their minds at rest: Julio César Arana.

Another man, too, awaited Arana's coming. On the evening of October 12, Captain Thomas Whiffen, a half-pay officer in the 14th Hussars, lingered nervously in the bar of the United Service Club on fog-shrouded Pall Mall. As always at this time of day, Whiffen craved a drink, yet his natural good manners constrained him to await the arrival of his guest, Julio Arana.

A quick-tempered 31-year-old, Whiffen drank to numb the pain that rarely left him; almost ten years earlier, in the Boer War, he had been left for dead on the battlefield at Colenso with a near-lethal wound in his femoral artery. Now, despite his dragging limp, his restless urge to seek far horizons seemed insatiable; his one day in the office of his father, a wealthy manufacturing chemist, had been passed reading *Sporting Life,* after which he had quit in disgust. "Get up and strike out for yourself," he would urge his younger brother, Stanley. "Pen pushing's no life for a man." But though his eight brothers and sisters came close to worshiping him, none had sought to emulate his roving, spendthrift life.

Often in debt, despite his father's £1,200 a year allowance, the footloose Whiffen was already a family legend: the youngster who had enlisted in the militia and won a commission when his father refused to put him through the Royal Military Academy, Sandhurst, the explorer who returned unannounced from far-off

Percival Farquhar, builder of the Madeira-Mamoré Railroad. (*Courtesy of Mrs. Percival Farquhar*)

To the Madeira flocked "tropical tramps" (*above*) of some twenty-five nationalities to contend with the jungle and malarial swamps like the 30-mile Abuna Strait (*below*), which is said to have cost a life for every crosstie. (*Photos: Author's Collection*)

For the building of the Madeira-Mamoré Railroad, termite-resistant eucalyptus-wood crossties (*above*) were imported from Formosa at a cost of five dollars per tie. Scores of bridges were built, as shown below, to span rivers teeming with electric eels and piranha fish. (*Photos: Author's Collection*)

In five years' building primitive survey camps (*above*) gave place to Amazon townships like Pôrto Velho (*right*) on the Madeira. (*Photos: Author's Collection*)

Above: During the construction of Farquhar's railroad, medical teams like this one, accoutered against yellow fever, battled some thirty-nine different tropical diseases. *Below:* On the Putumayo: Henry Gielgud, *third from left,* and Sir Roger Casement, *far right.* (*Photos: Author's Collection*)

The worldwide Putumayo scandals following Hardenburg's exposures involved such figures as Captain Thomas Whiffen (*upper left*), explorer framed on a blackmail charge; the Reverend John Harris (*upper right*), missionary-reformer; Sir John Lister-Kaye (*lower left*), a hapless British director of Arana's Peruvian Amazon Company; and Swift MacNeill, M.P. (*lower right*), one of fifteen parliamentary investigators. (*Photos courtesy of Stanley Whiffen; Lady Harris; Bassano and Vandyck; British Museum*)

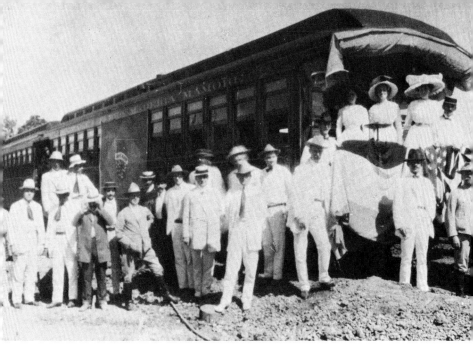

By 1912, year of the railroad's final inauguration, Asia's plantation rubber had surpassed the Amazon's — a crisis that brought ghost towns, bankruptcies, suicides and two million workless in its wake. (*Photos: Author's Collection*)

places to unfasten cage loads of monkeys, budgerigars and marmosets on the living-room carpet. "Never mind the old man," he counseled the others, as he spirited them off for exciting taxi rides and music-hall visits. "He'll pay up—he's paid up for me."

To Whiffen Senior's consternation, the most recent trip he had underwritten had almost cost his son's life. At the end of May, 1908, seconded from the Army through ill-health, Thomas had journeyed upriver from Manaus for a seven-month trip into Putumayo territory, along with guides supplied by the Peruvian Amazon Company. A gifted amateur anthropologist, he lived for months among the Bora and the Resigero tribes until he had compiled the only known vocabularies of their language. Stricken with beriberi he had returned to England more dead than alive, forced to lie for hours in sulfur baths to treat the boils that scarred his body.

But Whiffen bore mental as well as physical scars. Before even reaching Putumayo territory, he had heard from his guide, John Brown, a 32-year-old Barbadian, appalling tales of organized raids carried out to impress Bora Indians, of men starved, beaten and flogged to death. The Englishman, Brown opined, would see nothing of this; orders would have gone ahead to each section to "clean things up." But Whiffen had witnessed enough. At Abisinia, sickened to see an Indian girl trussed to the rafters of a storehouse and cruelly flogged, he had angrily demanded and secured her release from agent Abelardo Agüero. At other depots, Brown had shown him glimpses of prisoners under strong guard and hastily dismantled stocks.

In Iquitos, though weak from his travels, Whiffen had gone straight to Pablo Zumaeta to protest against the atrocities. Though Zumaeta seemed surprised, he admitted to having heard such tales before. Then, five days later, just before disembarking from the riverboat at Manaus, it was Whiffen's turn to be surprised. Up the gangplank, his hand outstretched in welcome, walked Julio César Arana, accompanied by the city's Peruvian Consul General, Carlos Rey de Castro.

Though the Englishman knew Arana only by name, the rubber

baron had greeted him as cordially as a long-lost friend. Explaining that he had recently built a small hacienda a mile downriver, he begged Whiffen to accept his hospitality until he boarded the oceangoing liner. Since Arana did not admit to English, French became the agreed common language.

Despite Arana's openhandedness, Whiffen had not shirked the issue. Everything he had seen and heard from John Brown was now related to the Peruvian. "Arana," he later recalled, "seemed horrified . . . however, he appeared to accept my word for it." Declaring he would dismiss all personnel responsible, including chief agent Victor Macedo, at La Chorrera, he still warned Whiffen: "Of course, such a change can't be made in one sweep."

At the time Whiffen had been satisfied of his good faith. As a matter of routine, he said, he had reported the facts to David Cazes, his host in Iquitos. He had arranged to hand the Consul a written report when Cazes reached London on leave.

Amicably enough, the conversation then turned to Whiffen's explorations. Pressed by Carlos Rey de Castro, Whiffen had shown both men his geographical and ethnographic notes and his draft maps. At once an idea struck Castro. Some years back he had edited the Peruvian edition of the French explorer, Eugenio Robuchon's book on Putumayo territory, which Arana had commissioned. It would be an honor to perform the same service for Whiffen. And Arana had added: the Peruvian Government had paid Robuchon a princely sum for his reports on the Putumayo and Japurá rivers.

"If you made over your notes to Señor Rey de Castro," he suggested, "it's possible you could get some return from my government for the money you have expended."

Though Whiffen refused to surrender his notes on the spot, he agreed to consider it. Arana then raised the questions of irregularities on the Putumayo. There were rumors that some of his employees were smuggling rubber from the region direct to Manaus by way of the Japurá River—defrauding both the company of revenue and the Peruvian Government of export tax.

Would the captain, in drawing up his notes, comment on such a leakage?

"I have notes to the effect," Whiffen replied, "but I never saw any irregularities of that sort."

"We shall meet again in England," Arana said genially, when the Englishman boarded the liner, at the same time pressing on him an introduction to Abel Alarco in London. "I hope you are leaving in good faith."

From this time on, Arana took infinite pains to keep in touch with Whiffen. Arriving in England at July's end, the captain had no time to present his letter to Abel Alarco; a letter from Alarco had already reached his club, offering help and hospitality. For six weeks, Whiffen was under treatment for the aftereffects of beriberi; he had no chance to take up the offer. But two further letters, this time from Arana, routed to the United Service Club, kept the memory green. The first solicited copies of photographs Whiffen had taken on the Putumayo for Arana's private album. The second informed him that by September's end Arana would have reached Paris, care of the Hotel Nouvelle.

By chance, Whiffen was just then leaving for France to try his luck at the gaming tables of Trouville's Casino. Moving on to Paris, he met Arana over lunch. It was the Peruvian, he later recalled, who first raised the subject of the *Truth* articles. "Are you too going to write for them?" he asked Whiffen directly.

"No, no," Whiffen assured him. "I'm not out for notoriety of any kind."

Abruptly changing the subject, Arana again stressed the importance of Whiffen's making his notes available to Rey de Castro. "They could be of great value to my government," he said. "They might do much to encourage foreign capital." Whiffen, scrupulous in such matters, was aware that he now stood greatly in Arana's debt for hospitality. A date was fixed for 7:30 P.M. on Tuesday, October 12, at the United Service Club.

Hence Whiffen's unease on this foggy night as he awaited Arana in the club bar—for on returning to London he had found a formal letter from the Foreign Office. As an explorer who had recently traversed the Putumayo, it said, he must render an immediate report on local conditions. Now it was plain Walt Hardenburg's allegations were being investigated at top-level, and Whiffen had no doubts as to what he must do. Though he had drafted a shipboard report for David Cazes, as yet he had not met the Consul. Now he must finalize the report and forward it direct to the Foreign Office—at the same time informing Arana what he planned to do.

The hot-tempered Whiffen, with the faults and virtues of his kind, saw no other choice. Though he would thrash a horse mercilessly if it shied out hunting, it was mandatory if a man had entertained him to return hospitality. He would spend his father's money without compunction—but if forced to report on a man unfavorably, he would tell him so in advance.

And on this memorable evening, the captain was too open to hold his guest in suspense for any longer than was necessary. In Monsieur Auguste Judah's Café Royal Restaurant on Regent Street, with its blue medallions, discreet pink-shaded lamps and fine Minton china, the menu was still under discussion when Whiffen, again speaking French, broached the subject. This request from the Foreign Office, he said, was akin to a command.

Arana neither expostulated nor seemed unduly concerned. "What do you intend to do in the matter?" was all he said. Once Whiffen had outlined his intentions, Arana asked, "Are you bound to do it?" Restrainedly, Whiffen nodded. "Yes," he replied, "I have no option."

Then, anxious that the evening should go smoothly, he was again the perfect host, the young blade who knew his way round town. A bottle of the Johannisberger '74 would prove a perfect complement to M. Judah's Chicken Pie Café Royal—prepared with bacon, mushrooms, onions and hard-boiled eggs. Quietly, Arana declined: he had what was virtually an allergy to chicken.

But he did not elaborate and Whiffen was too tactful to press him. Instead he tried to divert his guest with tales of the jungle life he had endured on the Putumayo . . . of the aching fatigue at the day's end, when the mind and body cried out for respite from the jungle smells and the constant laceration of thorns . . .

of the shouts of joy with which the Indians greeted his phono-
graph and records of the latest barn dances . . . they had called
the musicians "the little men in the bottom of the box" . . . he
himself had been known among the Boras as *Pimuc*, meaning Ibis,
because of his white bathrobe.

Arana nodded soberly, nursing his thoughts. The casual reference to chickens had taken his mind back to Yurimaguas, the
time he was stricken with "Yavarí fever," so near to death he was
forced to learn to walk again. It was chickens, above all, that had
built up his strength, for Eleonora had one by one killed all of
their twenty-seven chickens, rendering them into nourishing,
easy-to-digest broths and stews. Then she had gone on to buy up
the villagers' chickens and sent messages to relatives beseeching
still more.

"I think I ate every chicken in Yurimaguas," Arana was wont
to joke, but there was no true humor in his jest. It had been one
more bitter battle to secure his family's future, a battle in which
he had triumphed as always, and now this young fop with his
eyeglass and his Savile Row suits sought to jeopardize that future,
like the American, Hardenburg, because he saw it as his duty to
report to his Foreign Office.

He watched Whiffen refilling their glasses, too impatient to
await the sommelier, and he remembered those long evenings in
Manaus, and, more recently, the meeting in Paris. Whiffen had
been his luncheon guest, yet on arrival at the Nouvelle Hotel, he
had at once, without consulting his host, called for a bottle of
champagne. "He likes drink at all times," the ascetic Arana had
reported scornfully later, and it was now, with his memory fresh
in his mind, that it came to him what he had to do.

It was just on 11 P.M. when Whiffen and Arana
at last left the Alhambra Theatre of Varieties on Leicester
Square. Now, as they picked their way through the after-theater
traffic, the raffish clamor of late-night London swirled about
them through the fog . . . blind beggars with iron-shod staves

. . . the shrill voices of flower girls, wheedling "Buy a penny bouquet" . . . streetwalkers in pearl-buttoned velvet coats flooding out of the Café de l'Europe . . . hansom cabs, their lights glowing like fireflies, hemmed in by the newfangled taxis of the Motor Age.

To the fastidious Arana, the evening had proved almost intolerable. True, Whiffen had provided the best stall seats, at four shillings a head, but he had found America's Ethel Levey, who topped the bill with "Yankee Doodle Dandy" and "Give My Regards to Broadway," both crude and noisy. Hating the spilled drink, the mingled smells of cigar smoke and patchouli, the bawdy shouted choruses, he had thought resentfully of Covent Garden Opera House, nearby, where he had heard his favorite, Enrico Caruso, sing the Duke of Mantua in *Rigoletto*, with the incomparable Melba as Gilda. But at least the proximity of bar to stalls had kept Whiffen drinking steadily. Though Arana normally limited himself to two glasses of wine with a meal, tonight he had drunk more freely, prompting the Englishman to keep the champagne flowing.

And his patience was rewarded, for Whiffen now proposed to continue the evening across the square in the Motor Club, at 37 Coventry Street, of which he had recently become a member. "The night is young, señor, eh?" he encouraged Arana.

At this hour few members still lingered in the club's second-floor suite of rooms. Summoning a steward, Whiffen toyed with the idea of a nightcap, but Arana dissuaded him. Surely there was no better drink to follow champagne than more champagne? As Arana had guessed he would, Whiffen assented.

Now Arana once more turned the talk to Whiffen's projected report for the Peruvian Government. It would be best, he said, if he personally negotiated the transaction to ensure that Whiffen was well remunerated. The report must be exhaustive, dealing with every aspect of the Putumayo: geographic, ethnographic, economic. "What do you have in mind?" he asked, pouring more champagne for the captain. "What would you consider a fair price?"

Already Whiffen was trying hard to keep the Peruvian's face in focus. "My expenses were around £ 1,400," he said deliberately. "I would settle for a sum in that neighborhood."

"Very good," Arana approved. "Let us drink to that." Then, again, refilling their glasses, he became brisk and businesslike. It was important Whiffen's acceptance of these terms should be put on record. Whiffen agreed; a shade unsteadily, he retrieved a sheet of club paper from the writing desk and began to jot down some notes. "No, no," Arana intervened, "we must set it down in Spanish. Then we shall be sure my government understands the full implications."

Whiffen protested. French was no problem, but he was a very poor Spanish scholar—in fact, he spoke only a few words of the language. "But this is no obstacle," said Arana suavely, and with this he arose to fetch the captain a fresh sheet of paper. "I will dictate and you will write down the words as I say them."

At first Whiffen had no suspicion as to what was afoot. He was too busy grappling with the unfamiliar Spanish. *"Yo tengo como sabe Usted informacion que puedo dar al Gobierno—como Yo lo é dicho a Usted."* (I have, as you know, information which I can give to the government—as I have told you.) Feebly, Whiffen queried this. Surely they should specify that it was the Peruvian Government to which he referred? But Arana, impatient, shook his head. It was his intention to route the letter direct to the new President, Augusto Leguía. Obviously only one government was involved.

The captain stumbled on: "If I can receive £ 1,000 spent in the Putumayo, etc. during the year 1908–9, I am going to say that I have not seen any irregularities . . ." Uncomprehending, he laid aside his pen, blinking at Arana. What was the meaning of this word *irregularidades?*

Patiently, Arana refreshed his memory: surely he remembered how they had thrashed this out in Manaus, when Carlos Rey de Castro was present? The rumor that his employees were smuggling rubber to Manaus, defrauding both the company and the Peruvian Government, still persisted—moreover, some members of Leguía's cabinet believed Arana was in collusion with them. It was important to nail the lie before it gained currency. If Whiffen, as he had sworn in Manaus, had seen no such irregularities, he must put this on record.

His head growing foggier by the minute, Whiffen wrote on. "My expenses were £1,400. But I am agreeable and will receive £1,000. Nothing less."

Whiffen grappled with the sense of the draft. It seemed a strangely colloquial letter to write to the President of a republic. "That is all," Arana told him. "There is no need for you to sign it." Still, Whiffen stared at his own handwriting, bemusedly shaking his head. Though he was in no shape to define them, the words seemed to carry disquieting implications. He begged Arana to let him sleep on it; they could rephrase it in the morning.

"No, the phrasing is entirely correct," Arana disagreed. Then, seeing Whiffen still staring at the paper, he reached forward peremptorily to take it. The captain withdrew it just beyond his reach, and Arana stood up. "Come," he said softly, dangerously, "come. Let me have it now." For the first time the thought leaped into Whiffen's fuddled brain: *It's a trap.*

Without more ado, he tore the sheet of notepaper into fragments. "It's a mistake," he said thickly. "I'm sorry—let's forget about it. I want nothing more to do with it." For a long moment the two men stared at one another, saying nothing. "Then if our business is concluded," said Arana, at last, "the hour is late. I must make my way back to my hotel." Whiffen demurred: he was still the host. The porter should call a hansom and he would escort Arana back to the Hotel Cecil in the Strand.

He searched for the torn-up letter but it was no longer there. Afterward he could not remember whether he had put it on a side table or thrown it into a wastebasket.

Five thousand miles from London, on Manaus' Republic Square, the heat was a hostile force: it was as if an oven door had been flung suddenly open. From the shaded terrace of the Garden Chalet, beyond the green-and-gilt Aphrodite Fountain and the whitewashed Governor's Palace, Henry Lex Gielgud glimpsed steam suspended like a veil of gauze above the waters of the Negro River. Yet to Gielgud this exotic tropical life held the promise of a new unclouded future.

Seven months earlier, as an obscure £150 a year audit clerk, employed by a London firm of accountants, Gielgud had been assigned to reorganize the bookkeeping for their clients, the Peruvian Amazon Company, in Manaus and Iquitos. Unlike the clerk who had conducted the audit prior to Arana's incorporation in London, Gielgud, whose Spanish was competent, had spent two months on the Putumayo. At La Chorrera and El Encanto he had been the honored guest of Victor Macedo and Miguel Loayza and he had visited four subsidiary depots, too—Sur, Occidente, Entre Rios and Ultimo Retiro. In May, on his way through Manaus, Julio Arana had proved a courteous and liberal host.

The deference accorded him on all sides had by no means displeased Gielgud. In London, his life was shaped like that of most struggling clerks: a world of third-class season tickets, "office coats," cuff protectors and hastily bolted lunches of beef à la mode at Wilkinson's Dining Rooms on Coleman Street. Yet at twenty-eight, after four and a half years as an auditor, this six-foot Cambridge graduate had dreams that were still big and undiminished—and his patronizing manner with his fellow clerks, the advice he so freely tendered between puffs at his briar pipe, left no doubt he thought himself a man of consequence.

But within days now, his overhaul of the system accomplished, Gielgud was booked to return to England and obscurity, and the knowledge galled him. In Manaus, his probe had revealed that here the most junior clerks earned £480 a year, three times his own salary. Even office managers as incompetent as Lizardo Arana were paid £2,500.

And Manaus, too, was a living proof of the power that money could buy. Night after night he had watched the "colonels," immaculate in their white linen, loll on the green-painted chairs of the Chalet's terrace, complacently awaiting the arrival of their silk-clad women. Over all-night poker games, he had seen laborers lose £200 on the turn of a card without blinking an eyelash. This morning's issue of *Amazonas*, which showed top-grade wild rubber at 8/9d a pound, was packed with advertisements that set the keynote of the city . . . new consignments of crystal chandeliers, Omega watches and bench-made English shoes . . . a fresh assortment of "amorous postcards" had arrived at the Agencia Freitas . . . Dr. Geldhinho Ramos announced that he could cure syphilis even through the mail. Yet soon Gielgud must leave the one city that had ever accorded him his due to board the Booth liner, *Antony*.

Abruptly the Manaus branch's English accountant, young J. A. Meech, who had accompanied him up the Putumayo, dropped into a chair beside him. "Here's a rum go," he said excitedly, passing over a month-old issue of *Truth*. "This has just arrived in the mail." Gielgud, scanning the first article intently, now recalled hearing Hardenburg's name before. In Iquitos, a Dutchman named Janssen had spoken of the American's claim to have been badly treated and his plan to write a book by way of revenge.

Idly, he wondered: would the Peruvian Amazon Company be likely to ask his firm's permission for him to return upriver and prepare a report on the allegations? But Meech speedily disillusioned him. "There isn't a hope," he said. "They'd have no way of reaching you. The cable communication between Pará and Manaus is out—has been for weeks."

Gielgud resigned himself to the inevitable. On October 23, he would sail back to England and obscurity after all.

In fact, Gielgud had overestimated the British directors' sense of urgency. Their minute book had already recorded their decision: since the clerk was soon due to return they would await his arrival before formally seeking a written report through his firm.

Meanwhile, Gubbins and his colleagues were in a quandary. Though they sought to duck the searchlight of publicity by maintaining a dignified silence, Hardenburg's weekly disclosures in *Truth*—which were to be serialized without a break until November 17—had already seen tempers flare hotly. As early as September 25, the Peruvian Chargé d'Affaires, R. E. Lembcke, had publicly denied the allegations—complaining that Rocca's papers had been started "for dishonest purposes" and that individuals in Iquitos had tried "to obtain from persons of bad character false information for blackmailing purposes." On October 4, Lembcke followed up with another press release: Hardenburg's depositions were both "worthless and unfounded." Though editor Robert Bennett gave the letters space, he saw one question as unanswered. Why, if Hardenburg had concocted the evidence, had the Peruvian Government agreed to pay him and Perkins £500 compensation?

But the Reverend Harris and his colleagues of the Anti-Slavery Society were not to be put off. On October 13, secretary Travers Buxton took the company to task: their contention that the British directors bore no responsibility prior to December, 1908, had no foundation in law. The company had been incorporated by October, 1907, and at least two directors—Arana and Alarco —had controlled the vendor firm. Nor was there reason to believe that ill-treatment of the Indians had ceased even now. It was their duty, Buxton urged, to receive a deputation from the society.

Two weeks later, still firmly taking the stand that the Putumayo was nobody's business but their own, the directors rejected
Buxton's suggestion: "no useful purpose would be served by the
deputation which you suggest." And secretary Vernon Smith
went further: "We would have the Society to know that this
company is managed in the best traditions of an English company."

Under pressure, Henry Read did agree to receive Francis
William Fox, the society's vice-chairman, who called personally
at his office. But the banker stubbornly held out: to date there
was no proof *Truth*'s articles were anything but a tissue of lies.
Fox tried to reason with him: if the board agreed to see Hardenburg, he could furnish cold hard facts straight from the source.
At once Read arose to show his visitor the door. "Hardenburg?"
he blazed. "We don't go to a man of that sort for information, I
can tell you!"

Still, the growing public clamor demanded action, and John
Russell Gubbins hit on a solution of his own: if the charges were
valid, only the Peruvians could put their house in order. On
October 8, two days before the British directors again met Arana,
Gubbins used his acquaintance with President Leguía to write a
letter bringing the allegations to his notice. It was desirable "for
the credit of the company," he urged, "that things should be put
in their proper light." Though Leguía never acknowledged receipt, the Senate in Lima debated this question on November 22.

But Gubbins and the others were forced to tread warily.
Though Arana had only codirector's status, they held him in
much awe. At their October 20 board meeting, when the Peruvian first learned of the letter to Leguía, he was consumed with
cold deadly anger. "Your letter may well have given a wrong
impression," he told Gubbins harshly. "It does not do justice to
the efforts always made by the Peruvian authorities to maintain
order." Meekly, Gubbins and the others had accepted his censure. The letter had been mistakenly dispatched, the minute book
recorded, without awaiting Arana's approval.

Yet now, for the first time, Gubbins heard Arana's admission that such charges had already been leveled by *La Felpa* and *La Sancíon*. The old man was dumbfounded. Had he known this, he later went on record, he would never have accepted his directorship, for he felt that "Arana had concealed a very material fact." But still none of the British directors dared approach *Truth* to examine the evidence on file. To probe deeply into Hardenburg's accusations would incur Arana's implacable displeasure.

Thus all three set much store by an independent witness. On November 18, on behalf of the board, Abel Alarco wrote to the accountants: "Gentlemen, your Mr. Gielgud having now returned from our properties in South America, we should be exceedingly obliged if he would favour the company with his impressions regarding the attacks recently made in *Truth* on the company's operations on the Putumayo." But this, the auditor later admitted, was a formality. Within twenty-four hours of the *Antony* docking at Liverpool, on November 13, he had arrived unbidden in the Peruvian Amazon Company's office.

One of the first men he encountered on this afternoon visit was Julio Arana. "You have seen the allegations?" the Peruvian asked bluntly. "Do you believe them?" "I do not," Gielgud answered readily.

On November 24, the report of his visit was read and adopted by the board. At last Gubbins and the others heaved a sigh of relief, for this, all along, in unequivocal black and white, was what they had hoped to hear. "The charges brought by *Truth*," Gielgud assured them, "entirely misrepresent the conditions that prevail on the company's properties . . . the impressions I formed of the general conditions were decidedly favourable. The Indians had not that cowed and miserable look one would expect from the victims of . . . barbarities . . . [they] seemed to me in the main to be simply as children of rather happy disposition. . . .

"The officers of the company whom I met . . . did not appear to me the sort of men who would wantonly flog, maim or kill the people put under them. Messrs. Macedo and Loayza, in particular . . . are men whom I should not believe capable of the

alleged atrocities without the very strongest evidence . . .
instances of such wanton barbarity may have occurred, but I
have no hesitation in stating that they are not general or even of
fairly common occurrence. . . ."

He had completed it just in time. On the same day his report
was adopted, the Foreign Office stepped into the breach, as the
Reverend Harris had hoped they would, having considered
Whiffen's report in conjunction with Hardenburg's articles. At
least one director, was their official verdict, had been fully aware
the system was open to abuses for, as far back as June, Whiffen,
in Manaus, had secured Arana's promise to dismiss Macedo and
his hirelings. So what action did the company propose to take?

At this stage, the directors made no reply, though they discounted Whiffen's testimony entirely. Arana's painstaking col-
lage of the fragments of Motor Club notepaper seemed proof of
one more blackmailer who would accept "£1,000—nothing less,"
to suppress a report to his government. But now the Britons hit
upon an ingenious way of setting their house in order. Only with
difficulty had they talked the incensed Arana out of suing *Truth*
for libel; since Walt had made no direct personal accusations,
they felt their chances were slim. Nor did the Peruvian favor an
independent commission of investigation; the very suggestion, he
said, might mortally offend his government. But on one point, at
least, all found accord. Abel Alarco must go.

For months, the British directors' relations with Alarco had
been at snapping point; his vile temper had provoked countless
stormy scenes. Then, too, he neglected the business, making off
for weeks at a time to his rented house in Geneva, to strut the
boulevards in Inverness cape and deerstalker with his two prize
German wolfhounds. "If we had removed him before Arana
came back," Gubbins admitted later, "this would have incensed
Arana"—but now, to their undying relief, they found the Peruvian was the first to moot his brother-in-law's deposal from the
board.

To be sure, he had a five-year contract, at £2,500 a year, but, as
Arana saw it, it was cheaper to pay him this money in Lima than

retain him one moment longer in London. At the same time Vernon Smith was discreetly transferred to the Manaus office. Not easily would any among them forget the red faces resulting from that attempted bribe.

On December 13, Henry Lex Gielgud was offered—and accepted—the combined post of secretary and manager of the Peruvian Amazon Company at £1,000 a year, almost seven times the salary he had earned before his uneventful journey up the Putumayo.

In his rented room on Sandwich Street, Walt Hardenburg, by contrast, still awaited his share of the £500 promised him by the Peruvian Government. By now he had seen the last of his savings swallowed up. Soon after his arrival, pocketing his pride, he had written home to Youngsville to ask a favor of his father: he urgently needed to realize the cash value of the £78 which he had sent home earlier and which Spencer had put out for him on mortgages. But even this sum, paid to him in two installments through the Union of London and Smith's Bank, near the Mansion House, vanished swiftly.

By now, Walt's dramatic disclosures had cast him as a social lion, and the gatherings of wealthy philanthropists he attended along with the Reverend Harris and others demanded such formal additions to his wardrobe as white tie and tails. And to find work in this year of growing unemployment seemed next to impossible; no one wanted the services of an American railroad engineer. Calling at *Truth*'s offices, he confessed to Bennett and Paternoster that his resources were at an end.

"I've spent every red cent I have and I just can't hold out any longer," he told them. "If anything else is to be done it's up to your Foreign Office."

Both men urged him to reconsider. It was inconceivable the company would content themselves with their one tame rejoinder of September 27—"it's so feeble," said Paternoster incredulously. Knowing nothing of the confusion and indecision that beset the British directors, Bennett and his assistant believed they must either sue for libel—or follow up the sources of confirmation that were open to them.

"We've been getting letters from Manaus and Iquitos backing you up almost every week," Bennett encouraged Walt, "but we shall still need you in the witness box if it comes to an action."

Reluctantly, Hardenburg agreed to accept a £20 subsidy until his compensation came through. He was living as frugally as he had ever done, but this was not easy for a young man to whom London ways were strange and who was, moreover, in love.

Over the weeks he had come to realize that Mary Feeney's warm sympathy had brought him the truest happiness he had ever known—so that insensibly friendship had ripened into courtship. But this, too, could be costly when he wanted to give Mary a good time on the town, and though they often went to shows like *The Dollar Princess*, at Daly's, with Lily Elsie, and *Our Miss Gibbs* at the Gaiety, it was usually after queuing early for the cheaper pit stalls. Once, at this time, Walt, buying an evening paper, tendered a gold half-sovereign, asking the news-boy to get change. He was more angry than Mary had ever seen him when the lad failed to return—but she knew the sum represented a day's board and lodging.

One day, quite simply, Walt slipped from his little finger a plain gold wedding-type ring that he always wore. "A very close man friend gave it to me in South America," he told Mary. "I'd like you to have it from now on." Mary never knew whether this friend had been Perkins, nor did she then know she would wear the ring for all of her married life.

To Walt, their meeting was the one fine and uncomplicated thing that had happened to him since reaching London. As yet, he knew nothing of Arana's attempt to brand him as a black-mailer and a forger: he knew only that he had devoted almost two years to this crusade, spending every penny he had, and that it had degenerated into nothing more than a polemic interchange of letters to the newspapers.

Now Julio Arana, still in London, reached a crucial decision—crucial because it was one day to topple him from his hard-won pinnacle of power. Hardenburg's meddling had cost him almost £200,000. Not only was the publicity damaging, bringing him long, overwrought letters from Eleonora, in Geneva with the children, but his hasty departure from Manaus to London to oversee the British directors had caused certain rubber deals to fall through. Once for all he determined he would crush both the American and Captain Whiffen.

Since the Foreign Office had as yet taken no action, many men might have let well alone. But Arana's ego was massive, and he did not rank himself with the majority. All the evidence he needed, and more, was in his possession—not only the carefully-pieced-together "blackmail" note of Whiffen's, but also a whole dossier of depositions alleging Hardenburg's moral turpitude, gleaned painstakingly by Pablo in Iquitos and Lizardo in Manaus—statements from Borsa, the hotel proprietor, Garnier, editor of *Amazonas*, and a score of others. Pablo had forwarded them from Iquitos on November 18, at the same time cautioning his brother-in-law: "These are documents very proper for your secret archives." Arana had taken the hint; they were locked in his safe and the British directors had never seen them.

His success over the years had convinced Arana he was invulnerable: a pillar of Manaus society, a man feared throughout the Amazon Valley. Working his way from nothing, he had given his family advantages which he had never known: a fine chalet with a rose garden and a croquet lawn, good schools to educate them, servants to wait on them and brush their hair. No obscure American engineer or wine-swilling army officer was going to get the better of Julio Arana.

By Christmas of 1909, he was, Gubbins and the others observed, "wildly excited." He urged them to join with him in circularizing every shareholder and making public the facts: it was time the world realized the nature of the blackmailers who conspired against him. But one brief horrified glance at the draft he had prepared and the British directors showed unusual spirit:

they refused point-blank to support him. "You can make any report you please," Henry Read told him. "The accusations are against you, not us; you know the details, we don't. We're not associating ourselves with anything like libel."

Arana would not be deterred. On the evening of December 30, a few hours before the next day's annual general meeting, the shareholders were rocked on their heels by one of the strangest circulars ever issued by a company director: "Dear Sir (or Madam), On my arrival in London a short time ago, I read the series of articles that appeared in *Truth* . . . the alleged atrocities related [there] are entirely unfounded . . . the result of excited imaginations . . . in a region so remote . . . it is a matter for little surprise that certain disreputable characters, from mercenary motives, should lend themselves to swear to anything they are asked . . .

"In reference to W. E. Hardenburg . . . I can only inform the shareholders that this person whom *Truth* is taking under its protection is not worthy of credit . . . I doubt whether the shareholders will be of the same opinion [as *Truth*] when they know of the proofs which I have in my possession . . . amongst others, a cable, confirmed since by letter from Mr. Egoaguirre, Senator for Loreto, in Lima . . . to the following effect . . . it was to him that Mr. W. E. Hardenburg made the proposal that he should be paid the sum of £7,000 in consideration of his not publishing his so-called evidence . . .

". . . There yet remains something to which I feel forced . . . to refer . . . on 12th October last, an officer of the English Army who had called on me [in Manaus] disclosed to me . . . that he held in his hands the fate of the Company, which depended on his report, and which would be favourable to my Company, and all trouble avoided if I gave him £1,000 . . ."

PART FOUR

The Judgment Seat

ON April 12, 1910, Julio César Arana was 46 years old—but his children knew better than to commemorate the occasion with gifts or greetings cards. It would have invited only a baleful glance and the comment, "We should never remember when we are one year older." By tacit consent, the day passed like any other in the rented three-story London house at 42 Queen's Gardens, Hyde Park, in which Arana had recently installed his family, with a staff of fourteen to attend on them. It was the close-knit domestic life of Iquitos he sought to re-create, though with notable additions to the household—Gladys Holliday, the English governess, the French governess, Marthe, and Juan Aymena, a Huitoto lad Arana had on a whim brought from the Putumayo. Enrolling him as a pupil at Margate College, Kent, he planned he should become the first forest Indian ever to graduate as a doctor.

Despite his ever-present sciatica, his distrust of the advancing years, the family found him overtly more relaxed. Now he dined earlier than in Manaus, always quitting the London Wall office by 7 P.M. Ten-year-old Julio César, Junior, and Luiz, aged eight, ate separately with the governesses, but Eleonora was careful to hold dinner for the rest of the family until Julio's carriage was heard at the door; during school holidays he took much comfort that Angelica, eighteen, and Lily, eleven, both studying at the Convent of the Sacred Heart, Highgate, could join him for this leisurely meal, along with twenty-year-old Alicia. Sometimes their niece, Elena, Pablo's daughter and Julio's sister, Petronila, who were on a visit to Europe, made up the party.

Often they chaffed Julio that he was growing contented,

putting on weight, and the Peruvian had to admit it: even with his iron will he found it hard to deny himself such European delicacies as Whitstable oysters, young asparagus, frog's legs and meringues billowing with thick cream. But Rosalia, the Peruvian cook who traveled everywhere with the family, was reassured to find two old favorites still had pride of place: Peruvian chicken soufflé and bananas baked in the oven with cheese and butter.

This dinner hour, his family recognized as sacred. To discuss business or household worries was taboo: more than one of Arana's children, threatened with Papa's wrath by their mother, was thankful if Eleonora raised the subject of their misconduct at the dinner table. Whatever the peccadillo, Arana good-humoredly brushed it aside: "This is no time to talk of serious matters." Tackling his food with a gourmet's absorption, he would talk only of opera, current books or the new Royal Academy Exhibition, and with Papa at his wittiest the table was a constant ripple of laughter.

He seemed mellower in other ways. Once again he recalled Eleonora's love of flowers, and big copper vases of her favorite carnations and chrysanthemums filled every room. The smallest domestic detail intrigued him: rarely had he laughed as heartily as when Eleonora told him of the straw basket that Luiz had painstakingly fashioned in kindergarten. "Believe me, Julio," she assured him, "it was family talent coming out—every bit as good as we made at home in Rioja." At the office, his staff now found him as indulgent a boss as he was a father. Even priority letters would be pondered for three days before Arana committed himself to paper.

The one thing to anger him openly was loss of dignity: more than ever, it was the facade that counted. If he thought a photograph less than perfect he scrawled a scathing comment on the cardboard mount: "A third-rate picture of my delicious and beautiful Alicia." Once, accompanying his father to the Hotel Cecil, young Luiz was intent on shinning down the marble balustrade to the peacock-tiled main hall. Though his father, having summoned the elevator, beckoned, Luiz shook a mutinous head. Then he saw Arana's face darken with anger as his finger crooked imperiously: "When the general commands, a captain doesn't give any orders." In chastened silence, Luiz rode down beside his father.

Few suspected it, but Arana, beneath his unruffled calm, was more tense than he had ever been. Though his long-standing dream of putting down roots in Europe was at last a reality, and he explored the countryside surrounding London for a suitable dream house, it was still too early to relax. Had that audacious circular letter to the shareholders succeeded or not? As yet, more than three months after its dispatch, Arana did not know.

To be sure, Hardenburg and Whiffen had not taken legal action—for neither man was as yet aware that the circular existed. Walt, in any case, after at last receiving his money from the Peruvian Government, had tired of waiting. On March 1, 1910, along with Mary Feeney, now his wife, he had reached St. John, New Brunswick, on the liner *Corsican*, bent on putting the past behind him and starting a new life in Canada. But at the shareholders' meeting of December 31, Gubbins and the others had dumbfounded Arana. Señor Arana, Gubbins made plain, had issued this circular on his own responsibility. The board disclaimed any connection with it.

"It's a private circular," Gubbins had warned shareholders before dismissing the matter, "and anyone referring to it publicly may be had up for libel or slander, possibly both."

An unbroken front, Arana felt, would have kept the meeting tranquil—but Gubbins' open disavowal only lent fuel to the flames. One shareholder, Morgan Williams, a terse-spoken mining engineer, had publicly rebuked the directors: "I should have thought that by now, by hook or by crook, the board would have been able to send out an unbiased representative to obtain a correct version of the facts."

Again *Truth*'s allegations, the story of Alarco's attempted bribe had leaped into the headlines—and Morgan Williams had followed up his outburst with two personal visits to Gubbins at the company's office. On one occasion, Arana had heard him expostulating: "Here are these *Truth* articles, making the name of the company stink in everybody's nostrils! Here's one Peruvian director accused of bribery, and another Peruvian director mixed up with blackmailing charges, and a guerrilla warfare going on with company employees being used as soldiers. It seems to be an extraordinary thing for a rubber company to be employed on."

Though Gubbins sought to mollify the engineer, Williams replied spiritedly: "With all this before you, I should have thought one of you, or all of you, would take the first boat out to probe *in situ* into the matter."

Hence Arana's unease, for how much latent discontent was massing to destroy his carefully wrought enterprise he did not know. And the world was now at the peak of a rubber boom which might, at any moment, burst like a toy balloon.

Over three years, the world's hunger for rubber had not abated, and the back numbers of *The India Rubber Journal* piled neatly on Arana's office desk made the position plain. In 1909, the factories had swallowed up 69,000 tons of rubber: 15,000 tons alone for winter overshoes in New York, Moscow and Oslo, 3,000 tons for engine and boiler packing.

But it was the fast-booming Motor Age whose demands were inexorable—right from the October day in 1908, when the first of 15 million Model T's, the homely $825 car, that would "take you anywhere but into Society," chugged off Henry Ford's Detroit assembly line. From the privileged pastime of bluebloods like Baron Henri de Rothschild and Lady Randolph Churchill, motoring had captivated a grass-roots democracy, and the sky was the limit.

Now, in the rubber brokers' sample rooms of London and New York, it took five days to sample the goods before each auction—and five more to conduct the auction itself. Buyers were bidding land-office prices for strange grades of rubber with Alice-in-Wonderland names: hard-cure fine Pará, Niger Flake, Manaus Scrappy, Mozambique Balls, Gold Coast Lump. Within the year, 500 tons of rubber were ferried down the Amazon every ten days, and even *sernamby*, the despised scrapings from the tappers' tin cups, was fetching fifty cents a pound.

Out of Pará, on March 18, came the Booth liner *Antony*, with a cargo of rubber worth £1,200,000; three days later, from this same port, sailed the *Cearense*, her £1 million freight destined for New York, the market for 30 percent of all Amazon rubber. Weeks earlier, when the *Clement* left Pará for Liverpool with another £1 million cargo, Lloyd's underwriters demanded double premiums on this record shipment—then held their breath as the rubber's value soared all through the three-week voyage.

It was small wonder Julio Arana saw the red light. By March 5, 1910, the most disastrous rubber boom in history had overtaken the world. British brokers, snatching a few hours' sleep in hotels near their offices, paid telephonists and stenographers double wages to stay on the job, not daring to venture home for fear of the spiraling market. In railway carriages and smoke rooms, total strangers traded expertise on share prices and the latex yields of four-year trees. At Kew's Royal Botanic Gardens, horticulturists in the trial sheds were driven wild by a nonstop flood of company promoters, boning up on rubber lore. Shares changed hands like pieces in a game of Monopoly, and the city hummed with stories of lucky speculations; by April's end, one office boy, profiting by tips, had netted a £19,000 fortune. Within weeks, as two shilling shares soared to £2 in value, the chairman of the London Stock Exchange, Robert Inglis, made a radical but vain proposal: to close the exchange for one whole week to allow the frenzy to subside.

In London, Sir Frank Swettenham, former governor of the Straits Settlements of Malaya, cautioned: "A great many companies have been floated in which I would have thought no one outside a lunatic asylum would have invested a shilling." It was a timely warning. Between July and November, 1909, seventy-seven companies were organized with a total capital of more than £6 million; before the boom had petered out and shares plummeted, new flotations had reached an all-time high of £150 million. More than half, as Swettenham had prophesied, proved either valueless or fraudulent.

To the canny Arana, the shape of the future was plain. Within two years, rubber consumption would have upped steeply to 100,000 tons—and since the Amazon could never meet this world need, prices would fall and go on falling. By August, 1909, 250,000 acres in Malaya alone were planted in orderly groves of 40 million trees, spaced no more than twenty feet apart. For a skilled Chinese coolie, it was child's play to tap over 400 trees a day.

For as Henry Wickham's long-ago seed snatch began to pay off, it was plantation rubber that held the stage: estates whose initial costs had been a thrifty £9 an acre, now, after seven years, showed a book value of £700 per acre. On April 16, 1910, fine amber-colored sheet rubber from the four-year-old Highlands and Lowlands Estate, western Malaya, fetched an unparalleled 12/10d a pound—and trees on such estates were yielding from eleven to eighteen pounds each year as against the Amazon's three and a half. To Arana it was significant that in May, 1910, the United States Rubber Company, donor of Manaus' fine streetcar system, turned its back on Brazil and looked east, investing in what grew to be a giant 90,000-acre plot in northeast Sumatra.

But in Manaus' Chamber of Commerce, Arana was still a lone voice. Now, with a rubber exchange newly installed in their headquarters building, the barons basked securely in their seeming world monopoly: from 3 to 4 P.M. each day they gathered jubilantly for word of the latest quotations, relayed by direct telegraph service from London and New York. As top-grade wild rubber again touched 9/2d a pound, one bigwig went on record: "If it was not our duty to keep abreast of scientific developments, we could completely ignore these foreign plantations."

In the three years since Arana founded the Peruvian Amazon Company, Manaus' population had rocketed from 37,000 to

50,000. Not all were bent on living it up: many, through training and diligent effort, meant to make a place for themselves in the world. Shops now closed three hours earlier, at 6 P.M., to allow ambitious salesmen time for night classes. Two language schools, one run by Berlitz, were teaching English, French and German. The largest single item in the state budget was for education.

But for rubber there were still men who would take any risk, endure any hardship. Already in 1910, so many motormen had taken off upriver to get rich quick as tappers that Manaus' street-car system ground to a standstill. Mobs a thousand strong stoned, even burned, the stranded cars, until the governor ordered a cavalry charge to scatter them. At Remate de Males, on the Upper Amazon, the most malarial zone in all South America, would-be rubber trail barons sat it out through the rainy season in the half-flooded Hotel de Augusto, hammocks slung three feet above the water level, victualed by traders who paddled their canoes through the open kitchen door.

But in Manaus too many men who had made their pile were spending like Eastern caliphs. The talk of the city was the new £15,000 yacht that Carlos Montenegro had commissioned from the British shipbuilders, Cammell Laird; both its 40-seater saloon and deluxe bar were "designed for talking business." Birthday parties, with full-scale orchestras, staffed by waiters in white knee-length breeches, now sometimes lasted two days: free drinks for gate-crashers were a matter of alcoholic routine. No wish, while the money lasted, went unfulfilled. One "colonel," journeying to London, booked a box for the entire season at Covent Garden Opera House, solely to focus his binoculars on the comeliest bosoms in the stalls. By common consent, the palm for prodigality went to an up-country baron who was short of both ice and gasoline. To chill two bottles of champagne for his dinner, he rigged up a kerosene-powered refrigerator for £40, then used £9 worth of absinthe to fuel his launch for a half-hour jaunt up the Yavarí River.

Though most were slow to realize it, their greed was fast driving manufacturers into the plantation owners' arms. As early

as 1908, a tight ring of Brazilian barons had set out to restrict
Manaus' exports, cornering 4,000 tons of rubber on a valorizing
plan, determined to store them under lock and key until world
prices were driven to a peak. As a result, buyers like the United
States Rubber Company, taking as little Amazon latex as possible,
shipped even larger supplies from the Far East. Forced to liqui-
date its stocks before the year's end, the Bank of Brazil, heading
the ill-starred syndicate, lost £2 million.

But from April, 1910, the city saw a threat as formidable as the
plantations looming large on its own doorstep: Percival Farquhar's inimitable Madeira-Mamoré Railroad, christened by her
engineers "Mad Mary," was now, after three years' trial and
error, forging ahead. From this time on, the new wireless telegraph between Manaus and Pôrto Velho, the railroad's terminal
on the Madeira River, kept the Manauense all too keenly aware
of the Mary's progress. By May 31, traffic had been inaugurated
as far as Kilometre 90, at Jaci-Paraná; by October's end, the
engineers had pushed on to Kilometre 152. Now, wild rubber
could be borne within twelve hours from deepest jungle to the
Atlantic-bound steamers anchored at Pôrto Velho.

And if Farquhar's dream came true, Itacoatiara, a tiny shantytown port of 2,000 people on the Amazon's main stream, must
one day supersede the white city—for Ita, a direct port of call
for oceangoing liners, was sited nearer the Atlantic than Manaus,
nine miles up the Negro River tributary.

The achievement of the railroad would be a triumph of faith
and rugged individualism—a faith the Amazon's jungle hazards
never quite overwhelmed, though at times they came perilously
close to it. All through the early summer of 1907, the rodmen,
transitmen and locating engineers battled to establish a precarious
foothold on the jungle's edge, felling trees, slicing lianas, scoring
the deep red wound in the raw earth above the Madeira River
that became Pôrto Velho township. At last, aptly, on July 4, to
the sound of massed rifle fire, "Old Glory" fluttered to the top of
a makeshift flagstaff and the Americans settled in earnest to the
five-year task of whipping the jungle.

Many who came were roughnecks and roustabouts from the world's four corners—"down there for the good of their health," as one man recalled. Money was spent so freely on liquor that soon the paymasters confined them to scrip; on pay-night forays, a man, on a whim, might spend $200 to acquire a pair of bullet-riddled boots. As tough and sometimes tougher were the laborers —Barbadians, half-castes, Caribbean quadroons—hired for ten shillings a day to shift every cubic yard of dirt by hand. In Manaus and Pará, recruiting agents had standards all their own: a volunteer arriving at the center in a sober dark suit was rejected out of hand. Medicals consisted of one test: the iron a man put into his handshake with the doctor.

But a whipcord physique was essential. Before barracks were raised, survey crews on the first ten miles of track strung their hammocks between the trees, swathing themselves from head to foot in mosquito netting. Pioneer doctors brought their own instruments and bought their own medicaments—including quinine priced by profiteering druggists at £20 a capsule, often adulterated with starch and sodium bicarbonate. Other medicines were virtually nonexistent. Dysentery patients were dosed with calomel. Aluminum sulfate was the one water purifier. And no man injected with permanganate of potassium for snakebite survived to talk about it.

Working conditions were a nightmare. One hundred feet above the workers' heads wire-taut lianas held the treetops in a vise, so that even timber sawn through at the base could not fall. Often, in forest extending for 120 unbroken miles from the river's edge, an assistant was invisible three feet away through the tangle of vines and branches. As bearded as castaways, blanched with anemia, sand flies and mosquitoes tormented them until they looked "like criminals fresh from the whipping post." In the seconds it took a transitman to line a point ahead, two other men fought to keep his eyes clear of flies. "This is war," one man at breaking point sobbed; "we're just fighting to stay alive."

It was not surprising that the nerves of many broke. Not only disease stalked them, but hostile Caripúna Indians, adorned with moustaches of red wild turkey feathers, armed with nine-foot palm-wood bows and handfuls of poison arrows. And the first batches of recruits numbered thirteen-year-old boys and old men of seventy, 90 percent of them hospitalized within three weeks. Already the railroad was costing a life a day.

Mutinies were endemic. Some were sparked by rumor alone; of 350 Spaniards, imported from Cuba in January, 1908, all but sixty-five stampeded off the freighter *Amanda* in Pará, appalled by stories that had filtered 3,000 miles downriver from Pôrto Velho. Hard on their heels came a German contingent, 600 strong, dockwallopers from the cool salt fogs of the Baltic ports; following one glance at Pôrto Velho's tumbledown hutments, most refused to disembark. The few who did, sent to work up-country, rebelled within days; some, fashioning rafts from empty cement barrels, conceived the insane idea of floating downriver toward Manaus. A primitive catamaran bearing six headless torsos was the only later evidence of their fate.

Of the remainder, only seventy-five went back down the Amazon alive; beriberi slew them by the score. As the Germans fought the disease, no man in Pôrto Velho slept; their death cries echoed through the walls of the makeshift hospitals in this picket post of civilization.

It was small wonder that not only Germany, but Spain, Portugal and Italy now boycotted the railroad entirely, banishing the company's recruiting agents, clamping down on direct emigration.

A keen humanitarian, Percival Farquhar was shocked by these reports. "The costliest labor is underpaid, underfed labor," he argued, then set out to right the wrongs. From Guatemala, early in 1908, he imported three veteran rail contractors who abided by his standards—Robert H. May, Burt Jekyll and "King John" Randolph. From Panama soon after came Washington-born Dr. Carl Lovelace to build a 300-bed hospital at Candelaria, two miles downriver. A hawk-eyed sanitarian, Lovelace, with his fifteen interns, soon installed such Canal Zone-type trimmings as wide-screen, mosquito-proof porches for dormitories and office buildings. Drenching stagnant water with petroleum to prevent the development of tiger mosquito larvae, they wore protective head screens like fencing masks, gloves and heavy boots. Within a month of his arrival, Lovelace had treated all but 5 percent of Pôrto Velho's 1,000-strong populace for every ailment from yellow fever to ulcers.

Soon Pôrto Velho was a model of what a healthy, efficient frontier town could be. Pure water, electricity generators, telephones, ice mills and an automatic laundry became reality almost overnight. Then followed a steam bakery, a movie house, and a printing press, churning out on wrapping paper the town's own newssheet, *The Marconigram*. And there were other touches to gladden the hearts of homesick men . . . a cracker machine providing 2,600 pounds of fresh crackers daily . . . minstrel shows and masonic banquets . . . turkey and trimmings dinners on the Fourth of July . . . even Brazil's first baseball diamond for Sunday afternoon games.

As the town mushroomed, Farquhar looked to the commissary —not only for the men at base but for those at the far-flung survey camps. By August, 1910, the railroaders' time-honored diet of "sow's belly and beans" was just a dismal memory. Up the Madeira by the bargeload came herds of beef on the hoof destined for the new slaughterhouse. California oranges and pears, potatoes and onions, "the construction man's apple," were shipped in by the ton: even drinking water was imported in bottles. Menus now featured such hometown favorites as buckwheat cakes and syrup, liver and bacon and Irish stew. But this vitamin-rich diet was allied to a rigid system of prophylaxis. Quinine came in 25-ton lots, and bottles of it, in big yellow ten-grain capsules, stood on the mess tables, along with the tabasco and the Worcestershire sauce.

No one ever began a meal until he had swallowed that capsule —if need be under the rock-steady guns of the railroad police.

In Lovelace's wake came a new kind of laborer: men acclimatized to tropic heat, such as the 800 Spaniards shipped in March, 1908, from the Panama Canal. To secure their like, Farquhar upped his bonuses to recruiting agents: the scout who contracted sixty-eight Greeks on the tiny isle of Crete netted a sizable £8 a head for them—as against the earlier standard bonus of £1/10/0. Oxen replaced Arkansas and Missouri mules, which had perished in a sweltering heat of 120 degrees in the shade. And Farquhar's policy of discipline, hospital care and fair wages paid off. Even ten degrees below the equator, his newfound "tropical tramps" now rallied to the old railroaders' slogan: "The line must go through." Slowly but inexorably the "Mad Mary's" two slender streaks of steel pushed ahead into the green malarial hell.

And Farquhar made other changes. Earlier contractors had taken guns to rout the hostile Caripúnas, but Farquhar, of Quaker stock, recalled instead that sect's peaceful settlement of his native Pennsylvania. From this moment, every man recruited signed a nonmolestation contract: he would neither interfere with Caripúna women nor sell arms to their menfolk. Violation of the contract meant immediate discharge without pay. In place of guns, survey crews took beads and cheap mirrors to trade with the Indians. There was no bloodshed from that time on.

Determined to protect his workers from prostitutes and rotgut liquor, Farquhar put the pesthole of Santo Antônio, a rubber port two miles downriver, off limits—unaware that many, to compensate for the ban, swilled the cheap sugarcane rum used to salve the sore backs of the pack mules. But often camp bosses found ingenious ways to restrict the liquor intake. The man who ran the most temperate outfit had trained his pet cheetah to sleep atop the cases of rationed Scotch.

But even Farquhar's enlightened approach to tropical engineering never cut the death rate to zero. On his orders, men who had suffered two bouts of malaria were invalided from the zone, but all through 1910, despite a monthly intake of 500 men, only 3,000 were fit to work at any one time: a man's total working span on "Mad Mary" averaged ninety days. On many nights, when jaguars were abroad, the whistles shrilled in vain for the missing —"El Tigre got him" became their somber epitaph. And as the line pushed ever onward to Bolivia's Mamoré River, construction camps were so isolated that many sick men were shipped to Candelaria too late. Half of those who rode in the hospital vans were dead on arrival—and up country instant burials in mass graves became implacable daily routine.

In some sectors, like the dread thirty-mile Abunã Strait, laid through malarial marsh, conditions were worse. Toiling up to their knees in water, men twice saw the high "fills" (embankments) clawed away by washouts, leaving the metals looped and twisted in midair. On Abunã, a man who fell sick could hope for no other operating table than a rubber blanket on the jungle floor—so that one four-mile stretch of track cost a life for every crosstie.*

At peak, Candelaria Hospital saw twenty-five nationalities battling thirty-nine disease. Most lethal by far were beriberi and blackwater fever—a malignant disease that attacks the red blood cells—but malaria, hookworm, dysentery, nephritis and cirrhosis of the liver also took their toll.

Daily at Candelaria there were sights to touch the heart. Though the death rate had diminished, male nurses still toured the wards at 5 A.M., checking to see who had survived the night by lifting the eyelids, feeling the toes. One carpenter alone did full-time duty constructing coffins; only 600 yards distant, in the cemetery, the merciless tide of white crosses flowed on toward the jungle's edge. One survivor still recalls: "From far off, it was as if they were laying out a plantation."

But Farquhar grew daily more determined to slash the death rate and to finalize his project on a cost-and-be-damned basis. Already winning lumber and ties from the dripping malarial

* Popular legend has saddled "Mad Mary" with the reputation of claiming a similar toll along every mile of track, a blood-chilling thought and a statistical impossibility. Official estimates of the crossties laid have ranged from 615,000 to 549,000—and no more than 30,000 men (21,717 according to one source) labored on the railroad during the five years of its construction. No one knows with any certainty the total casualties, since the company's contemporary statistics did not allow for deaths outside the Amazon Valley theater. But even the most liberal recent estimate—6,208 deaths—demonstrably falls a long way short of legend.

forests had proved too costly in terms of lives; in the wake of fresh beef and vegetables there now came termite-resistant eucalyptus-wood ties, routed all the way from Formosa at five dollars a tie. To power the twelve Baldwin locomotives already operative, coal was routed from as far afield as Swansea, Wales, on freighters like the 3,000-ton *Capella*. From the docks of New York and Mobile came steel from Pittsburgh, lumber from Georgia. Now it was plain that the original estimate of £2,250,000 was likely to be trebled—but still rubber-boom optimism declared: The line *must* pay for itself.

Weekly, as each installment in this drama of life and death, of courage and heart reached Manaus from Pôrto Velho, one factor was plain: the pioneer spirit of Farquhar's men must in the end prevail. Each report from Lizardo Arana to his brother in London emphasized this above all: the day was in sight when Itacoatiara might supplant Manaus as the arrogant white city.

As shrewdly as ever, Arana was laying his plans. Despite his wish to remain in Europe, a return to the Amazon was mandatory. He must secure his empire up the Putumayo, review the position in Manaus, take steps, if necessary, to transfer the branch to Itacoatiara. It was now, late in July, 1910, that news like a body blow reached him.

To the commission of inquiry which his company, following constant Foreign Office pressure, had appointed to investigate Hardenburg's allegations, Sir Edward Grey, the Foreign Secretary, had, on July 21, attached Roger Casement, now British Consul General in Rio de Janeiro. The whole framework of Arana's empire would now be subject to nothing less than a full-scale probe at top government level.

Until the day of Casement's appointment Arana had grown increasingly sure he had stifled all opposition. True, ever since December, 1909, he had raised every conceivable objection to the company's dispatching a commission, and to every delegate proposed. This man lacked experience, that man's name carried no weight, the Peruvian Government would see the whole venture as a slight. But the British directors, despite their patent indecision, went on seeking suitable candidates: men who knew Spanish, who had some commercial experience and who could hold their own in any conflict with Peruvian authority. Faced with Sir Edward Grey's insistent pressure, they saw no other choice.

At last, grudgingly, Arana had assented: the task of compiling a short list began. Colonel the Honourable Reginald Bertie, a mining engineer and a personal friend of Sir John Lister-Kaye's, was chosen to head the commission, for a fee of £2,500. Other final selections were Louis Barnes, a tropical agriculturist who knew both Brazil and Africa's East Coast; Walter Fox, botanist and rubber expert; and Seymour Bell, a merchant. As company secretary and manager, Henry Lex Gielgud would hold a watching brief, his salary, including overseas allowances, now increased to £2,000 a year.

Still Arana felt he had the situation in check. Time and again he reassured John Russell Gubbins. "Every Indian represents a capital value to the company. It is absurd for people to think they are being killed." No sooner were the members selected than he routed a gentle threat to David Cazes, now back in Iquitos: "The commission is coming to enquire into the present, not the past."

In Manaus, he knew, few took the accusations seriously. As recently as February, a Commercial Congress held in the opera house had awarded his company a silver medal for their photographic display of "groups of civilised Putumayo Indians with their overseers." True, Bertie and the others were briefed to spend six months in the region, from September, 1910, to the spring of 1911, and visit every depot, but Lizardo and Pablo knew what to do. The stocks and whipping posts would be dismantled, badly scarred natives moved out of sight, just as when Whiffen and Gielgud had passed through.

Arana knew the British directors were disturbed, though not unduly so. They still disbelieved in Hardenburg's disclosures—and all had benefited from the steadily prospering business. From January's end, Gubbins' salary as chairman had been increased to

£600 a year; once Gielgud departed for the Amazon and the old man became acting managing director, it would be doubled. The others felt no scruples about drawing their £200 a year directors' fees, and the company had paid four half-yearly dividends.

Arana had no dark intuition that his luck was running out. But no sooner was the commission appointed than the Reverend John Harris and his fellow crusaders—among them powerful industrialists like George Cadbury and Joseph Rowntree—sent a deputation to Sir Edward Grey. A commission selected by the company, they objected, could never furnish an impartial report; their own interests were too much at stake. Only a body with official government backing could hope to uncover the truth.

A conscientious eagle-faced man, whose eleven troubled years as Foreign Secretary were to cost him his sight, Sir Edward saw no way to achieve this. The company had London offices and British directors, but its zone of operation lay outside his jurisdiction. Then the solution dawned on him: in deliberately selecting Barbadian employees as smoke screen, Arana had been a shade too clever. These men, recruited in the West Indies, were all British subjects—and this one factor gave Sir Edward the loophole he needed. Within days, Casement's seconding to the commission was accomplished fact.

Now Arana scented trouble. As recently as February, 1908, en route to Manaus from Liverpool, the Peruvian had, as always, been a guest of honor at the captain's table on the liner *Clement*. At Madeira, a distinguished newcomer had boarded the ship, and, joining the select assembly as a matter of course, was seated next to Arana: 44-year-old Roger Casement, journeying to take up a post as Consul in Pará. Already famed for his investigations on the Congo, the tall, bearded stranger, with his kindly gray eyes and musical voice, had impressed Arana not only by the breadth of his knowledge but also with his penetrating intellect. Casement was a man likely to uncover every vestige of fraud, and with his appointment, Arana felt, all the seeds Walt Hardenburg had sown were at last bearing fruit.

The commission had been only three months on the Putumayo

before the stormy and memorable annual general meeting of December 16, 1910. Fully twenty newsmen were present to hear the troublesome shareholder, Morgan Williams, raise the vexed question of the company's title deeds, and Gubbins' guileless reply, as chairman: "I presume they are in our safe at Iquitos."

At once Williams rose, outraged, from his seat. "*Presume* they are in the safe?" he countered sharply. "Have the auditors seen them?" Confused, Gubbins now turned to Henry Gielgud, asking, "Do you remember seeing them out there?" To the listening newsmen, Gielgud's reply was inaudible, but at length, following a muttered conference, Gubbins told the dumbfounded shareholders: "In the Putumayo district, you know, we have no titles; we only hold those by squatter's right."

Worse was to follow. Shareholder after shareholder now rose with trenchant questions—pressing, above all, for an interim report on the commission's findings. To pacify them, Gubbins went on record: "Any report that we receive . . . will be communicated as a matter of duty to the shareholders." Then to Arana's fury, Morgan Williams, backed by another disgruntled investor, arose with a fresh resolution: on the grounds of the Peruvian's connection with the alleged atrocities, they opposed his reelection to the board. Only a technicality—Article 103 of the company's statutes, which laid down that any such motion required one year's notice—saved Arana's skin.

"We shareholders still think the matter of the atrocities should be cleared up for the good credit of the company," was Williams' parting shot, as the meeting broke up in a buzz of furious comment.

Arana knew he must work fast: time was running out. The year 1911 was less than two weeks old before he had proposed steps to improve the company's finances—launching a claim against the Colombian Government for damage to property and suspension of business during the affrays of 1908. Now Gubbins and the others could scarcely believe their eyes. The Peruvian demanded as compensation an unheard-of £898,000.

"It's perfectly absurd," Gubbins protested, "a claim of almost a million. It's more than the total capital of the company, more than the whole capital value of the place." In vain Arana tried to explain: "But the Colombians are going to make a counterclaim against us. We must ask more in order to come down." But once again he failed to carry them with him.

The Peruvian did not know that four days earlier, on January 7, Casement, returning to London ahead of the commission, had submitted a preliminary report to Sir Edward Grey fully vindicating Walt Hardenburg's charges. "The condition of things," he confirmed, "fully warrants the worst charges brought against the agents of the Peruvian Amazon Company and its methods of administration on the Putumayo."

In fact, Casement's visit to the region had enabled him to dissect Arana's whole intricate plot—even taking note of Pablo Zumaeta's approach, as intermediary, to Michel Fabre, chairman of the Franco-Dutch Syndicate, who was just then visiting Manaus. Pablo, Fabre had reported to Casement, was authorized to sell out Arana's entire shareholding "as a very good bargain"— for whoever held these shares held the Putumayo. Angrily Casement confided in his diary: "This confirms Cazes' opinion that J.A. wishes to clear out and has been rushing the rubber . . . what a murderous ruffian. By God's help I'll unmask him."

Four months later, on May 13, each director received through the mail from the Foreign Office a report marked "Private and Confidential" which stunned them: Casement's terrible 135-page exposé of conditions on the Putumayo. Though Hardenburg's articles, the Consul said, had been largely instrumental in persuading men to talk, neither he nor any commission member, Gielgud included, had found difficulty in establishing that the forests were "battlefields of bones"—or that the Indian population, in five years, had fallen from 50,000 to no more than 8,000.

Fearing his West Indian witnesses might suffer vengeance at the hands of Arana's men, Casement had spirited fourteen Barbadians, their Indian wives and children away from the region, securing work for them in Pará.

On May 31, to a packed and silent House of Commons, Under-

Secretary of State for Foreign Affairs, McKinnon Wood, announced baldly, "Consul-General Casement fully confirms the information received."

Before the British directors had even recovered from this shock, they faced another: a letter from Pablo Zumaeta, in Iquitos, drafted after the tenor of Casement's report had been made known. On behalf of his siter, Eleonora, he said, for whom he held power of attorney, he had that day mortgaged the Putumayo estates for £60,000.

At first Gubbins, for one, could not grasp the implications. "What is the meaning of this?" he challenged Arana hotly. "You should never have done it, you should never have consented to it." But Arana, suavely, disclaimed all responsibility. It was not his doing, nor yet Eleonora's. It was Zumaeta's, acting as her representative.

Now belatedly the truth dawned on the three Britons. Back in 1903, when Arana Brothers was founded, the Peruvian had hived off £40,000 to Eleonora to invest in the company under her own name. Mulling over the books, the board had taken this sum to be a holding in the company, until Arana disillusioned them. His wife was, in fact, a company creditor whose dues, with interest, had gradually risen to £60,000.

Until this moment there had been no pressure for repayment—yet Pablo's unexpected coup, mortgaging company estates to recover Eleonora's money, at once made her the preferential creditor. Saddled with a debt of this magnitude, it would be virtually impossible to obtain further credit in England.

In fact, this was Arana's intention—for lacking credit the Peruvian Amazon Company must soon cease to exist. Bitterly impatient with the directors' code of honor, with government interference, with a press that could not be bought, he was now determined to oust the board and regain full personal control of the Putumayo.

Following their initial consternation, the directors' reaction was violent. Tempers flared like tinder; the old white-bearded Gubbins thundered and pounded the boardroom table. Furious that his puppets were displaying a will of their own, a flush rose to Arana's sallow cheeks. He lashed back at Gubbins: "It's you all along who've led this campaign against me. You're nothing but a Colombian agent."

There was good reason for Gubbins' agitation. Though the Foreign Office had released no details of Casement's report to the public, the House of Commons announcement had told enough. The company's business was almost at a standstill. Already the commission had cost the company £8,000; the running costs of the Manaus and Iquitos offices were never less than £10,000 a year. And no longer were shipments of rubber keeping pace with the revolving credit. The current debt to the London Bank of Mexico stood close to £20,000.

On the Putumayo, many section chiefs, alarmed by Casement's visit, had claimed £10,000 in credit balances before defecting—and now had come Eleonora's disastrous £60,000 mortgage. From July 17, to Gubbins' alarm, their bankers, Lloyd's Bank, would no longer honor their bills. On August 31, with less than £3 in the petty cash drawer, he reluctantly circularized all shareholders: "I regret to inform you that not having received expected remittances of rubber the company is unable to meet its engagements."

At this moment, the unsecured debts of the Peruvian Amazon Company amounted to £272,470.

Then there ensued a scene so incredible that Walt Hardenburg might never have journeyed down the Putumayo, nor Roger Casement traveled 5,000 miles to check his findings. On September 27, 1911, a meeting to confirm the winding-up resolution was convened at Winchester House, in the City sector—and the man unanimously elected as liquidator was Julio César Arana. Though Casement did not attend, he had already, at Sir Edward's suggestion, held four private meetings with the British directors, urging them to reject Arana and sacrifice everything to secure just treatment for the Indians. "But I very soon realised," he reported later, "that they were much more preoccupied with their financial position."

In any case, the directors had been powerless. The principal creditors—the London Bank of Mexico and the Anglo-Mercantile Finance Company—were adamant that Arana was their choice.

Not that the British directors disbelieved Casement's findings—but to a man they stoutly rejected any suggestion that Arana himself was implicated. Then, too, as Gubbins saw it, he was "a sort of symbol of Peruvian sovereignty in the Putumayo"—and most of the outstanding debtors were his personal friends. Did any man have a better chance of putting the company back on a sound business footing? The directors did not think so—"we were very much impressed with his quiet reserved manner," Henry Read recalled later.

"I will arrange all these things, put everything straight and then I hope to make some proposal to you," Arana assured all three men, shaking them warmly by the hand. Such was his personal magnetism that none of them thought to raise the question of that crippling mortgage—and Gubbins, in his final address to the shareholders, hinted that all too much emphasis had been laid on the atrocities.

"On the whole, the efforts of the company to improve the lot of the Indians have met with a fair measure of success," he told them, "though much still remains to be done before the primeval savage is converted into a civilized human being."

At the last meeting of all, on December 12, 1911, shareholder Morgan Williams was the lone voice challenging Arana's fitness to be liquidator. "The management of the company was rotten from the beginning and is still rotten," he told the board defiantly —but no man rose to second his resolution.

Of this final meeting, Arana had only long-distance reports. Though it was a wrench to move his household from No. 42 Queen's Gardens, the Putumayo scandals had received much lurid publicity—and he could no longer stay to bear the brunt. After renting his family a chalet on Geneva's Avenue Florian, he returned to Manaus along with a deed box crammed with un-identified documents. But as the months stretched out he felt he had moved too fast. So far the Foreign Office had released no details of Casement's report.

Arana had no means of knowing that high-level diplomacy was

involved. From the moment the Consul General had confirmed the facts in March, 1911, Sir Edward Grey was resolved on vigorous concerted action. Cables from the Foreign Office sped weekly to Charles Des Graz, Envoy Extraordinary to Peru, and James Bryce, Ambassador in Washington—seeking not only prompt action from President Leguía's government but also America's rock-ribbed support. And, at first, news from Lima was heartening: as early as March 15, a commission under Judge Romulo Paredes had left Iquitos on a gunboat, determined once for all to clean up the Putumayo. Three months later, on his return, Paredes had issued 237 apprehension warrants, summarizing his evidence in a 1,300-page report. "So many warrants out, gaol will be too small," ran an early estimate from Iquitos.

But Leguía, though a tactful and adroit peacemaker, had moved too slowly. Scores of the worst killers—Fonseca, Agüero, O'Donnell—had already fled to Manaus, and no extradition treaty then existed between Brazil and Peru. Though a draft treaty was, the President assured Charles Des Graz, being drawn up, this would take time—and at this moment his government lacked means even to enforce their authority in the far-flung Putumayo.

Sir Edward chafed impatiently. From October, 1911, to January, 1912, Casement, now knighted for his work, had again returned to the Amazon to check on the Peruvians' good faith. His report was disquieting: though Paredes had issued 237 warrants, only nine men had thus far been swept into the net. Many had fled the country, shanghaiing Indians by the score to work fresh rubber trails. Often corrupt police officials in Arana's pay had failed to swoop until the criminals "escaped."

Meanwhile, from Washington, Ambassador Bryce reported, American concern was quickening. Before returning to England, Sir Roger Casement had spent days closeted with President Taft and State Department officials—and all were firmly resolved the outrages must be checked. Already Secretary of State Philander Knox was coming to share Sir Edward's viewpoint: the one sure way to force the Peruvians' hand was to publish Casement's report.

It was by no means standard Foreign Office practice but Sir Edward's keen personal indignation had driven him to this. In a private letter to C. P. Scott, famed editor and proprietor of the *Manchester Guardian,* he confessed: "The one thing I should deprecate would be any action on our part that would make us lose touch with the United States or alienate their sympathy . . . it is American public opinion that must be the most potent factor in either American Continent."

From now on, messages to Leguía from both great powers contained a gentle hint of steel. "His Majesty's Government attach the greatest importance to Peru giving visible proof . . . that she is determined to eradicate the present abuses," Grey cabled Lima. "Failing such proof they will have no alternative but to publish Sir Roger Casement's reports."

To Ambassador Bryce, too, Sir Edward stressed the urgency: "Sir Roger Casement had heard that Arana . . . was saying that as soon as what he called 'this fuss' was over, the natives would be set to work again, which meant that the remnant would be exterminated."

At first the State Department agreed to publish—then, in May, 1912, as Leguía proposed a comission of reform, counseled a postponement. But Sir Edward was inflexible. The commission was not scheduled to make its first report until January, 1913— and meanwhile word came from Iquitos that in April alone over 75 tons of rubber had been shipped downriver, "one of the largest single consignments derived from the Putumayo." From January through April, rubber leaving that port had totaled three-quarters of its shipments for 1911.

"These figures can only have been rendered possible by a continuance of the old system of forced labour," Sir Edward informed the Washington Embassy on June 27. "I am unable to fall in with Mr. Knox's view that publication might with advantage be deferred." Perhaps with tongue in cheek, he added: "The facts cannot but assist the Peruvian Government in their reforming efforts."

In July, 1912, after more than a year's delay, Casement's report was at last published. It caused an international furore. To Walt Hardenburg's graphic depositions, the Consul had added telling statistics: every ton of Putumayo latex had cost seven human lives, in an era when top-grade wild rubber had passed £700 a ton. In twelve years, 4,000 tons of Arana's shipments had fetched almost £1,500,000 on the London Market—but 30,000 forest Indians had died to make that possible.

All over the world public indignation reached boiling point—among laymen and clergy alike. Men like Sir Arthur Conan Doyle, Lord Rothschild, Count Blücher and the Duke of Norfolk were prime movers, along with Sir Roger, in setting up a £15,000 Putumayo Mission Fund to ensure the Indians permanent sanctuary—taking as their watchword Casement's motto: "Christianity means schools and missions as well as dreadnoughts and dividends." From the Vatican, Pope Pius X exhorted the prelates of Latin America to spare no efforts to protect the Indians in their dioceses. At President Leguía's request, the Pope was establishing mission stations all over the Putumayo "where the Indians can find safety and succour."

And in London, on Sunday, August 4, Herbert Hensley Henson, a hard-hitting Canon of Westminster Abbey, basing his sermon on the Casement report, not only named the British directors from the pulpit but demanded their immediate public trial. "It is . . . a disgrace to civilisation," he blazed, "that adventurers of the type of the Arana brothers should be able, uncommissioned and uncontrolled, to set up over a great territory an infamous despotism. . . ."

From Iquitos, British Consul George B. Michell reported that trade had slumped disastrously: most European houses now refused all credit to local firms. At a Berlin trade congress, German rubber manufacturers voted unanimously to boycott all Putumayo rubber from this time on. But the Reverend Beresford Potter, Archdeacon of Cyprus, and a lifelong crusader against slavery, trod on stonier ground with the Booth Steamship Company. To his suggestion that they ship no more rubber until the atrocities ceased, the Booths replied: "The directors of the company are quite satisfied that the evidence you have put before them is impracticable."

There was action, too, where it counted most—on the Amazon itself. In Lima, the Peruvian society Pro Indigena sprang up to champion the Indians' rights—in the footsteps of Brazil, which two years earlier, following Walt Hardenburg's revelations, had set up its own unique commission. Under 45-year-old Colonel Candido Rondon, the republic's small, smiling Commissioner for Telegraphs, an Indian Protection Service now worked to establish friendly relations with tribes hitherto regarded as intractable—staffed solely by unarmed men, working from "attraction posts" stocked with primitive ornaments, in the heart of the jungle.

Already, in twenty months, Rondon and his men had overcome the initial hostility of a dozen tribes—winning them over with presents and provisions, crying their message of peace from crow's nests built in tall trees, instructing them in elementary agriculture, providing free medical treatment. As communications chief, Rondon spun a spider's web of 15,000 miles of telegraph line through dense jungle; as the Indians' friend, he entrusted these once-hostile tribes to guard it. The spirit of the service was vividly summed up by Rondon's instructions to his subordinates: "Die if necessary, but never kill."

On the Upper Amazon at this moment Julio Arana felt no cause for alarm. Only recently he had successfully foiled all attempts by Stuart Fuller, newly appointed American Consul, and Britain's George B. Michell to conduct a fact-finding tour along the Putumayo. Briefed by their governments to report on prevailing conditions, the two consuls had found the launch *Liberal* the only means of transport—and during the frustrating eight-week journey, Arana and Carlos Rey de Castro, had never once let them drop from sight. So zealously did spies and informers dog them, Michell complained bitterly, "It was like walking about in another man's garden and being expected to admire the flowers."

And Arana savored other proofs of his power. On November 5, Iquitos' leading merchants gave a banquet in his honor at the Hotel Continental—an expression of sympathy for the "unwarranted attacks" that had been made upon him. Even the one voice raised against him he had been able to turn to his own advantage. Dr. Gamarra, editor of *La Occidente*, had observed sharply: "It's all very well to be presenting bouquets, but we should bear in mind that Don Julio's name is connected with very reprehensible practices."

For Arana, this was too good an opportunity to miss. "The investigations undertaken by Parliament and foreign ministries have not resulted in anything that can prejudice my good name," he told the assembled diners. "The fact that I was sent out as liquidator is clear proof no reflection has been made on me in England." Admiring onlookers noted now that his eyes shone with tears as he continued: "The faith of you sympathisers has given me strength to go on with my struggles, though sometimes they were so hard I thought I hadn't the constancy or will-power to continue. . . ."

On this day, 5,000 miles away in London, government agents were just then swooping on the Peruvian Amazon Company's London Wall offices armed with a unique search warrant. Signed by the Speaker of the House of Commons, it empowered them to remove the company's records for perusal by a committee of fifteen Members of Parliament nominated by the government. The powers of these men were absolute: to send for any persons, papers or records that might pertain. Their terms of reference were far-reaching: to probe the motives and secrets of the men Walt Hardenburg had arraigned.

At twenty-seven, Hardenburg was as fully occupied as he had ever been. In the past two years life had offered many challenges to Walt and his bride; to eke out a living as Canadian pioneers with their young son James had not at first proved easy. For one year, based in Toronto, Walt had taken whatever odd jobs he could find; most of the young couple's income was derived from making shop awnings to order on

Mary's small portable sewing machine. Finally, lured by the stories of Alberta's abundant wheatland and dairy cattle, the Hardenburgs headed northwest for the township of Red Deer.

Finding work as a surveyor on the Canadian Pacific Railway, Walt set to work in his spare time building his own home, first spading the earth for a basement, then constructing an airy four-room house of Douglas fir, before insulating it with felt and layers of wood against the sub-zero winters. He had learned his carpentry, as he learned everything else, by reading and application.

But despite his newfound happiness as a family man, Walt was still puzzled and indignant. True he had received his half share in the Peruvian Government's £500, proof positive they admitted the justice of his claim—but as far back as February, 1910, just prior to leaving London, he had heard a vague rumor of charges that Arana had leveled against him in Iquitos. Promptly, he wrote to Dr. Guy King, asking of what he stood accused.

The dentist's reply left him speechless: forgery and blackmail in collusion with a man named Muriedas, now serving a jail term in Pará.

Bemused, Walt had no time to do more before boarding the *Corsican*—though no sooner had he reached Toronto than he again set inquiries on foot among his remaining contacts in Iquitos. But as he confessed to the Reverend Harris in a letter of June 28, 1910: "I have repeatedly written to Iquitos, but rarely received answers." Walt, in any case, was himself a reluctant letter writer. Not until a month later did he follow King's advice and route a letter to George Pickerell, American Consul in Pará.

But with Pickerell's reply the mystery only deepened. Muriedas was indeed in jail, on another charge of forgery, and if ever a man was afraid for his life it was the Spaniard. At no time would he admit to having known Hardenburg. Briefly, he admitted, he had met an American whose name he had forgotten but he had never borrowed money from this man. On the contrary, he had lent him money almost daily.

Doggedly, Walt wrote to Pickerell yet again: would the

Consul please return to Muriedas and obtain a statement exonerating Hardenburg from any charge of forgery? But again the Consul drew a blank. How, Muriedas asked, could he exonerate a man of whom he had never heard?

Hardenburg's mind was in a whirl. Had Muriedas somehow altered the bill he had received from the man named Bazan, the purchaser of his rubber estate? Had he drunk so recklessly in Manaus to incapacitate himself, to force Hardenburg to take possession of the bill? So had he borrowed that £20 deliberately, knowing Hardenburg would demand repayment? As the months passed, Walt was still no closer to solving the riddle.

The charge of blackmail puzzled him, too—though again he had heard only rumors. In London *Truth*'s editor, Robert Bennett, had referred vaguely to Arana's circular letter—but neither Bennett nor his staff had been able to lay hands on a copy. "If the company makes any statement against you," the editor advised, "it would be as well for you to take action against them." But nobody could furnish proof that Arana or the company *had* made any statement. In impotent fury, Hardenburg saw himself labeled as blackmailer and forger—yet denied any chance to clear his name.

At first he could do nothing but follow reports of the parliamentary committee from afar—and these told him little enough. From Harris he learned that M.P.'s active in the Anti-Slavery Society had pressed Sir Edward Grey to appoint this official inquiry—among them the Member for Leicester, James Ramsay MacDonald, a tall gaunt Scot with challenging brown eyes, later Britain's first Labour Premier. A procedure as old as Parliament itself, these select committees normally rolled up their sleeves and went to work for two distinct purposes—to mull over a proposed bill or as a behind-the-scenes fact-finding commission. For the most part, given such terms of reference as the management of the British Museum or the adulteration of wine, they were affairs of yawning tedium, whose deliberations rarely hit the headlines.

But at 10 A.M. on Wednesday, November 6, as the committee's

fifteen members took their seats on the dais in Room No. 11, a lofty, paneled green-and-brown chamber overlooking the Thames on the House of Commons' first floor, newsmen were already packing out the tiny press enclosure close to the witness entrance—and the public seats, at the rear of the oblong room, were jam-packed, too. For these M.P.'s, determined to uncover the truth behind Arana's empire, were akin to a tribunal, unhampered as in a courtroom by laws of evidence that might shield the guilty as often as the innocent. In the task that lay before them—to assess the British directors' share of guilt—there would be harder-hitting and harsher truths than were ever heard in the Commons' debating chamber.

For this reason, the House had granted selected witnesses the rare privilege of being represented by black-robed, white-wigged barristers—and today the formidable battery of legal skill assembled with their juniors at the counsel's table told the newsmen something big was about to break. Foremost among them was John Astbury, K.C., known to lawyers as "Honest Jack," a Chancery "special," with burning ambitions to become a judge, his services only obtainable by a special additional fee of fifty guineas. Backing Astbury was the Prime Minister's eldest son, Raymond Asquith, a handsome, sardonic 34-year-old, already marked out by his work in the *Titanic* inquiry. Soon they would be joined by Douglas McGarel Hogg, stocky and combative, later Lord Hailsham and a future Lord Chancellor.

But the commission also numbered several qualified barristers, men skilled in rapier-witted cross-examination. Already Charles Roberts, M.P. for the City of Lincoln, clutching his familiar black portfolio, had taken his seat in the chairman's leather-padded armchair; a stooping giant with penetrating blue eyes, Roberts was now busy mastering Spanish to equip himself for the task. Close at hand sat another formidable figure, the earnest, frock-coated William Joynson-Hicks, later Lord Brentford and Home Secretary-to-be. Of a different stamp were 40-year-old Lord Alexander Thynne, youngest son of the Marquis of Bath, an elegant old Etonian, and Douglas Hall, wealthy clubman, yachtsman, and lord of a Sussex manor.

By contrast Scots-born William Young was a man of the people, a farmer's son who had worked his way from office boy to merchant banker. Since his business interests lay in Mexico, Young's Spanish was already fluent. Prominent, too, was the municipal reformer Willoughby (later Lord) Dickinson, whose relentless interrogation would reduce at least one eyewitness to tears.

Yet all among them were overshadowed by 64-year-old John Gordon Swift MacNeill, K.C., M.P. for South Donegal, Irish wit and firebrand, lover of courtroom histrionics, with a tongue like a lash where injustice was concerned. Once the First Sea Lord of the Admiralty, Lord Fisher, had summed up his spirit with this impulsive tribute: "Mr. MacNeill, you are a damned good fighter. I wish to God I had you with me in the Navy."*

But at first the tribunal's spectators, many of them share-holders, packed densely on green leather-backed chairs stamped with the Beaufort Portcullis, featured in the Palace of Westminster's coat of arms, were conscious of disappointment. Few of the committee's initial witnesses contributed evidence that was not already known to press or public alike. Foreign Office officials Gerald Spicer and Gilbert Grindle testified weightily on the visits of Arana's recruiting agents to Barbados and on their own efforts to goad the company into positive action. Sir Roger Casement filled in on his report to Sir Edward Grey. Reporter Horace Thorogood and secretary George Tickton reconstructed minute by minute the astounding episode of Abel Alarco's attempted bribe. Both the Reverend John Harris and editor Sydney

---

* The remaining members of the Select Committee on Putumayo were Hubert Carr-Gomm (Southwark); James Hastings Duncan (Yorkshire, West Riding, Otley Division); Sir Thomas Esmonde (Wexford North); Frederick Jowett (Bradford West); Joseph King (Somerset North); Ian Malcolm (Croydon); Henry Fitzherbert Wright (Hereford, Leominster). Following the death of Sir Clement Hill (Shrewsbury), Arnold Ward (West Herts.) joined the committee in April, 1913.

Paternoster spoke of Walt Hardenburg's first vital impact as a man of honor—and of how they, at least, had found little difficulty in swiftly corroborating his evidence.

For Hardenburg, in Alberta, news of his old friends in the witness seat brought renewed hope. He learned that when Raymond Asquith, for the directors, had asked Harris point-blank: "Supposing you had good reason to believe Mr. Hardenburg was a criminal and had been guilty of blackmail and forgery, would that have altered your attitude towards him?"

"From the internal evidence I should have said the story was a true one," was Harris' reply—but to Hardenburg what counted most was that this charge had at last been voiced. Somehow he must now find a way to clear his name before the world.

Not until the morning of December 11, 1912, did the public feel a subtle quickening of the tension. Breaking for a muttered consultation with his colleagues, Chairman Charles Roberts asked them: "Are we ready for Sir Roger Casement again?" Upon a nod, the doorkeeper, resplendent in ceremonial black tailcoat and white dress tie, flung wide the witnesses' door to the cathedral hush of the Committee Corridor: "Recall Sir Roger Casement."

As the lean, bearded Casement, his carriage marked by a pronounced stoop, loped swiftly to the witness seat, there was a subdued buzz of interest. He had returned, as Roberts made plain, at his own request, to give evidence on points omitted from his earlier testimony.

"I have here the original Hardenburg documents which I took out with me," Sir Roger told them, stressing, "The Barbadians confirmed in more than one particular that testimony." And he elaborated: having gone more deeply into Hardenburg's allegations on the spot, he had collected important additional evidence, photographic as well as documentary, on the company's labor policy.

From the dais, Lord Alexander Thynne spoke for all: "I think it would be of great assistance if we could see some photographs."

Now, as Sir Roger unrolled a set of prints, heads were craning all over the chamber. Rising from the witness seat, which faced the committee squarely, counsel and spectators massed behind him, Sir Roger gave a staccato running commentary as the pictures sped from member to member along the committee table: "*That* wretched one was flogged; *this* creature was flogged . . . they appealed to me and showed me the marks . . . *that* man's head was cut open." From his inside breast pocket came more photographs to travel the long dais. "These are photographs showing how the rubber was carried down, and these are important—a great many deaths took place owing to the long journeys and the heavy weights imposed. They had to carry sometimes from fifty to sixty miles these very heavy loads."

The bearded, benign-seeming Swift MacNeill showed keen interest. "I understood you to say you saw a woman in the last stages of starvation and threw her load away from her."

"Yes." For a moment Sir Roger could say no more.

"I take it the general system was by hook or by crook to get the Indians into debt and to keep them there?"

"Yes—*these* are some of the things which I bought from the company's store at La Chorrera."

Now the spectators gasped. At a murmured aside from Sir Roger, the doorkeeper, aided by a helmeted bobby, had returned to the chamber, weighed down by a load of bizarre properties. At this moment, the bright bank of coals in the stone fireplace, the tugs hooting on the Thames beyond the mullioned windows, seemed strangely unreal. It was as if London River had abruptly given place to the warm, sulfur-smelling world of the Amazon.

Aloft above his head Sir Roger was brandishing a single-barreled shotgun. "I paid for that gun forty-five shillings in La Chorrera. The alleged cost to the company was twenty-nine shillings." Recalling his journey to Arana's territory, he was, the members saw, literally trembling with indignation. "That weapon there would have to be paid for by an Indian with two years' work."

"And no food?" asked Willoughby Dickinson incredulously.

Sir Roger was succinct. "No food and frequent floggings."

In swift succession a pathetic pile of trade goods cascaded onto the polished exhibit table below the dais, checkered shirts, pantaloons, cardboard belts, fishhooks, strings of colored beads, a flask of gunpowder—strange items in the sober House of Commons.

"I do not want these things which I have produced here back," Casement told them. "I suggest they should be sent to the Board of Trade as specimens for their museum. They represent more than three years' work to an Indian."

But had the Indians, Sir Thomas Esmonde queried, no civil rights? Did an overseer on the Putumayo have no regard for them? For answer, Casement snapped his fingers: the crack was clearly audible in the silent room. "No more regard than you or I might have for a parrot or a monkey. He would shoot it or tame it."

By now, the committee were visibly shocked. How alerted had Arana and his British representatives been to this system? How much had it been possible for them to know? Back to the witness seat came the one company official who had set foot on Amazon soil, Henry Lex Gielgud, former secretary and manager.

The lean, frock-coated William Joynson-Hicks craned forward for the opening questions. At the time of Gielgud's appointment had copies of the Manaus and Iquitos accounts been kept in the London office? But the accountant could not be certain. During his six months' term as secretary he had several times sent hasteners to the Amazon branches for their current accounts. Whether these accounts had ever reached London he did not know.

Joynson-Hicks' examination was striving to establish a foundation of direct knowledge. "Surely these accounts, if they had come over properly, would have disclosed the whole labor position?"

"As to that," Gielgud hedged, "I am not quite certain."

To some spectators it now seemed that Gielgud scented danger. For every point he was willing to admit, he was swift to disclaim another. Yes, he had given the directors his written impressions. They had asked for them and made full use of them.

But, he added, "They attached considerable weight to that letter which it did not deserve."

Joynson-Hicks recalled to him his own wording: " 'I was able to see something of the company's dealings with the Indians.' " The accountant sought to minimize this: "I did not investigate them. I made a little trip round. I did see a fairish number of Indians and a couple of big Indian dances."

"Was not your investigation really of a very perfunctory character?"

Gielgud was only too ready to agree. Unfortunately, although he had found Macedo, Loayza and Fonseca "very amiable," his impressions had turned out to be wrong, and the directors had relied on them too heavily.

Now, as Lord Alexander Thynne took over, it was plain the committee had burned some midnight oil in studying the company's accounts. "Did not the sum put down for rifles in the invoices strike you as rather high?" Gielgud thought not, but Lord Alex persisted: "In one case, it was £3,200 and in another case it was £2,165, wasn't it?" The accountant had no exact recollection. "You regarded the spending of several thousand pounds on rifles as incidental to the expenditure of a rubber company?" Lord Alex taxed him.

But Gielgud would not be drawn: that would depend on the company's sphere of operations. "I would not care personally to walk about unarmed," he said; "there are a number of jaguars about."

It had fallen to Gielgud to provide the needed break in the tension. Both committee and spectators now exploded into laughter. At last, when the mirth subsided, Joynson-Hicks blew his nose and resumed. Did he seriously ask them to believe the company acquired £7,000 worth of rifles to protect themselves against jaguars? Hastily, Gielgud said no.

The questioning switched back to Lord Alex. Surely Gielgud must have realized that some of those rifles were for use against the Colombians? The accountant modified it: "In the Colombian troubles, yes."

"Did it strike you as a normal proceeding that a commercial company should arm itself and march out in battle array against a friendly state?"

Again Gielgud sidestepped the implication. If a company was attacked, it was normal that it should defend itself.

Lord Alex came with force to the crux of the matter: "And yet I suppose there is hardly an English shareholder here who would not have sold out if he had known what was going on?"

Doggedly, Gielgud retreated to his terms of reference. Whether conditions had been normal or not, he had seen it as no part of a chartered accountant's duties to investigate them.

Swift MacNeill was quick to pounce on his point. "In fact, the treatment of these natives did not enter into your mind?" his soft Irish brogue interposed, and Gielgud had to admit it.

"They were negligible quantities?"

"I will not go so far as to say they were negligible quantities," Gielgud retracted, "but it never occurred to me."

"You went to the Amazon forest largely for financial purposes, completely ignorant that the atrocities, as we heard from Sir Roger Casement, were common talk in Iquitos—a little financial babe in the wood."

"If you like that description, I will accept it," the six-foot Gielgud answered coldly.

Swift MacNeill was warming up. "In this momentous report of yours, you give a high character to three gentlemen—to Julio Arana, to the gentleman Loayza, and the brother-in-law Zumaeta. Do you know that few documents have had such great effect as your report, and do you know that it produced a considerable effect in the Foreign Office?"

Unwarily, Gielgud fell into the trap. "I do not know that," he answered, "but I am very pleased to hear it."

"And we have it from the Foreign Office," Swift MacNeill whispered, "that on the strength of your report the company had a good excuse for withholding the commission—that all these horrors went on for six long months. I am glad I have not your responsibility."

Conversationally, as man to man, he put it to Gielgud: "You went out as an accountant, and you occupied yourself as an accountant, and you thought moral considerations were blotted out."

Now Gielgud made his most damning admission to date. "From a legal point of view, I think they were," he said, then, attempted swiftly to cancel out the statement. "Of course, I have not the least doubt I was made use of by these people . . ."

"Really," Swift MacNeill reproved him, "you do injustice to your own intelligence. Were you a mere decoy duck?" He flourished Gielgud's report. "One would imagine you were at a tea fight in the Crystal Palace from this account."

But Gielgud was alerted to the trend of the cross-examination; he made no more unguarded admissions. He had not stressed to the directors that payment by trade goods was open to abuse; it had never occurred to him that this was the case. True, the company had paid him a larger salary than his predecessor, but then he was a chartered accountant with Amazon experience. Moreover, without a seat on the board, he was doing Vernon Smith's work and Alarco's besides.

No, he was not aware that section chiefs on the Putumayo were paid solely by a commission on the rubber. If the directors had examined the books kept in London, they themselves would have been none the wiser. Only the Manaus and Iquitos accounts dealt with matters of local management. The London books were limited to the company's general position and finances.

"What about the badly scarred natives?" Willoughby Dickinson asked. On his second Amazon journey with Casement, Gielgud had seen the marks of flogging—but how was it that he had been blind to them on his first visit? Almost primly, Gielgud replied, "They were on a part of the body that one does not usually look at."

Puzzled, the committee adjourned. Despite the mounds of company papers impounded, the firm's solicitors were still searching the files for the Putumayo cashbooks that Charles Roberts had demanded. Unless these came to light, it would be hard to determine how much any man had been party to Arana's system.

But when they reconvened, in the New Year, on January 8, 1913, one fact began slowly to emerge: few among the Peruvian's colleagues had made concerted efforts to elicit the truth. And the newsmen took due note of a solemn moment; no sooner had the white-bearded John Russell Gubbins, in the witness seat, been sworn by the Clerk to the Committee than Charles Roberts leaned forward from the dais.

"You are entitled to refuse to answer questions in your discretion," he told him, "if the answer would in your opinion tend to incriminate you, or to render you liable to a criminal charge, to a penalty or a punishment." He added meaningly: "On that ground you may refuse, but otherwise you will be good enough to give us explanations on the points we want."

Chastened, Gubbins nodded. In truth, he and his codirectors had had little choice as to whether they would appear. A refusal to testify, construed as contempt of the House, was at once punishable by imprisonment during the term of Parliament, followed by an admonition from the Speaker before the Bar of the House of Commons.

Quietly, skillfully, Roberts began by taking Gubbins through his commercial career in Peru: his knowledge of Peruvian institutions and public men, his mastery of Spanish. Now, for the first time, the shareholders realized that the company's 1908 prospectus had misled them. Despite his knowledge of the country, Gubbins had never in thirty-eight years set foot in the Amazon Valley—and his lifelong experience had been as an exporter of sugar.

Thus the only Peruvian Amazon Company directors who had ever visited the Putumayo region were Julio Arana and his brother-in-law Abel Alarco.

Courteous, but intent, Roberts delved further into the mind of the ex-chairman. Was it true that during his term of office a photograph of Amazon Indians had hung in the boardroom at Salisbury House? Then had not this ever encouraged him to ask about the actual way in which these Indians were paid—into the cost, say, of producing a pound of rubber? Gubbins hesitated. The directors had it on Gielgud's authority that when rubber was selling at 3/9d per pound, the cost of landing it in Liverpool was 1/9d per pound.

"And you never asked how much of that 1/9d went to the laborers?"

"No, it would be almost impossible to determine," Gubbins maintained, "very difficult indeed."

"Did you ask anything about the labor conditions before you accepted office?" But Gubbins' answer was negative.

Roberts was insistent. "Not a word?"

"Not a word."

Now, in the long paneled room, it was so quiet a man could have heard a handkerchief flutter to the floor. The newsmen were scribbling furiously; at the barristers' table the clerks had laid their tomes and documents aside. And Roberts probed on. Among the company's papers he had unearthed a copy of the Frenchman Eugenio Robuchon's book, *On the Putumayo and its Tributaries*. Though it was a work of exploration, Arana had plainly commissioned it as a commercial brochure in 1903. The illustrations included photos of him, his brother Lizardo and Abel Alarco.

"I never studied it," Gubbins said. "I read it in a very hurried manner. Alarco handed me that copy but shortly after he asked for it back."

Even so, Roberts challenged him, he must have been aware of at least three factors which the book revealed: that the heads of sections were paid by commission on the pound of rubber, that the forest Indians were in revolt and that armed men watched them day and night. "I do not remember that," said Gubbins blankly.

Roberts turned to another item: Article 169 of the company's articles of association. He now read slowly and deliberately from the printed record: "No shareholder, or general or other meeting of shareholders, shall be entitled to require discovery of, or any information respecting, any of the details of the company's operations or trading, or any matter which may be or is of the nature of a trade secret, or which may relate to the conduct of the business of the company which, in the opinion of the directors, it may not be expedient in the interests of the share-holders to communicate."

His keen blue eyes trained on Gubbins, Roberts asked: "Did it strike you, reading it, that that was very curious and unusual? Surely that article was put in by someone who was afraid of discovery?"

"Well," Gubbins had to confess, "probably I did not read the articles of association."

Moving on, Roberts revealed other incidents that had in no way struck Gubbins as strange. The steady increase of rubber production in the three years prior to 1908 had, he said, suggested no cause for anxiety to him. In August, 1909, even before Hardenburg's revelations, word had reached the London office that Arana's brother-in-law, Bartolomé Zumaeta, had been cut down by the Indians—but Gubbins had not given it more than passing thought. Pressed by Roberts, he did not think the office inventories would have revealed that every company employee was armed.

Roberts began to lose patience. "But here is an inventory," he said, lifting it peremptorily from the papers piled before the members, "pages of it, and you must have seen it. Did it not strike you to look at a large inventory of some twenty pages?"

Gubbins, as bluff and jovial as a favorite uncle, mistakenly tried a joke for the spectators' benefit: "The larger the inventory, the less likely would I be to go through it."

With a steely glare, Roberts brought him down to earth with a bump. "You have an item of paying £10 to a chief of section for hunting fugitive Indians. What right had you to hunt for Indians that owed you money? British law would not sanction it."

"Yes, but we were working there under Peruvian law," Gubbins retorted with a show of spirit.

"You would also," said Robert grimly, "be liable to British law. I am advised so, and the penalty is not light—fourteen years' penal servitude—because it would amount to slave raiding if you knew it."

He paused to let this sink in. "But it did not happen to strike you?" "No, no," Gubbins assured him, chastened once more, though he was moved to add a tactless rider: "The subjection of Indians by commercial companies is the condition prevailing in the whole of the Amazon Valley." Outraged, Roberts lashed back: "That does not make it any better!"

Now, as Gubbins' cross-examination gathered pace, one astounding factor became apparent. In the nine months that the directors, as Roberts put it, "fought and fenced with the Foreign Office," twenty-five murders, by Sir Roger Casement's reckoning, had been committed on the Putumayo—yet even this could not dim the old man's blind faith in Arana's integrity.

This became clear once William Joynson-Hicks had struck the first blow in defense of the absent Hardenburg. Why, he asked, should the bill the American was alleged to have forged have been sent to London? It had never been charged that Hardenburg had swindled the Peruvian Amazon Company—so how could a possible fraud on the Bank of Brazil concern them?

Gubbins had to admit it: a satisfactory explanation escaped him. It was possible the Manaus office, knowing of Hardenburg's charges, borrowed the bill and forwarded it to prove the American's perfidy.

From among the piled papers, Joynson-Hicks extracted a letter that Lizardo had routed to London on August 31, 1909: "Our chief, Don Julio, is leaving for Europe by the ship conveying this letter." Had it never struck Gubbins as coincidental that Arana was in Manaus at the same time as the alleged forgery was committed? Or that the accusations by Garnier, editor of *Amazonas*, had been forwarded to London by Arana's Manaus office?

"What you mean is perhaps," said Gubbins naïvely, "that he influenced the evidence of Mr. Garnier?"

"I mean further. I mean that he got up the charges against Hardenburg because he knew Hardenburg was coming to England with the full description of his infamies on the Putumayo. It looks very like it, does it not?"

"That is a matter of appreciation," Gubbins submitted.

Now Joynson-Hicks lost his temper. "And that is all you can say," he raged, "and you treat the Anti-Slavery Society, you treat *Truth*, you treat the Foreign Office in exactly the same way—you will not have anything to do with them, you are so satisfied, and your only evidence was Arana, Arana, Arana! That is so, is it not?"

Gubbins had to admit it. "Practically so, now."

For Lord Alex Thynne's benefit, the ex-chairman tried desperately to clarify matters. "We had to rely on Mr. Arana; we had to have confidence in somebody."

"Mr. Arana, I suppose," suggested Lord Alex suavely, "was more or less in the position of being able to insist on your relying on his word."

"Well, he could have turned us all out if he had wished," was Gubbins' telling admission. "He had the absolute control of the company."

Now Lord Alex faced Gubbins with a nonstop volley of questions. "If you had said, 'We are not satisfied with your explanations,' Mr. Arana would have had you off the board at once."

"I am afraid he would."

"If you had probed too deeply . . . I suppose it would not have been impossible for him to do it?"

Gubbins agreed. Arana and his friends had owned 83 percent of the voting shares.

"You could not have made enquiries through independent sources . . . without placing your position in jeopardy, could you?"

"Well, everything filtered through sources over which he had control."

Lord Alex hammered home his point to its logical conclusion. "You could not do *anything* unless you had the willing cooperation of Arana and his consent?"

Gubbins did not deny it. "That was the difficulty of the whole situation," he explained, and now as he elaborated, an incredible picture emerged—of the British directors' strange servitude and the almost hypnotic power Arana had exercised over them. In London, the Peruvian had conducted much of the company's correspondence in private, routing letters to Pablo and Lizardo which his associates never saw. Sometimes, at a board meeting, he would read extracts from these letters, but they were never permitted to examine them more closely—nor were copies placed in the company's files. Only as managing director and then chairman had Gubbins achieved the status of a desk. Until then he and the others had studied documents or signed checks at any vacant table.

From the outset, though, Arana had occupied his own private desk in the office. He had constantly written and received letters which the others never saw.

Proof of the British directors' ineptitude now seemed so damning that leading counsel, John Astbury, K.C., attempted a diversion. Rising with an important rustle of papers, he pleaded a pressing engagement in another court—but first he begged the chance to clarify some important items with Gubbins. Before Charles Roberts could even reply, the impulsive Swift MacNeill seemed to overrule the Chair. Glaring at Astbury he answered hotly, "This is a matter of life and death and is of far more importance than that."

Then, taking over the cross-examination, he asked Gubbins: "The company was mitigating murder. Why did you not go out personally?"

Gubbins protested. Had he been thirty years younger he would have boarded the next boat. As it was, he had taken every feasible step to set the business to rights. There had been his personal letter to President Leguía. And instructions he had routed to the Manaus and Iquitos offices in the autumn of 1908 had stressed that in future Indians must be treated with "great kindness and justice." His briefing to Colonel Bertie's commission had even outlined a plan for each estate to set up cottage gardens, with facilities for rearing guinea pigs.

"I mentioned guinea pigs," Gubbins explained, "because it is a little animal of cleanly habits, very easily reared, and which makes a dainty dish."

"Yes, yes," Swift MacNeill assured him, gesturing rudely in the direction of the House's debating chamber. "We have got a lot of them downstairs." Again the committee rocked with laughter.

But Swift MacNeill would not be deflected from the truth. "Why didn't you leave the company? The charges of murder and rapine were a byword throughout the country."

"Because under those conditions it would have been a cowardly and dishonorable act. The moment we were faced with difficulty I was not going to back out of it."

Swift MacNeill cast his mind back to January, 1910. "And at the same time you received a salary increase of £600 a year?"

John Astbury was back on his feet in an instant. "That is not an accurate statement. The witness should be treated fairly."

"I do not think we can have interruptions from counsel," Charles Roberts overruled him. "I think it is a question of fact." Again MacNeill repeated the question, and again Astbury cut in hotly: "The witness ought to be treated fairly."

"Sit down!" Swift MacNeill shouted at him, and in this moment of electric angry tension, Roberts, too, rose from his seat—the parliamentary chairman's time-honored method of restoring order. Suddenly Gubbins' hoarse-voiced admission broke the silence: "I do not dispute the fact."

Then an astonishing thing happened. Almost as if the spell of Arana persisted in the paneled room, Gubbins now spoke up for the absent Peruvian as spiritedly as any defense counsel. From the outset, he said, Arana had been vitally concerned regarding the allegations. Following Sir Roger's commission, it was plain that atrocities had taken place—but no evidence had ever linked Arana with them.

Once, when Gubbins had broached the subject, he had confided his ambition to see both Pablo and Lizardo make their pile; this accomplished, they could be eased into retirement, along with Alarco. Then, and only then, could the company be put on a sounder business footing. For this reason alone, he maintained, Arana was the ideal choice as liquidator. He had proposed him at the final meeting; he would propose him again today.

Trembling with emotion, the old man urged: "I don't say Arana is a saint . . . but he has never shown the white feather. He holds up his head and he says he is honestly going to try his best to put the thing straight. He is the man who has been pilloried; he is on his honor today . . . and Arana now is willing to come back to London to face the music here. . . ."

There was sensation among the spectators. Every man darted a swift interrogatory glance at his neighbor, and again, to subdue the buzz of voices, Roberts half rose from his seat. Incredulously, William Joynson-Hicks asked: "Are you authorized to say that Arana is willing to come *here?*"

Now Gubbins asked permission to confer with his friends, and amid a low hum of speculation made his way through the close-packed seats to where Henry Read sat with Sir John Lister-Kaye. All eyes were trained on their muttered consultation, then Gubbins returned to the witness seat.

"I am told the exact state of things is this," he reported to the committee, "he expressed his willingness to come and appear."

Hastily, as the sonorous notes of Big Ben reverberated through the chamber, tolling 4 P.M., the newsmen were scrambling through the witnesses' door. By early evening the headlines were on the streets and the newsboys were bawling on the frosty air: "AT THE MERCY OF ARANA . . . PUTUMAYO DIRECTORS' THRALLDOM . . . AMAZING ADMISSIONS OF EX-CHAIRMAN . . ."

As the committee's day-by-day revelations filtered through to Manaus via the world's press, Julio Arana knew he must return to London. The whole future of his empire was now at stake.

As far back as October, 1912, he was aware that trouble threatened, even before the Iquitos banquet when only bluff had saved his face. It was with difficulty then that he had obtained an adjournment in a High Court action brought, after the promptings of the Anti-Slavery Society, by the zealous Morgan Williams and another shareholder. Pressing for the company's compulsory winding up, they based their petition on three counts: cruelty to the Indians was continuing and the original sale of the company required investigation, as did Eleonora's mortgage. But to enable Arana's evidence to be heard, the case had been put forward to mid-March.

If the verdict went against him, Arana knew, the implications would be far-reaching. When in 1907 the government had requested written evidence on his rights in the Putumayo, his link with a British company had been his strongest suit. Even now, his appointment as liquidator told in his favor—but President Augusto Leguía, by nature a peacemaker, had already patched up boundary disputes with Bolivia and Brazil and sought to resume friendly relations with Chile. If a High Court decision ousted Arana from office, Leguía might contrive a solution for the Putumayo, too—and Arana's position would be precarious indeed.

Aides like Carlos Rey de Castro noted that at times he now lost all control. Most often in the past, when the cards were stacked against him, Arana had chuckled richly—knowing he would find another way to worst the opposition. Now his insults against the men who had frustrated his designs were blistering. Hardenburg was "a North American adventurer"; Whiffen, "a cheap failure"; Casement, "a morbid megalomaniac." After scanning one press report he burst out: "Have you seen Gubbins' evidence? The Colombians are paying him to lie, to get control in the Putumayo."

By January 24, 1913, he would delay no longer. He was Arana the unique. Once he appeared in person no High Court judge or parliamentary commission could fail to see that he was not one more illiterate ex-rubber tapper but a man of power and distinction, whose true roots lay in Europe. "To sail not later than the 11th day of February for London; impossible before," ran his decisive cable to his lawyers. "I will take important evidence for Committee and petition shareholders."

On the face of it, Arana's was the wise decision. As the inquiry gathered momentum, his codirectors only conspired to damage his cause still further—through their unwitting demonstration of how skillfully he had pulled the strings. Though Sir John Lister-Kaye strode confidently enough to the witness seat, Charles Roberts' opening questions were enough to establish the baronet's profound ignorance of the company's dealings.

No, Sir John had not thought it his duty to inquire into the Indians' wages. He was never aware the company was employing Barbadian overseers. He had no idea how Arana felt about the allegations; since he did not speak Spanish, they had never exchanged so much as a word together. True, board meetings had been conducted in this language, but Gubbins or Read had translated anything they felt he should know. This service, he admitted, had not included even a précis of the company's Spanish correspondence.

Warmly, Sir John disputed the suggestion put forward by more than one member: that the underwriters, Bellamy and Isaac, had been eager to secure his title for the prospectus. M.P. Frederick Jowett went so far as to posit that once Bellamy's had managed to dispose of the shares the baronet would have quit the board.

"What is your point, sir?" Sir John rapped out. "I do not see your point. Why should I resign because they had asked me to go on and because they might sell their interests. What is your point?"

Typically, it was Swift MacNeill who made the point crystal-clear. "Take a simple-minded fellow like myself," he invited Sir John, "and I saw at the top of the list of directors, 'Sir John Lister-Kaye, Baronet.' Should I not at once, in giving my few hundred pounds, think I was giving it on the faith of a gentleman's name who knew all about the business and was a gentleman in a high position in society?"

Sir John was haughty. "I knew as much as I could know, and the point was this, first of all in my mind, 'How does the commercial record of the enterprise stand before I have connection with it?' "

With this in view, he had sent the company's articles and

prospectus to his solicitor, not the Foreign Office—though in other business dealings abroad he had always consulted that department. At last, under the relentless probing of Willoughby Dickinson, who combated all his suggestions that the Britons had favored a commission prior to Foreign Office pressure, Sir John broke down completely.

"Cannot you understand the horror I felt at the situation?" he cried out, in a scene that made next day's headlines. "I expect a certain amount of sympathy for the hideous position I was dragged into in utter ignorance. . . ."

And banker Henry Read, despite twenty-odd years in Peru and Chile, showed himself as ill-informed. Though his Spanish was fluent, he had never been nearer the Amazon than Lima, then 1,200 miles distant by the overland route. Prior to joining the London Bank of Mexico as manager, he had been an expert on nitrates.

Had he ever, the chairman asked, inquired about labor conditions?

He had made general inquiries from Alarco, Read testified. "He told me that the Indian went into the company shop, took a knife or gun, and went into the woods for three or four months for rubber. It struck me as a free-and-easy life."

Now Roberts brought into sharp focus the question of the company's dealings with the Foreign Office. Delving into the mountain of correspondence, he had come upon three crucial letters. The first, a reply to Sir Edward Grey's request for action, dated December 30, 1909, had been signed by Vernon Smith, as secretary, on behalf of the board.

"It is not the case that the Indians are compelled under a system of forced labor to supply the company with rubber," Roberts read out, "nor are the managers of the estates paid according to the amount of rubber they are able to compel the Indians to collect. In all cases they are paid by salary."

Was it significant, Roberts mused, that the company's solicitor had overseen the draft? Had the company been anxious that a lawyer should view the phrasing of this particular letter?

Now Roberts turned to the second letter, entered in the

company's Spanish mail book on June 17, 1909, which clearly the lawyer could never have seen. Then Abel Alarco had written: "The management here finds the system of granting to the heads of sections a bonus on the amount of rubber brought in by Indians and allowing to the higher officers a certain percentage of the profits . . . thwarts its own object . . . it encourages . . . quantities of rubber, not quality."

The third letter was passed to Read for his scrutiny. From Iquitos, on August 11, Pablo Zumaeta was replying to Alarco. To the packed and silent room the chairman read aloud: "We have cancelled the contracts of Aurelio and Aristides Rodriguez, managers of the Santa Catalina and Sabana sections, who got 50 per cent of the gross yield . . . there still remain the other sections, the managers of which get . . . not exceeding 7 per cent, though these contracts will be revised before long."

Roberts challenged the banker sternly: "So you knew that the system of paying commission on the output was in existence?"

"I did not know," Read maintained.

"Judging from your minute book, these letters coming from Manaus and Iquitos were submitted to the board."

"I think they were generally laid on the table," said Read cautiously.

"I put it to you that the board must have known."

"*I* certainly did not know," Read was careful to stress.

"And that in spite of that, in December, you made a statement to the Foreign Office which is entirely false on an important point."

"Yes," Read agreed readily, "but we were told so by Alarco and Arana and we believed them."

Joynson-Hicks switched to another aspect of the directors' responsibility. "When you came on the board, you knew that shares were ultimately going to be issued to the public. Did you make any enquiries as to whether the property was worth £780,000?"

Read was equivocal. The shares issued to the public were preference shares—whose dividends had priority over ordinary stock—and there had always been assets in hand to cover these. "The value they put on their own company they could have made what they liked," he said. "They could have made it £2 million or anything."

"You and I have been in the City long enough to know that that will not do," said Joynson-Hicks, profoundly shocked. "If a company agrees to buy for £2 million, the directors surely are responsible for seeing that there is property to represent that £2 million?"

The banker would not admit it. How could you assess the capital value of land up the Amazon? It was hard enough to do so in England. In such cases a director must abide by what an auditor told him. If Arana, as the prospectus stated, claimed to have spent £500,000 developing the Putumayo, why should he have doubted this? "I did not go through the accounts, you know," he reminded the committee.

The scrupulous Joynson-Hicks reproved him: "But, Mr. Read, you are a City man, and you were a director of the company, drawing fees?"

Obviously what Read saw as his niggardly £200 a year re-muneration rankled more than any factor. "Yes," he sneered, "precious little of them."

Then, seeing the stony faces of the committee, he tried un-successfully to redeem his lapse with a man-of-the-world ap-proach: "You know, a gentleman who goes once a week, and is only paid for going once a week—you know the rest."

Patiently Willoughby Dickinson harked back to an earlier calculation of the chairman's: if the cost of landing rubber at Liverpool worked out at 1/9d per pound, then the Indians had been paid a bare fivepence-halfpenny at most. "You never knew that?" he prompted.

"Never. The first I heard of it was before this committee."

Dickinson made one last effort to understand Read's thinking. "What *did* you think the natives were being paid?"

It was the breaking point. Exasperated, Read stormed back: "I did not know what the natives were being paid. I never entered into the question. I went on the board to look after the financial interests of the bank I was concerned with, and I looked after that."

Bitterly, he wound up with what might have stood as the Peruvian Amazon Company's epitaph: "I knew nothing about rubber."

On Tuesday, February 4, came a thunderbolt. Three weeks earlier, with the inquiry already looming large in the headlines, Charles Roberts had once more taxed the company's solicitors. Why had they failed to produce the Putumayo cashbooks, twice referred to in letters signed by Abel Alarco? He was determined to find out how far the directors were sheltering behind Arana. But to Roberts' unconcealed anger, the solicitors again drew a blank. The vital accounts had vanished—and, incredibly, the company had kept no register of incoming letters to pinpoint the date of their arrival.

In fact, there was no chicanery, as Roberts at first suspected— only dire confusion. As far back as December 3, when the chairman first demanded the cashbooks, the solicitors had reported none could be found. On January 13, once more goaded by Roberts, the solicitors' managing clerk went back to the company's offices for another vain search. Desperate, he turned to the original auditors, but they, too, found no trace. Next day, attending before the committee, he assured the fuming Roberts that nobody was being obstructive. Every company document still extant was at the members' disposal.

The committee hardly knew what to think. Until the company's liquidation Gubbins had attended the office daily. Had he and Read conspired to destroy documents that might incriminate them? Then again, a clerk had testified that back in October, 1911, Arana's secretary had removed a deedbox full of papers. No record now existed of what this had contained.

On January 15, Roberts, galled, sent the managing clerk back to Salisbury House again, this time in company with an audit clerk from the accountants'. Their instructions: to toothcomb every document until the missing cashbooks came to light. During their search the two men overhauled the company's safe—to find not cashbooks but two green files of notes made by Henry Gielgud. "I think these must be what he's looking for," the audit clerk decided.

The managing clerk hardly thought so. Returning to the committee chamber after that day's hearing, he raised the question with Gielgud who had just sat through the long humiliating examination of Sir John Lister-Kaye. "No, no," Gielgud had assured him with some urgency, "these are merely notes I brought back, not the Putumayo accounts at all."

Nonetheless, the solicitor, to whom no blame was ever remotely attached, passed them to the committee as fresh exhibits on January 16. On behalf of the company, Raymond Asquith now apologized: confusion had arisen because the search had focused on cashbooks, not files, but these were undoubtedly the long-sought Putumayo accounts. By February 4, after studying them intently, Roberts and his committee recalled Henry Gielgud to the witness seat.

What Roberts now proposed was nothing less than a grim stocktaking—a stocktaking that centered on three harmless-seeming sets of figures. The first set, which the chairman marked "A," was set out in Gielgud's own handwriting—a manuscript balance sheet, plus rough notes, for the trading post La Chorrera in the six-month periods ending July 1, 1907, and December 31, 1908. The second set, labeled "B," was a typescript copy of this, minus amplifying notes, made in the company's office sometime after Gielgud became secretary.

But it was the third set of figures to which Roberts drew prior attention: the combined accounts, marked "C," which Gielgud, then still an obscure audit clerk, had laid before the directors on December 14, 1909. The accountant could not deny that this balance sheet, a simplified breakdown of the earlier calculations, included an entry of £87,853 for "Rubber and Agricultural Estates, including Development Expenditure."

Yet in Accounts "A" and "B," Roberts pointed out, the value of the estates was shown separately to development expenditure.

These privately prepared sheets had contained one item missing from the combined accounts placed before the board: "Gastos de Conquistación—Expenses of Conquest— £11,400."

"You lumped together 'properties' and 'expenses for conquest' and put it at one round figure?"

"Yes."

"In other words, you concealed £11,400 under the head of development expenditure which was really 'expenses of conquest'?"

"No," Gielgud said, " 'Conquest' is an error. 'Conquistación' is the regular term for recruiting labor, used all over South America."

Roberts let fall his bombshell. "Then were you misrepresenting it in your manuscript notes, when your explanation is, 'This represents further expenditure of a capital nature incurred in reducing the Indians to subjection'?"

"These notes, I must remind you," Gielgud blazed, "were made for my own use."

"Yes, but they also show what your explanation of 'conquistación' was."

"For my own use!"

Roberts was inflexible. "I put it to you that you knew this was not expenses incurred in recruiting labor, but expenses incurred in reducing the Indians to subjection by means of rifles."

"Of course, I know now that the method of getting Indians to work was not what I originally believed it to be," said Gielgud, growing confused, "but at this time I am absolutely certain that my view was not what it is now."

Question by question, Roberts drove the unlucky accountant back against the wall. By whom had these manuscript notes been amended in red ink? Both Arana and Alarco had talked them over with him, Gielgud admitted, but he was not prepared to say who had made the amendments. Had Read seen the manuscript accounts? Or the typewritten ones? Had Gubbins? Gielgud thought not. The only figures presented to them had been the final combined accounts.

But, he added, the accounts marked "A" and "B" had been in the company's office all through his term as secretary. The directors could have examined them if they had wished. Sir Clement Hill's plaint summed up what many members now felt: "Can you give me any reason for what one may call the directors' almost extraordinary ignorance of what was in the office correspondence? The impression on my mind is that nobody appears to have known anything as to what was going on."

At once John Astbury, K.C., tried his utmost to sugar the pill—and as swiftly drew a spirited objection from Swift Mac-Neill. "Does Mr. Astbury appear for the directors or for Mr. Gielgud?"

"I do not appear for Mr. Gielgud," Astbury said, "but . . . as these reflections have been made upon him he should have an opportunity of explaining his point of view."

"Then the directors and Mr. Gielgud are in the same boat?"

Astbury was chilling. "Mr. MacNeill's idea seems to be that a witness is to come here and have grave reflections made on him, and the counsel for the directors is not to be allowed to go into them."

"Then that looks as if you do appear for him?" Swift MacNeill persisted.

"I do not," was Astbury's meaning reply. "It is quite consistent with my case that Mr. Gielgud may be a rascal and the directors may not."

Nonetheless, Astbury handled the accountant as gently as might be. Gielgud had surely not used "conquistar" in the military sense, but as referring to labor? Now, as clerks were sent hastening to the ground-floor library for dictionaries, a fine confusion of semantics ensued. Turning to the entry, Charles Roberts found no mention of the definition "to recruit." "To conquer, to overcome, to subdue, to acquire, to win another person's affections," he read out. And Astbury's dictionary by contrast showed only "to win over, to win round." "She stoops to conquer," volunteered Swift MacNeill, by way of light relief.

Skillfully Astbury phrased his questions to obtain for Gielgud the maximum benefit of the doubt. "You were not such a fine Spanish scholar that you thought in Spanish instead of English?"

"Not with regard to this matter," Gielgud assured him.

"Where a Spaniard, speaking to you, was using expressions which, if you translated literally, would convey a wrong impression, you tried to think with regard to these words in the Spanish sense, not the literal translation sense?"

"That is the case."

"You used an expression, which, in the light of today, looks very suspicious—'Reducing the Indians to subjection.' What did you really mean by it? You are on your oath and you are entitled to say."

"I meant that they were getting the Indians from their wild and uncivilized state to a condition of being prepared to work—in return, of course, for payments which I understood were made to them."

"Had you any idea that this 'reduction to subjection' had been effected by murder, or rifles, or massacre or brutality?"

"No, I had no idea of that sort."

And Gielgud stubbornly maintained his denials to the end. He had firmly believed that Arana's object on the Putumayo was to set up bona fide trading posts. Once more reaffirming his oath, he swore he had never sought to withhold information from the British directors. It had been merely a matter of presenting the accounts to busy men in an easily assimilable form. All along Arana had struck him as a man with a genuine mission to civilize the Indians—though, admittedly, while making a profit on the side.

How much Gielgud, whom newsmen christened "the blindfold witness," had seen or known, no committee member was prepared to say—though later their official summary recorded: "He is liable to be called on for explanations in the course of a judicial enquiry." Had Read, Sir John or Gubbins, "a guileless old gentleman," as Astbury pictured him, nourished even the faintest suspicions? How much was ignorance and to how much had they turned a blind eye? Even now, it was no easy decision, but one thing was plain: Julio Arana had known. For his bold flourishing hand had made those red-inked amendments.

On March 4, 1913, as Arana stepped off the Booth liner *Lanfranc* at Fishguard, Wales, newspaper subeditors aptly recalled John Russell Gubbins' assurance of a few weeks back. Across the country the headlines bannered: "ARANA COMES TO FACE THE MUSIC."

The breakfast coffee had grown cold. Abstractedly raising his eyes from the newspapers that scattered his suite in London's Hotel Cecil, Julio Arana bade a secretary to ring for a fresh pot. Then he turned once more to the headlines. At last, in the cool dawn of Wednesday, April 9, 1913, he began to see fresh hope after one of the most grueling months he had ever known.

The press, as an aide whose English was fluent agreed, had reported his first session before the committee as cordially as might be. *The Daily Telegraph* noted that he had given his evidence "with perfect readiness and composure." *The Daily Mirror* had found him "so calm, so confident." To *The Daily Mail* he had radiated "an instinctive impression of energy and determination." *The Daily Express*, visibly impressed, had seen him as "like the President of a South American Republic . . . a master man . . . a kind of Peruvian Hannibal, capable of leading an army over the Andes." The reporter had noted, too, that he had "the bullet-head of a fighter and the commanding air of a master of legions."

But it was from *The Daily News*, formerly *The Morning Leader*, that Arana derived most comfort. Though long anti-Arana in its views, his bearing yesterday had won him only that paper's unstinted praise. At first, arriving at the House of Commons before the doors of Room No. 11 were even unlocked, he had been plainly unnerved by the electric stares of the crowd thronging the Committee Corridor. Yet no sooner had he taken

This cartoon from *Tropical Life* was captioned: "Wake up, John Bull, and make Uncle Sam help you to stop these atrocities before your investments become mere waste paper." (*British Museum.*)

the witness seat than his old confidence visibly flowed back into him. Undaunted by the members massed below Wilfred Lawson's vast oil painting of "The Speaker Entering the House of Commons," the day-long traffic of society beauties and M.P.'s who tiptoed in to gape, Arana had conducted himself from first to last like a born parliamentarian.

As, with an aide's help, he now sifted the press reports, he could forget, if only briefly, the humiliation he had endured three weeks back on March 19, when he had sat in the Chancery Division of the High Court of Justice on the Strand and heard Mr. Justice Swinfen Eady grant the petitioning shareholders a compulsory winding up of the Peruvian Amazon Company. The short but trenchant summing up had stripped Arana of his position as liquidator.

"In my opinion, Arana and his partners sold a business to the company whose profits were derived from rubber collected in an atrocious manner," was the judge's crushing verdict. "If Arana did not know, then he ought to have known. Having regard to this, and to his position as vendor, he is the last person in the world to whom the winding up of the company should be entrusted."

Still Arana was battling to salvage something from the ruins of his enterprise. If this committee exonerated him completely, there was still hope—and who could say that they would not, if all the newspapers' coverage was on the order of the *News?* "A rain of questions which would have broken any English witness," ran the report, "was met by an imperturbable and unruffled courtesy, never irritated or shocked but armed at all points with a tolerance almost Christian."

"Such a man," summed up *The Daily News*, "is Arana; this yesterday, was the scene at his ordeal . . ."

Sipping fresh coffee, Arana crumbled a hot croissant and read on. The *News* had faithfully reported every twist and turn of that crucial first session—even Roberts' explanation to Arana and his counsel, Douglas McGarel Hogg, that, though the committee had no jurisdiction over him as a Peruvian, "the conclusion to

which we may come . . . on the grave charges which have been
made against you . . . may conceivably affect your reputation
indirectly."

Attentively, Hogg had listened to the committee's proposals
for taking his client's evidence and pronounced them wholly fair:
questions and answers, rendered through Dr. Mascarenhas, the
interpreter, would be noted down by two shorthand writers,
then printed in both English and Spanish, to give Arana opportunity of correcting them. As the interrogation proceeded, newsmen noted, the eager Roberts' questions often came too fast for
Dr. Mascarenhas to keep pace—yet so keen was the understand-
ing between chairman and witness that Arana was rarely at a loss
for the meaning.

His voice "low and musical," Arana had made no attempt to
deny the attacks by Benjamin Saldaña Rocca's papers—though he
disclaimed them as "periodicals of the lowest type." His account
of dismissing the rascally Ramon Sanchez was rated "prompt and
plausible," though Arana courteously refuted the earlier testimony of Iquitos' British Consul, David Cazes. Certainly he had
not dismissed him for whipping two women to death; he had
known nothing of the whipping. He had fired him because he
was of doubtful moral character, an inveterate gambler. His
successor was Armando Normand, a man more infamous still, but
why should Arana have suspected this? The Bolivian had been
educated at an English public school.

It was charged, Roberts said, that Indian boys and women had
been sold for money. Arana clarified this: these were orphans in
need of homes. Were the women also orphans? Roberts asked.
Arana had shrugged massively, his delicate hands spread wide:
"Ah well, gentlemen—you cannot prevent rubber traders adopt-
ing native women as wives."

Turning again to the explorer Robuchon's book, Roberts had
pressed: did not the Indians hold festivities in memory of their
lost liberties and in bitter denunciation of the white man? Arana
hinted mildly that they were merely yearning for their old tribal
wars—hardly an attitude to be encouraged in the second decade

of the twentieth century. Had not shocking reports been made by Capuchin friars to the heads of the Catholic Church? But all the priests, Arana claimed, were intimately known to him; he met them often on the streets of Manaus. They had made no such complaints to him.

Only one point of dissension had briefly troubled Arana. More than once Swift MacNeill had insisted Dr. Mascarenhas should give Arana's answers in the first person—not in the third, which the Peruvian so often affected. Spanish-speaking William Young had complained, too, that the interpreter did not put the questions accurately—and had cut in with his own version.

Mascarenhas protested: the chairman had asked about the hunting of fugitive Indians. The word suggested by Mr. Young applied to the hunting of wild animals. It was then that Swift MacNeill, his eyes fixed unwinkingly on Arana, had remarked: "That is the word we want."

From the first, MacNeill had displayed a marked aversion to the witness, but his questions during the first day's hearing had been few enough. As the committee adjourned for the day, most spectators felt that the Peruvian had stolen the honors.

In truth, Arana needed such crumbs of comfort. From the moment of his setting foot in England, on March 4, he had known nothing but anxious moments. First, on March 19, had come that bitter High Court verdict—and on the same day he had been forced to attend the committee chamber with his solicitors, to hear them plead for an extension. Originally, the solicitor said, his client had been scheduled to give his evidence on March 26. Now word had come that Señora Arana was gravely ill in Switzerland. Don Julio begged leave to hasten to her without delay.

After some deliberation—for in four months the committee had examined more than twenty witnesses, some on six separate occasions—Roberts had agreed to a postponement until April 8. By then, he hoped, Arana would have both instructed counsel and sent a précis of his evidence.

Distraught, Arana had hastened across the Channel to Paris, to

catch the night express from the Gare de Lyons. By late on
March 20 he had joined his family at the Villa Salisco in Geneva.
There the doctors had explained to him that Eleonora was under-
going the change of life, a condition much aggravated by her
current emotional stress. For days, Arana had lingered guiltily in
the darkened room close to her bedside, shocked to find her so
weak and overwrought. "Mama can eat nothing but Melba toast
and chicken soup," fourteen-year-old Lily announced gravely;
"even croissants are too rich."

And though Julio and Eleonora conferred only behind closed
doors, out of earshot of the children, he wondered how often
they heard her cry out: "Now it's too late, Julio—I warned you
back in Yurimaguas and you would never listen, and now it's too
late. The rubber and this terrible Casement have poisoned our
lives—why didn't you get out before it was too late?"

And the bulletins arriving by every mail from Lizardo and
Pablo only served to confirm Eleonora's premonitions, though
the truth had been apparent even before Arana left Manaus.
Overnight the white city was crumbling, and the first fatal flaws
presaged the imminent collapse of the entire Amazon rubber
boom.

Yet for two years now the signs had been clear to all who
cared to interpret them. All through 1911 and 1912, the price of
top-grade wild rubber had been virtually stationary at around
4/8d a pound. And though even in 1913 more than 10,000 tons
were ferried down the Amazon, most of it, traveling 3,000 miles
by portage, took one whole year to reach the manufacturer and
commanded a cash value of less than £1,700,000—almost half that
of 1912. Yet the 1912 crop, while outstripping that of 1910, had
still involved the rubber barons in a cash loss of £9 million. At
long last, Malayan rubber, now produced for less than ninepence
a pound, had triumphed over the Amazon.

What followed was a landslide to disaster. The women of the
town, scenting trouble, were the first to flee: daily, in the Booth
Steamship Company offices, they clamored for passages to Europe, often in lieu of banknotes, pressing rings and bracelets on

Señor Maracci, the Spanish cashier. Soon every liner was crammed to capacity as the dandies and the cardsharpers, then the old-established families followed, too—some of them so hastily that last good-byes to friends were made through the personal columns of the *Jornal do Comercio*. And the stage of the opera house was dark.

Not all got away in time. In Pará alone, this one year saw £4 million worth of bankruptcies—and Manaus was swift to follow in its wake. All too soon Alfredo Arruda had to quit his fine marble-fronted town house; his rubber in the harbor's warehouses was declared confiscate by the Bank of the Amazon. Another early fatality was Carlos Montenegro's £15,000 yacht, seized by the Bank of Brazil; soon after its owner fled to the northeast and died of beriberi. Waldemar Scholz, too, found the Babylonian orgies were over; another rubber baron had secured a mortgage on his fabulous Municipal Street palace and Scholz, ruined, made tracks for the Putumayo and took his life. Most spectacular of all these failures was João Antunes, whose fourteen riverboats had between them ferried more than 1,000 tons of rubber each year. Bankrupted for £700,000, he remained for years—as a lottery ticket vendor—a familiar sight on the streets of Manaus.

And the suffering was universal. Though the 226-mile Madeira-Mamoré Railroad had been triumphantly inaugurated back in 1912, the world had found cheaper standbys for Bolivia's "black gold." Itacoatiara, the town that had hoped to surpass Manaus, saw its chances vanish in space. Overnight, as the town's population shrank from 2,000 to 300, the hard-pressed municipality set wreckers to work on the half-completed city hall for the cash value of the bricks.

In Iquitos, the fine riverside promenade, the Malecón, crumbled by degrees into the Amazon below: all day the sidewalk outside the three-story Malecón Palace Hotel swarmed with painted teen-age girls, out-of-work servants, soliciting the guests, while their mothers controlled the bids like auctioneers. The crisis left almost two million people stranded along the riverbanks, and many smaller towns—Gurupá and Almirim on the Amazon, Santo Antônio on the Madeira—were literally engulfed by the jungle.

But it was Manaus, the fabled white city, that was hardest hit. Now, in the cafés on Eduardo Ribeiro Avenue, no man was more bitterly reviled than Henry Wickham. Seven years later Wickham would be knighted by Britain's King George V for his services to the plantation industry, but to Manaus he had become "the executioner of Amazonas," as men saw for the first time the havoc he had wrought thirty-seven years back. All day long in the nearby sale rooms of Agente Leon, the auctioneers' hammers sounded like a knell: on hoarding after hoarding posters blazoned: "Sale Fully authorised by Family Leaving for Europe." Among 140 auctions held in that black year, every one featured "prices that can't be repeated" and with reason . . . the Casa 22 department store and the gentlemen's outfitters, Havana House . . . the Golden Globe jewelers . . . house after fancy house on Joaquim Sarmento Street . . . luxury carriages . . . sparkling crystal . . . Steinway grands, chinoiserie tables, panther-skin rugs . . . the Paris in America fashion store, slashing £20,000 worth of perfumes to half-price.

In the space of years, a visiting British Consul would report: "The city is like a ghost town."

Hence Arana's deep-seated unease: although for years he had predicted the cataclysm that would overtake Manaus he had never admitted it as possible that his own ruin might be encompassed therein. Yet at the Hotel Cecil, on the morning of April 9, nothing of this showed in his face as he donned sober dark suit and black silk necktie. One impecunious rubber baron, Marcial Lopez Montero, who had followed him from Paris in the hope of negotiating a loan, never forgot the Peruvian's impassive calm as he was ushered into his suite.

Without a tremor, Arana remarked: "You know, Marcial, at 10 A.M., I am in the judgment seat before the English Parliament."

It was a masterly display of indifference. Even if Arana escaped the committee's censure—and they could visit no other punishment on him—there was no escape for Manaus and the Amazon. Though the President of Brazil, Marshal Hermes de Fonseca had belatedly, in January, 1912, launched an ambitious Defense of Rubber scheme, promising premiums to all pioneers who would establish scientific plantations and open up rubber factories, time had run out for the monopolists. Within a year, despite an initial £350,000 outlay, the scheme was abandoned—and on January 28, 1913, a last-ditch effort by Arana and other Manaus barons met with no greater success.

Vainly urging the State Governor of Amazonas, Jonatas Pedrosa, to grant the Chamber of Commerce a one-year £1,800,-000 loan to bolster rubber's falling fortunes, they overlooked one salient factor: after seventeen years of prodigal spending the state, too, teetered on the edge of bankruptcy. Already Amazonas owed £3,850,000 to French bankers—and Manaus, too, was £214,000 in debt. For eight long months, the city's civil servants were denied their paychecks. As the students ran riot, colleges and schools closed down altogether. Soon pickets of troops were posted outside every rubber baron's office, to protect them from the blind fury of the mob.

Thus, at 10 A.M. on April 9, passing through the St. Stephen's entrance of the House of Commons and climbing the long flight of stone stairs, lined with marble busts of long-dead prime ministers, Arana was in a cautious mood. Despite his inner elation at yesterday's success, he felt it prudent to be wary. Perhaps too wary, for scarcely had he resumed the witness seat, clasping his hands on the table before him, than both newsmen and examiners noted a subtle change in his manner. His open, man-to-man approach of yesterday had evaporated. On many issues he was now devious and evasive.

When Arana claimed he, too, was unaware his overseers were paid by commission until he studied Casement's report, most exchanged meaning glances—and his claim that the abuses were all originated by the Colombians whom he had bought out made Roberts lose patience. "I am bound to tell you," he rebuked Arana sharply, "that I am not impressed by that theory."

From this moment, Arana sensed that the mood of the chamber was against him. Somehow he had failed to gauge their temper, but how, he could not tell. He, too, did his best to explain his company's frequent use of the word "conquistar." "The object was to send a commission carrying food, tools, and so on, to give the Indians in exchange for rubber," he explained. "It was a pacific conquest."

"Conducted by persons armed with Winchester rifles?" asked Charles Roberts blandly, and the spectators rocked with laughter.

Abruptly, dropping his stoic manner, Arana became heated. "In all the woods of the Amazon, every person has to take a rifle. It is possible that they may meet a tiger." To his unconcealed anger, laughter filled the room again.

It was now, some noted, that Arana became haughty and aloof; his eyelids drooped until they half-closed. Never in all his years on the Amazon had he been exposed to the indignity of ridicule. "Did you notice that Saldaña Rocca accused your employees of flogging the Indians?" Roberts asked now, and Arana's reply, given in the third person, was distant. "At that time his publications were contradicted or disbelieved in the whole region."

Swift MacNeill was growing restive. "This witness never answers a question yes or no. The first thing, I submit, is to tell him to answer yes or no and make his explanations afterwards."

Roberts turned to Casement's report and the later independent verdict of Dr. Romulo Paredes. Putting aside any question of personal knowledge, did Arana accept the fact of the atrocities? "In the main," the Peruvian conceded, the thumbs of his clasped hands jerking impatiently upward, "but at the same time there is a great deal of exaggeration in them."

Willoughby Dickinson joined in the cross fire of questions. "In what respect do you say the report is exaggerated?"

"There are so many things described in a peculiar and fantastic manner."

But Dickinson would not let the matter drop. "Give me any instance to which you take exception." Noticeably, Arana began to hedge and stumble. There were many instances which he personally had been unable to prove. Pressed harder, he could recall only the story of a woman soaked in kerosene and burned to death. No, Arana admitted, he had not succeeded in disproving it; he had not interviewed the Barbadian who had told Casement this. "Mr. Casement was sent by the King of England," Arana charged. "He has only taken his statements from Barbadians. They lend themselves to give any kind of declaration."

"Do you deny the truth of this evidence that was given to Sir Roger Casement?" said Dickinson, puzzled, but once more Arana was evasive. "I do not deny it, but I say there has been exaggeration."

Dickinson was implacable. "I want you to understand that we want the information which you have which shows this to be exaggeration."

"I will send these proofs to the committee," said Arana, his head tilted disdainfully. "At the present moment I cannot remember, but I will send written details."

"Then the charge that you make, that they are exaggerations, breaks down?"

"I will send written proof tomorrow."

Later the shorthand writers who prepared each day's evidence for the printers, enabling members to refresh their memories, were to note: "This information was not sent to the Committee." It would hardly have surprised the newsmen, already scribbling busily, Arana, they saw, was making some very important admissions and withdrawals.

And more were to come. Following the lunch recess, M.P. Joseph King was one of several who sought to probe the allegations against Walt Hardenburg. Though Arana might conceivably have been unaware of the happenings up the Putumayo, his hand in the campaign to vilify the American seemed all too plain. Again, the newsmen noted, due to Arana's unwillingness to give a direct answer to any question, this cross-examination alone took forty-five minutes.

"Do you say that Hardenburg negotiated a bill wrongly?" King asked, first.

"Yes, and the bill is in my possession."

"It was forged by Hardenburg?"

"I do not know by whom," Arana sidestepped. "The bill was negotiated in the house of Wesche and Company, Iquitos. It was bought in the name of Estanisláo Bazan. Mr. Hardenburg bought it from Bazan and sold it to the Bank of Brazil and it was protested here in London by Rothschild."

"But how did it inculpate Hardenburg? What had he to do with it?"

"I do not say that Hardenburg was the forger, but that the bill was false."

"What name was forged on it? Was it a false name, accepting, or was it falsely drawn?"

"The whole bill was forged, and the amount altered by chemicals," Arana maintained. "Instead of £10 they put £830."

For answer, King handed the Clerk to the Committee Arana's circular letter to the shareholders, requesting the witness should study it afresh. "Look at it, please. I put it to you that it was an attempt to make out Hardenburg as a mere adventurer, if not a criminal."

"I make no reference in this to the bill of £830," said Arana, with truth.

King, not to be outdone, at once turned to the affidavit Arana had presented to the court through his counsel, Douglas Hogg. "Let me take you to paragraph 22 in your statement: 'I produced to the Board the evidence of forgery on the part of Hardenburg.'"

Now Arana's reply was inaudible even to Dr. Mascarenhas beside him, and the Spanish-speaking William Young cut in. Then, turning to the chairman, he complained: "He says these proofs will be something to ventilate, produced to the tribunal. He refuses to answer the question; I put it to him, but he goes off to something else."

"Answer the question, please, directly," Charles Roberts rapped out. "Do you charge Hardenburg with having committed the forgery or not?"

"That is entirely another thing," Arana dodged the question.

"I understand you to say the bill was forged; is that right? What I want to know is, do you charge Hardenburg with having done that?"

"I say this is a mistake."

"Do I understand then that you do not charge Hardenburg with the act?"

"I do not know who was the forger—Hardenburg or somebody else."

"I will only ask you one more question on the subject," King resumed. "You do not now charge Hardenburg with forgery—do you or not?"

At last, with an effort, his eyes again half-closed, Arana answered, "No, I do not accuse him now."

From Douglas Hall came a series of searching questions on Arana's management on the Putumayo. How close had been his liaison with his section managers? How often had they come to Iquitos on leave, and how often had Arana visited the Putumayo? Once more Arana's replies were equivocal. His sciatica had rarely permitted him to visit the Putumayo, though he had maintained close liaison with every agent. But each time Hall named an agent whom Hardenburg or Casement had arraigned, he drew a blank. These men had not availed themselves of leave—or Arana had missed them in his journeys upriver.

Hall's fancy led him to envisage how Arana had briefed his agents. "Is it a fact that the company simply said they wanted rubber? They wanted plenty of rubber, cheap rubber, and did not want to ask any questions as to how it was got."

"That is not true," said Arana impassively. "If you take into account the number of Indians in the Putumayo, you will see that the quantity produced is very small."

"I don't think that answers my question at all," said Hall, exasperated. "If the Indians lasted as long as the rubber, that is all you wanted: so many rubber trees, so many Indians. As long as one lasted as long as the other, that was all you cared about?"

Now to the committee's surprise Arana grew strangely wistful.

As he strove to paint a brighter picture of his forest domain, it was as if he recalled nostalgically his first days as a river trader, before the self-imposed burden of power and corruption had warped his soul. "The Indians who live in the woods or in the country are more free than we who have to fulfill certain obligations to our families and commercial undertakings," he told the rapt spectators, "all of which we consider sacred—but they have no knowledge of these obligations."

His hands widespread, he tried to make the assembly share his vision. "For them, the woods and the mountains are the same as the streets are here to us—they do not consider themselves slaves in any way."

William Young remained skeptical. If Arana had these details at his fingertips, how was it that he remained blissfully ignorant of the slavery and the atrocities—when Sir Roger Casement, coming fresh to the Putumayo, had uncovered the truth within weeks?

"It is necessary to have the experience of Sir Roger Casement, who had been in the Congo," Arana reminded him, "who had knowledge of the methods there and who went to meet the Barbadians who spoke English. They looked upon him as a man sent by God."

Mr. Swift MacNeill stood up decisively. "The first time God has been mentioned in this transaction," he said dourly, then his manner became silky, for the denouement that he had awaited was at hand. "You are very anxious to see that witnesses are persons of good character. When the charges were made against the company, of murder and so on, you did not think it right to go into them because Hardenburg was a forger."

Once more, Arana's reply was oblique. "The reports which I received from every source were to the effect that the Indians were well-treated."

"But was not the evidence in *Truth* discountenanced on account of your belief that Hardenburg was a forger?"

"The information that I have is that Hardenburg obtained money from a company by means of this falsified draft."

"Did Hardenburg tell you what was going on in the Putumayo?"

"He spoke to me with great seriousness about his lost baggage."

"And nothing more?"

"This was the object of his visit."

"He never said a word about the sufferings of the natives in Putumayo?"

"I asked him about his impressions of what had happened in Encanto, and he said that as I was going there I would know better."

"Did he say anything about blackmailing?" But Arana shook his head.

"Do you call him a forger now?" asked Swift MacNeill very softly.

"I have to repeat that the suspicion falls on two persons, on the buyer and on the endorser."

"Then," said Swift MacNeill, in a voice of thunder, "turn round—turn round and see Hardenburg before you."

Slowly, as if mesmerized, Arana turned to scan the sea of faces—and there, risen from his seat no more than four yards away, his keen brown eyes blazing with indignation, was the man he hated more than any other: Walter Ernest Hardenburg.

"Do you not know him?" mocked Swift MacNeill, relishing the drama.

After an eternity, Arana recovered. Then he answered suavely: "Yes—I am very pleased to see him here. Because we can then enter into other details."

To Walt Hardenburg it was barely credible that all through this day, unseen by Arana, he had sat beside the Reverend Harris in the public enclosure, almost 4,000 miles from his home in Red Deer, Alberta, and heard the Peruvian use every lie and subterfuge to blacken his name. Arana's face, as Swift MacNeill engineered his dramatic confrontation, was a sight he never afterward forgot. It was as if the rubber baron at last realized that his deep-laid scheme had recoiled with boomerang force.

In fact, for more than a month, the Reverend Harris had been working for this moment. Following an extraordinary meeting of the Anti-Slavery Society, the young minister had urged its leaders—among them Noel Buxton, M.P., and Lord Henry Cavendish-Bentinck—that they should back Walt to the hilt in the effort to clear his name. But even earlier than this, he and a group of committed M.P.'s had waited on Charles Roberts as chairman. "It's scandalous that this man should be vilified day after day with no chance to hit back," Harris declared. "We believe he should have the right to appear before you and answer these charges."

Roberts agreed readily. "The company have made so much of the charge of forgery," he said, "we simply can't refuse to receive his evidence."

On March 8, following Roberts' decision, Harris wrote hurriedly to Walt to break the good news: the society would pay his passage, £40 third class return, and £5 a week expenses during his stay in London. "If you accept this offer, please cable at once," Harris stressed. "Arana's evidence before the committee will probably take some little time . . . it is quite uncertain what development may take place . . . it will be of considerable importance that you should be in London at this juncture."

Walt talked it over with Mary, though she did little more than listen and steer him tactfully toward the decision he had already made: once her independent young husband set his heart upon a project, it was a thankless task to try and deter him. Both knew the risks involved too well even to voice them. Harris wanted Walt in London for at least three weeks; if he stayed longer, his job with Seymour and Dawe, the railroad contractors, might well be in jeopardy. And Walt, no longer the lone wolf of Iquitos and Manaus, had liberally given hostages to fortune. The snug home he had built with his own hands now housed not only Mary and two-year-old James but also their second son, Gerald, born one year earlier.

But in the end he could not pass up this chance to clear his name and confront Arana. As the S.S. *Mauretania* churned across the Atlantic in the last weeks of March, he recalled soberly that in preparation for this moment he had traveled many thousands of miles, endured poverty and obloquy and known death as a constant companion. On the morning of April 8, as he strode down the gangplank onto Liverpool's dockside, at the very moment Arana took the witness seat for the first time, it seemed fitting to find Harris and eager newsmen awaiting him at the end of this long and lonely crusade.

And on April 10, as Walt, alert with pencil and paper, sat intently through his second committee session, he had proof that his journey had not been in vain. Agog, the newsmen now saw Arana, two days before his forty-ninth birthday, make blunder after blunder—contradicting himself, stumbling, retracting. Plainly the presence of the young American, so close to the witness seat, scribbling absorbedly, passing notes to Swift MacNeill and other examiners, unnerved him badly. And it was seen that whenever Arana hesitated over a date or a personality, Hardenburg, with his intimate knowledge of the Amazon, was swift to supply it.

Walt's evidence on his own behalf—cool, factual, laconic—stood him in good stead, too. His account of his first meeting with Muriedas, of the Spaniard's unaccountable orgy in Manaus which had obliged him to take possession of the forged bill, prompted few questions—nor yet did his explanation of how he had set about documenting his proofs against Arana.

Had he, as Arana charged, bribed those witnesses in Manaus and Iquitos? The American drew attention to one unassailable fact: he had never had sufficient funds with which to bribe anybody.

Questioned about the raids on La Reserva and La Unión, allegedly provoked by Colombians, he drew laughter. Had he seen bloodthirsty Colombian troops massing? "All I saw," Walt drawled, "were fifteen peons planting crops."

If he had never, as he claimed, approached Dr. Egoaguirre with the threat of blackmail, how did the company know that he had documents that could be used against them? Again Walt's explanation was simple: "I occasionally approached people who would not give me information. It might be that they were in the pay of Arana."

His bewilderment concerning the journal *Amazonas*, and the deposition of the editor, Lyonel Garnier, was patent, too. Evidently he had never known such a newspaper existed.

Nor did the charges that Walt had absconded stand up in the light of proven fact. True, he had left no address behind on leaving Iquitos, because he had not known his final destination— but on reaching London he had at once routed postcards back to Dr. King, young Valderrama and others, and their replies were proof of receipt. Then again he had stayed for seven months with the Grahams at Sandwich Street, and the Reverend Harris and the editors of *Truth* had always known his whereabouts.

Now the committee saw clearly that, though during all this time Hardenburg had been at the company's disposal, the directors, restrained by what Roberts called "the unaccountable hold Señor Arana had established over their minds," had never once tried to contact him. But did a man guilty of forgery and blackmail, the examiners asked, leave forwarding addresses everywhere?

And despite all the evidence they had digested, Hardenburg's answers to their questions brought home, as no printed testimony could, the stark reign of terror that had prevailed in the Amazon Valley.

"Was it common knowledge in Manaus and Iquitos that Indians were being done to death by torture and starvation in thousands? Was it common talk in the streets?"

"Yes."

"Did you gather that men were afraid to talk because the company and Mr. Arana were so powerful?"

"Yes, I derived that impression shortly after I got to Iquitos."

"Would you say it was as much as a native's life was worth to talk too much about these things?"

"I would not say he would lose his life in Iquitos, but if he went back it might be a different question."

"Did you see the healed scars on the backs of the Indians—the *marca de Arana?*"

"Yes," said Walt, staring challengingly at the Peruvian as he answered, "Arana's trademark."

Perhaps wisely, Douglas Hogg did not challenge this statement on Arana's behalf—nor did he, from first to last, question any of Hardenburg's assertions. For the directors, Raymond Asquith contented himself with putting questions as to the shotguns and six-shooters Walt and Perkins had carried—an evident attempt to justify the company's arsenal of Winchesters. Yet no sooner had Arana resumed the witness seat than some perverse instinct seemed to goad him on to court his own destruction. For having previously retracted the charged against Walt, he now returned to them.

"According to the papers I have, Hardenburg is a forger and he tried to blackmail the company," he announced, producing a voluminous dossier of thirty-one sworn depositions.

And now Hardenburg saw little by little the complex web of intrigue that Arana and his hirelings had spun between them over five years. Besides the imposing testimonies of handwriting experts, confirming the forgery, there were depositions from many whom he only dimly remembered: men like Rodrigues Lira, the Iquitos photographer, who had refused to make photocopies of Saldaña Rocca's documents, and Borsa, the Manaus hotelier. Now Walt saw that even Borsa's inability to supply more than a single-bedded room at the Grand had been a scurrilous trick to brand him as a pervert—for the deposition hinted slyly that he and Muriedas "had stayed together in the most intimate manner possible."

But one among these depositions he had no reason to doubt: the affirmation of the Iquitos police that "Estanisláo Bazan," the shadowy purchaser of Muriedas' rubber estate, had never even existed.

Though Walt never succeeded in plumbing the full mystery of "Bazan," certain factors were plain. Perhaps Muriedas' original desire to help him round up eyewitnesses had been genuine enough—but somewhere along the line, before the two men had ever left Iquitos, he had defected to the enemy. It was he, acting under instructions, who had bought the £10 bill from Wesche, in the fictitious name of "Bazan," using his skills as a forger to transform it to £830. Then, having traded on Hardenburg's good nature for a £20 loan, the rest had been easy. To recover the money Walt had been forced to present the bill to the Bank of Brazil—because Muriedas, again working under orders, had drunk himself to the point of delirium.

Plainly, after this his brief had been to part company with Hardenburg as soon as possible—which explained that unconvincing offer of a job from a friend in Pará. Only on one point did Hardenburg remain forever undecided. Was the Spaniard's subsequent jail term in that city a frame-up by Arana—or had Muriedas deliberately staged a second clumsy forgery to secure the comparative sanctuary of prison walls?

But to Arana's unconcealed chagrin, the committe made only a cursory inspection of those collected depositions. The suspicions that were clarifying in Hardenburg's mind were common to them all. "You may keep them as far as I am concerned," said Swift MacNeill contemptuously when Arana proffered them to him.

It was then, one eyewitness always recalled, that MacNeill's behavior and words became "deliberately insulting" as he moved in for what was virtually the kill. "What do you mean, in your affidavit, that the Indians of the Putumayo resist the establishment of civilization?"

"I mean that they did not admit of exchange, or anybody to do business with them."

"I want to know more about this civilization. Didn't you mean, when you said they were becoming more civilized, that they were becoming more amenable to floggings and outrages and murders—more broken-spirited?"

"I think they are more civilized," said Arana flatly. "They have relations between each other and have stopped practicing cannibalism."

"Are you aware that the report of the commission of your company defended the Indians from that attack, saying that they were a kindly people—that instances of cannibalism were few and far between?"

"For that reason I maintain what I said before about great exaggeration," Arana retorted.

Swift MacNeill was indefatigable. He flourished the draft prospectus over which Arana had labored so painstakingly six years back. Though the public had never glimpsed it, it had not escaped the watchdogs of the committee. "In this original prospectus you say—and this relates to 1907: 'There is an abundance of labour, the Indians being naturally submissive, and eight or ten civilised men can control 300 or 400 of them.' Was the control carried on by means of Winchester rifles?"

Now Arana made a telling admission. Unguardedly, forsaking the fiction that the company's armament had been dictated by the hostile terrain, he replied: "In order to make themselves respected it was necessary that each employee should carry a Winchester. On various occasions, when they were off their guard, they were attacked."

"Did the outrages occur because these people were resisting a gang of murderous ruffians?"

Arana's veneer of impassiveness was wearing thin: again his eyes were half-closed. "During the whole domination of Spain, for something like three hundred years, these Indians have resisted in the same way."

"Cortés and Pizarro," sneered Swift MacNeill, "was that the system?" With the deliberation of a man faced with a willful child, yet keeping his temper in check, Arana answered: "Our system is taking merchandise to them and carrying on barter."

The implacable MacNeill turned to Arana's motivation. So

shrewd were his thrusts it was like stripping the man naked in public. "I come to the establishment of the great Arana company in 1903," he mused. "Lizardo was your brother, Pablo Zumaeta a brother-in-law, Alarco another brother-in-law." He smiled without humor. "You *are* a good family man." Then, sharply: "Why did you want to make an English company out of it? Did you think it would be useful to have a company trading under an English name in case of political complications between Colombia and Peru?"

"The principal advantage was I meant to retire from business, as I had spent twenty or thirty years in the valley of the Amazon."

"Yes," rejoined MacNeill astutely, "having provided for your own family. You were on your way home to see the advantages of having an English company when Hardenburg unmasked this great iniquity."

"I admit it was an advantage," Arana repeated. Even the newsmen, knowing nothing of Arana's obsession with dignity, could see how little he relished the personal tenor of these questions—often now he flung both hands in front of him, as if to push MacNeill's words away. And the alert presence of Hardenburg, so close to the witness seat, rankled more keenly by the minute.

"Many attempts have been made to blackmail you," MacNeill went on. "I will go through the list. First of all Hardenburg attempted to blackmail you. Is that true?"

Arana hesitated perceptibly before replying: "Yes, I have got all the proofs of that. I have not brought them today, but yesterday I had them."

Now the committee exchanged baffled glances. Barely an hour back, Arana had handed in that formidable sheaf of depositions. Was he referring to other proofs yet—or were they another figment of his megalomaniac imagination?

MacNeill's next question was a masterstroke. "Then a Captain Whiffen attempted to blackmail you?"

"Yes, it is true," Arana agreed, unsuspecting. "He did try. On that occasion, if I had wished to deceive the public, I might have done it."

Still Arana had no realization that MacNeill had sprung the last trap of all. Until this moment the British directors and their counsel, in referring to the "blackmail" note, had referred scrupulously to Whiffen as "Captain X." Though Whiffen's name had more than once been mentioned by Sir Roger Casement, as a Putumayo explorer, no attempt had been made to link the two. By letting drop Whiffen's name, allowing Arana to make his accusation public, MacNeill had opened the door to further investigation. The committee could not now refuse to hear Whiffen's refutation. To the evidence of Muriedas and the trumped-up forgery would be added now the story of that drunken evening at the Motor Club.

"You know Captain Whiffen is a commissioned officer of the army?" MacNeill continued. Then, as Arana nodded, "Do you know, if the statement were believed, that Whiffen would be expelled the army—dismissed with disgrace?"

"Yes, that appeared so to me," the Peruvian agreed.

"And if he is *not* expelled," whiplashed Swift MacNeill, "do you know what *your* position will be—a public liar!"

A shocked hush descended on the chamber—broken at first only by the interpreter's steady monotone. As the import of the words went home to Arana, he colored and half-rose, as if to fell his tormentor, black eyes blazing, his face working uncontrollably. Briefly, the spectators saw Hardenburg crouched forward on his chair, his fists clenched, then Douglas Hogg was on his feet. "Do I understand, however offensive and outrageous a question may be, I am not entitled to object—because really it is very difficult to sit still and hear the witness insulted. I submit the question is a most offensive one."

"I think the question had better not be put," ordered Charles Roberts quietly, "and that language had better not be used."

Deceptively meek, MacNeill apologized. "I think the words 'public liar' were an expression I should not have used." Nonetheless, he still returned to the impressive list of blackmailers. There was Saldaña Rocca, was there not? His eyes wary now, Arana agreed—"but knowing the immoral character of the man I did not take much notice of it." Finally, there was Sir Roger Casement. Arana hesitated palpably, and MacNeill refreshed his memory. Had not a friend of his, Carlos de la Torre, the Peruvian Senator, charged that Sir Roger, too, had attempted to blackmail Arana?

The rubber baron nodded restrainedly: he had heard this rumor in London but never in Lima.

MacNeill affected to be shocked. It was distressing how many of the witnesses against Arana emerged as men of bad character, whose evidence must be discounted. Did he know Sir Roger Casement had sent a selection of private papers to the committee, which included the Consul General's assessment of the company and its key men? Unsuspecting, Arana shook his head.

MacNeill's swift efficient fingers plucked the relevant statement from a pile of papers. He read slowly and with emphasis, giving Dr. Mascarenhas ample time to grasp his meaning: "The impression produced on Sir Roger Casement was that the directors did not know what to do, or had any ability to carry out any scheme of reform, being, as it seemed to him [Casement] entirely in the hands of Arana, whom they had allowed to rob them right and left through the Manaus and Iquitos head agencies."

All stoicism gone, Arana shouted: "Who can prove this? If that statement has been made, I should like to meet Sir Roger Casement on some other ground."

Affecting to notice nothing, still with the same deliberate stress, MacNeill read on: "In reporting his impressions of a meeting of the company on June 28, 1911, Sir Roger Casement writes: 'Their affairs seem hopeless. The business incapacity at this end has been on a par with the criminal neglect in Manaus and Iquitos.' "

He paused, before driving home Casement's somber conclusion: "The only men equal to their task were the murderers."

Now the spectators, watching with bated breath, saw Walt Hardenburg's tension suddenly relax. With a quiet smile of triumph, he leaned back in his chair beside the Reverend Harris. Soon they realized why: he had recognized more swiftly than any the total collapse of his enemy's ego, the flawing of his assured facade. To the final rain of questions, Arana's only replies were clumsy and desperate evasions.

"Do you now believe that numerous murders were perpetrated by the agents of your company in the Putumayo?"

"There was no information on that point at the time."

"I ask you—yes or no—do you believe it now?"

"I believe they do not commit them now."

"Do you believe they did commit them?"

"Yes, before they did."

"Do you believe in former years women were burned, mutilated and tortured by the agents of your company?"

"I do not believe they were mutilated. I believe there were certain cases of flogging and murder."

"And burning alive?"

"These cases have been described in various ways. It has not been possible for me to prove them because I have not met these persons."

"You do not deny that these are proved, but you say they have not been proved by yourself."

"Not proved by me. I have not been able to prove them."

"You have taken no steps of your own accord to find out whether they are true or not?"

"If these persons who have been denounced are no longer in the region, how is it possible to prove it?"

"That is not an answer to my question. Have you taken any steps?"

"What I have occupied myself with is to find out whether they still commit the crimes."

"*That* is not an answer to my question—I repeat my question. Have you taken steps to find out whether the statements in Sir Roger Casement's report are true or not? I want an answer—yes or no!"

The silence in the chamber seemed to stretch forever, broken

by degrees by a stifled babel of comment. Arana and the interpreter seemed locked in a silent battle of wills, though their frantic
muttered colloquy was inaudible from first to last. The murmur-
ing of the spectators rose, then Dr. Mascarenhas turned helplessly
toward the members on the dais, immobile beneath the vast oil
painting.

"The reply is exactly the same as before," he reported. "I
cannot get him to say yes or no."

But Hardenburg and every man present could see that no
answer was needed: the question had been rhetorical. The answer
lay in Arana's face. Some, now that his edifice of fraud had
collapsed, could find it in their hearts to pity the Peruvian; his
brazen self-assurance had deluded him that he could win this last
battle, as he had won all his battles, and thus he had charted his
own self-destruction. All his life, for what he had seen as the best
of ends, he had chosen the worst means possible, and now his
humiliation was both public and universal.

Too soon, the Peruvian Government would learn that he was
no longer the company's liquidator—and that the committee's
final report to the House of Commons declared roundly: "Señor
Arana, together with other partners . . . had knowledge of and
was responsible for the atrocities perpetrated by his agents and
employees in the Putumayo." His British codirectors, though
absolved of the direct complicity which would have justified
prosecution, did not get off lightly either. They stood before the
world as men whose "negligent ignorance" was "deserving of
severe censure."

Already Arana's empire was toppling. Profiting by the time
lapse which Sir Roger Casement's visit to the Amazon had
allowed them, thousands of Indians had struck out through the
forests, beyond the reach of the Peruvian Amazon Company's
hirelings. The whole eastern sector of the Putumayo was deserted: only abandoned tribal huts, sunken dugouts and mounds
of broken pottery marked where the Indian encampments had
stood. On scores of rubber rivers, the pattern was the same—
though at La Chorrera and elsewhere mission stations and out-

posts of the Indian Protection Service marked a giant step toward the future of the Amazon: the end of boom-or-bust psychology, the planned and humane development of the world's richest storehouse of natural resources.

Nor did Arana's thugs escape retribution. All along the Amazon, word of their current hideouts, the aliases they had adopted, reached the Reverend John Harris in London, for onward transmission to the Foreign Office. Soon the manhunt had spread through six rubber republics: Andrés O'Donnell, hunted from Manaus to Barbados and back again, was finally run to earth in Caracas, Venezuela, before being returned to Lima for trial. By October, 1913, Iquitos' British Consul reported to Sir Edward Grey that Armando Normand, in jail under armed guard, awaited the same fate. A year later, Abelardo Agüero and Augusto Jiménez, working rubber in the Beni territory, were arrested by the Bolivian authorities and returned to Peru.

Stripped of his Indian labor force, his hired gunmen and his Barbadian overseers, Arana no longer had the means to terrorize the Putumayo—and the rubber manufacturers, in any case, were still resolutely facing east. What Walt Hardenburg and his fellow crusaders had concluded in humanity's name had in truth begun with Henry Wickham's long-ago seed snatch. On July 27, 1914, one month after Julio Arana closed down his Manaus office for good and all, and the armies gathered in Europe, top-grade Amazon rubber had slumped to 2/9d a pound. And rubber was one of the few commodities whose price was not driven up by war. On Armistice Day, 1918, it stood at exactly this same level.

The final crushing blow came from on high. Determined to put an end to frontier strife, President Augusto Leguía, during his second term of office, contrived a noble solution. He ceded over 24 million acres of Putumayo territory, including all the land claimed by Arana, to Colombia. There was no border bloodshed from that time on.

All this lay in the future. On this warm April day, with the chestnuts budding along the river, Arana could no longer face the House of Commons. Presently a soft-spoken Irish K.C. named

Vesey Knox arose: he had been instructed to appear on behalf of
Captain Whiffen, who had been mentioned during the course of
the proceedings and who wished to give evidence as soon as was
convenient. At the hour when Whiffen, bronzed and soldierly,
limped into the committee room, heads were craning all over the
chamber to see Arana's reaction. But the Peruvian's chair stood
empty: Arana had gone.

On Tuesday, April 15, as the committee, follow-
ing their final public session, rose for the day, Walt Hardenburg
passed through the St. Stephen's entrance of the House of
Commons for the last time. Threading his way through the jam
of red London buses, he struck north across Parliament Square.
There were still items of unfinished business awaiting him before
he returned to Red Deer. Mary had entrusted him with many
messages to the Grahams—and in eight days' time he was star
guest of honor at the Anti-Slavery Society's annual meeting,
when notables like the Archbishop of Canterbury, the Ranee of
Sarawak and the novelist Israel Zangwill flocked to heap congratulations on him.

Meanwhile, he was bound for the offices of *Truth*, overlooking
St. James's Park, to pay his respects to his old friends Bennett and
Paternoster. All three men would shortly rate a tribute in the
committee's published report, which went on record that
"Thanks to the public spirit of a chance traveller and an English
journal . . . able to present a strong *prima facie* case for enquiry . . . the truth has been established, the worst infamies [of
the rubber boom] have been terminated."

Yet the boom had brought much positive gain in its wake. In
their quest for rubber, men had found and explored scores of
rivers hitherto unknown to the cartographers. All over the
Amazon Valley, electric lines, telephone systems, adequate sewer-
age and steamboat services had arrived to stay. Percival Farquhar's Madeira-Mamoré Railroad had proved that the key to the

Amazon was the well-being of the worker, which in turn paved the way to health centers and mammoth drainage projects. Candido Rondon's 15,000-mile network of telegraph lines linked with his Indian Protection Service had shown that in this land of tomorrow progress must march hand in hand with respect for minority rights.

As Big Ben boomed 4 P.M., and clattering flights of pigeons rose upward from the sooty stones, Hardenburg recalled again the sweet-toned clock that had chimed the hours in faraway Manaus. Overnight, that bubble world had been pricked like any rubber balloon: the slaves were free, the warehouses silent and shuttered, the glittering tiled mansions of the rubber barons stood empty. It had been a bitter unequal struggle to bring home to the world the price it paid for so much of its black gold, but not a vain one. He had pitted his faith in humanity against the powerful tyranny of Arana's empire and he had won.

On the north side of the square, he paused to face the House of Commons. For a long time his gaze remained fixed on the rambling building, the stage on which the final act of his personal drama had been played out. Words that Abraham Lincoln had uttered more than half a century earlier had never seemed more apt than at this moment: *Let us have faith that right makes might; and in that faith let us, to the end, dare to do our duty as we understand it. . . .*

Acknowledgments

THIS STRANGE STORY emerged by degrees in the course of a 25,000-mile journey. From London, my route led me by way of Rio de Janeiro to Manaus, on the Amazon's Negro River tributary, where some of the facts were gleaned; thence to Pôrto Velho, down the length of the Madeira-Mamoré Railroad to Guajará-Mirim, over the Andes to La Paz. By then the story was assuming discernible shape, though there were still many interviews to conduct and records to examine in places as far-flung: in Lima and Iquitos; in Panama City and the highlands of Guatemala; in Yucatán State and Mexico City; finally across the United States in locations as far removed as South Carolina and New York. The way was devious, and along the route I found no one person who knew all the facts as I have set them down.

That it was possible at all is due primarily to three men. From the first, Professor Arthur Cezar Ferreira Reis, then Governor of the State of Amazonas, ensured that my researches in Manaus were some of the most rewarding I have ever undertaken. As fruitful and enjoyable was my trip through the wilds of Rondonia Territory; for General João Carlos Mader, former Governor, and his warmhearted family, nothing was ever too much trouble. And to Graham Watson, my friend, counselor and agent for many years, goes my undying gratitude. The entire project originated in his mind and he never lost faith that I could pull it off.

Others, too, joined with me wholeheartedly in unraveling threads of the narrative—above all, Mrs. Deborah H. Bressi and Mary and Wesley Hardenbergh. Without their help, and the collated memories of James A. Hardenburg, Gerald C. Hardenburg and William A. Hardenbergh, I doubt that this book could have been written at all. Almost as invaluable were the tireless and unselfish labors of Sr. L. A. Navarro Cáuper, Dr. Mário Ypiranga Monteiro and Dr. Geraldo Pinheiro, who collaborated in my investigations from first to last.

So much of my information was derived from personal memorabilia, or came from archives in Spanish and Portuguese nowhere available outside the Amazon theater, that I have dispensed with a bibliography. And so many men and women added one telling fragment to the completed jigsaw that it would be unfair to single out individuals. I would like instead to name them in alphabetical order, with my assurance that none of them is forgotten: Sr. Yegislau de Araújo; Sr. Walter Bartolo; Burton N. Behling; Sr. Jacob Benoliel; George M. Booth, Chairman, Manaus Harbour Board; Sra. C. Bosaconia Bovel; Mrs. Pippa Boyle; Norman Carrick, Liverpool Record Office; Leora and George Craswell; George R. P. Farquhar; Mrs. Percival Farquhar; T. S. E. Figgis; Dr. Charles A. Gauld; Sra. Helena Gentil; G. C. Grantham; R. L. Grayson, Secretary, The Booth Steamship Co. Ltd.; Lady Harris; Sr. Victor Israel; T. H. Jeffery, Secretary, Rubber Trade Association of London; Dr. Andre Jobim; Grace and Frank Jonas; L. H. Kennaway; Helen and Frank Kravigny; Major G. V. S. Le Fanu, Deputy Assistant Serjeant at Arms, House of Commons; Sra. Maria Luisa; Bodil and William McDermott; Malcolm Matheson; Colonel Patrick Montgomery, Secretary, Anti-Slavery and Aborigines Protection Society; Sr. Pablo Morán; R. C. Morris; Brigadier A. Leslie Newth; Dr. Waldemar Pedrosa; Sr. Eduardo Barros Prado; Sr. Fernando Sabinho; D. H. Simpson, Librarian, The Royal Commonwealth Society; Peter Singleton-Gates; Mrs. Emma Smith; J. B. Steadman; Sr. Dn. Nicolás Suárez; Winston Suárez; Sir George Taylor, Director, and R. G. C. Desmond, Librarian, Royal Botanic Gardens, Kew; Stanley Whiffen; Frances and Colonel Robert P. Waters. To these and many, many others, my most sincere thanks.

What of my researchers, who from first to last saw a forgotten fact or an elusive personality as no more than a series of irresistible challenges? Without the staunch support of Joan St. George Saunders and her team in London, the inexorable sleuthing of Pamela Hoskins, the pioneer translations of Nadia Radowitz, I should indeed have been lost. In New York, Amy Forbert, Robin McKown and Sheila Whitney never failed to yield up the clues just when I needed them most. The Amazon leg of the journey fell to Maria Teresa Vasta, who despite heat, insects and the dizzying perils of trans-Andean flights followed every factual lead to the bitter end. The finished work would have been poorer without her help, her courage and fortitude.

But as ever, my deepest debt is to my wife, who besides conducting many interviews, typing the final draft and offering the moral support that saw it through, doggedly followed the trail of Walt Hardenburg and the veterans of "Mad Mary" across the length and breadth of the United States. But for her efforts, this story of a brave man who took no thought of self might well have remained forgotten forever in the limbo of the past.

Index